McGraw-Hill Publications in Psychology
CLIFFORD T. MORGAN, *Consulting Editor*

INTRODUCTION TO
EXPERIMENTAL METHOD

McGraw-Hill Publications in Psychology

CLIFFORD T. MORGAN, *Consulting Editor*

John F. Dashiell was Consulting Editor of this series from its inception in 1931 until January 1, 1950.

INTRODUCTION TO
EXPERIMENTAL METHOD

For Psychology and the Social Sciences

JOHN C. TOWNSEND, Ph.D.

Associate Professor of Psychology
West Virginia University

New York   Toronto   London
McGRAW-HILL BOOK COMPANY, INC.
1953

THE MAPLE PRESS COMPANY, YORK, PA.

Dedicated to

Roger W. Russell
Head, Department of Psychology,
University College, London,
my friend and former
professor

PREFACE

This is a book that should appeal to three overlapping categories of individuals. First, the undergraduate student who is undergoing his first exposure to the rigors of the experimental method in psychology and the social sciences. Second, the student who, with an inadequate background in the application of the experimental method, finds himself faced with the necessity of "doing a piece of research" to satisfy thesis requirements. Third, the social science worker who discovers that his job in industry, the clinic, the prison, etc., is one demanding the execution of research projects.

At the outset, I would like to state my main purpose in writing this book. It has become increasingly clear to me, and to other teachers in the area of experimental psychology, that there is a need to develop in students an early appreciation of the theory of scientific method and statistics. In the past, laboratory courses in general experimental psychology offered, largely, a type of training based on what may be known as a "cookbook" method. The students were given complete directions for performing a certain experiment and were required only to follow the directions given, fill in the blanks with the appropriate words and phrases, and write their conclusions. Such experiments, if they can be called that, did not call upon the student to demonstrate his ability to design experiments but only to carry out those already designed. He spent most of his time in the laboratory serving as a subject for experiments and not as an experimenter. In a sense, such a program trains the student to be a good subject and does not further him toward the supposed ideal of receiving training as an experimenter.

The emphasis in this book is placed on preparing the student to think along lines of the development of sound research designs rather than the successful execution of standardized traditional experiments. In this way, it is believed that the beginning student may be exposed to the elements of theory and method necessary for the understanding of the performance of experiments. Equally important, the student will be given the opportunity to become sensitive to the ways of critical thinking early in his contact with science and not be forced to labor in darkness and boredom until he becomes a graduate student. I believe theory and content can be successfully taught simultaneously.

This book, an introductory text, is written for the student, in his language, and in line with his preparation for beginning a course of study in research design and statistical methods. No attempt will be made to cover completely all the methods or statistics used by the more advanced students in experimental psychology. Often, as is true when concepts are greatly simplified, much of the preciseness and beauty of the topic discussed will be lost. This is the inevitable consequence when anything less than the whole of a topic is presented; however, since I wrote this book for the purpose of making my subject matter clear to the student, I offer no apology for simplicty and repetition.

Appreciation is expressed to Drs. Raymond J. Christman, Ann Greenhut, and Quin F. Curtis of West Virginia University who read and constructively criticized parts of the manuscript. To my brother, George W. Townsend, goes my thanks for his contributions to the chapter on apparatus. Dr. Roger W. Russell, University College, London, will recognize many of his contributions as he reads this book, for it was he who first told me the story of the experimental method. For his thought-provoking lectures I am eternally grateful.

I am indebted to Prof. Ronald A. Fisher, Cambridge, and to Messrs. Oliver and Boyd, Ltd., Edinburgh, for permission to reprint Tables 3, 4, and V.A. from their book "Statistical Methods for Research Workers" and to the many other publishers and authors who granted permission to use their materials.

Last, but not least, I thank Mrs. Barbara Boggs, who deciphered and typed the manuscript.

JOHN C. TOWNSEND

MORGANTOWN, W. VA.
March, 1953

CONTENTS

PART A
THEORY OF EXPERIMENTATION

CHAPTER 1

PSYCHOLOGY AND SCIENCE

Since the earliest recorded event in history, man has attempted to inquire into the what, how, and why of not only his existence, but also the existence of almost all things with which he has come in contact. From man's experience, driven by insatiable curiosity, has come the bundle of facts we call knowledge.

Science and Mysticism

The most exacting, direct, and efficient means by which facts have been collected and organized is by the use of tools of thinking and acting which have come to be known as scientific methods. But man has not always been scientific in the way he went about attempting to explain phenomena in nature. He has often, when baffled as to the cause of an event, resorted to attributing power over natural events to pagan gods.

If a primitive man saw lightning strike a tree and a fire result, he would be at a loss to explain the phenomenon in terms of the source of lightning and the chemistry of combustion. Because of lack of knowledge, he would not be able to explain the event satisfactorily in terms of the factors involved in the event itself. Instead, to find the cause, he would turn away from the event and go outside it to some hypothesized external agent. He would probably invent a god of lightning and a god of fire as the cause of the occurrence.

As man has progressed in his knowledge of the relationships of nature, he has felt less and less need to hypothesize mystical external agents as causes of natural phenomena. It is through the gaining of more and more facts of nature that man has slowly replaced ignorance, governed by superstition, with systematic scientific knowledge. A further discussion of this line of thought is to be found in the writings of Zilboorg and Henry (15, p. 27).[1]

Let us notice Fig. 1.1. The scientist works only within areas I and II. When he attempts to deal with area III, he becomes a mystic and a scientific renegade. Science attempts to enlarge area I and eliminate

---

[1] Numbers in parentheses throughout this book refer to the bibliography found at the end of each chapter.

areas II and III.   Since the work of the scientist is to find answers to problems by the method of determining the truth or falsity of testable hypotheses, he spends most of his time in area II.

The following example may further clarify the concept of the legitimate areas of scientific endeavor.   Suppose a scientist's attention is called to an unexplained event which we will name event X.   He is asked to find an acceptable scientific explanation for event X.   Just where is event X located in the chart, Fig. 1.1?   Event X cannot be in area I, for this area

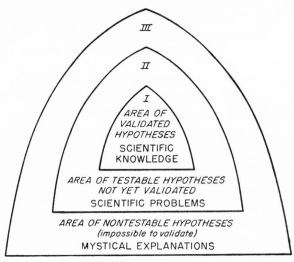

FIG. 1.1.   The relationship of scientific knowledge, scientific problems, and mystical explanations.

contains only that knowledge which has been gathered through the technique of validating hypotheses, and we said we have no known scientific explanation for event X.   Event X cannot be located in area III, for this area contains only nontestable hypotheses or mystical explanations for events.   The scientific explanation of event X must rest in area II, for this area is reserved for problems in need of scientific explanation and whose explanation is to be discovered by the process of testing the validity of hypotheses.

During the history of mankind and his search for meaningful explanations of events, area I has increased in size while area III has decreased. Area II has also expanded.   Although area II represents man's ignorance of the causes of events, it has become larger for two reasons: (a) area I, our present knowledge, has made us more conscious of the need of looking for explanations in terms of testable hypotheses, and (b) the answer to one problem most often suggests another problem. Northrop's (11) discussion of the analysis of the problem facing the scientist is relevant here.

Definition of Scientific Psychology

Psychology itself grew from a varied background. It progressed from the mystical to the scientific stage during its long history. One of psychology's most prominent ancestors was philosophy. It was not until 1879 that psychology became dignified by having a laboratory dedicated to psychological research. See Bartley (2, p. 3) for a good, short history of psychology.

Regardless of the strides made by scientific psychology there are many today who would deny that psychology is a science. *Psychology is a science*, but only under certain conditions. Let us see when psychology is and when it is not a science.

Almost no one will disagree with you if you affirm that chemistry, physics, and biology are sciences. Now it is obvious that the subject matter of each of these sciences is different. Chemistry treats of the composition of substances and their changes. Physics deals with the phenomena of inanimate matter involving no changes in chemical composition, and biology is the science which treats of living organisms. Therefore, we can say that science, whatever it is, is not defined in terms of the subject matter with which it deals. What, then, is a science?

The definition of science does not rest on what is accomplished, but how it was accomplished. The important factor present when science is present and absent when science is absent is the factor, scientific thinking. To define science as "any body of organized knowledge which has been gathered through the use of systematic methods of investigation" is close to the true definition, but only if the emphasis is placed on the method of investigating and not the materials investigated.

Scientific thinking is a particular kind of thinking. It has two major characteristics. These are *direction* and *control*. Above all, scientific thinking represents organized, orderly, methodical thought concerning the issues at hand. The common factor, then, running through all accepted sciences, is the method by which facts concerning a certain class of phenomena are gathered. If this is so, then there is no reason for excluding psychology from the list of sciences just because its subject matter is often of an intangible nature. So long as facts concerning the consciousness and behavior of organisms are gathered in accordance with the rules of scientific methodology, then such facts form an organized body of knowledge that meets every specification of a science. Conversely, psychology is not a science when its data are gathered and evaluated by unorthodox methods which break the rules of logic. Ruch

(12, p. 3), Munn (10, p. 3), Cruze (8, p. 6), and Bugelski (4, p. 3) discuss psychology as a science.

Common Sense and Scientific Thinking

The layman when presented with a problem will often attempt to answer it by "common sense," while the scientist would prefer to use scientific methods.   Is the common-sense approach really different from the scientific approach?   The answer is that the scientific methods grew out of the common-sense approach.   In the growing process, Stebbing (13, p. 235) believed two major changes took place.   First, common sense became organized to a high degree, and, second, there was a change in the type of order with which it dealt.   The common-sense approach is usually an attempt to solve a problem by simply ruling out those factors which do not form an acceptable answer and taking as the answer that factor or circumstance which most completely accounts for the incident. The following is an example used by Stebbing (13) in a discussion of common-sense thinking:

Suppose that a man, having left his flat empty, returns in the early evening to find his front door bolted.   He knows that he left no one in the flat.   How, then, account for the bolted door?   That burglars have broken into the flat is the first idea likely to occur to a Londoner.   The suggestion springs into his mind almost before he has had time to reflect.   But then a difficulty arises to check the acceptance of this idea.   How could a burglar have left the door bolted on the inside?   The flat is on the third floor of a straight-faced block, so that it is improbable that the entry should have been made through a window.   Perhaps the bolt has slipped.   But that idea is immediately rejected, since it is a stiff, horizontal bolt rarely used.   Some one inside must have drawn the bolt.   Having succeeded in forcing the door, he inspects the flat, looking for confirmation of his suspicion.   There is no one in his study, but he finds the drawers of his desk open and their contents scattered.   There was, he knew, no money in the desk, so he does not pause to examine the drawers, but goes at once to the dining-room to inspect the silver.   He finds that two silver cups have gone and also that the table silver has disappeared.   These facts are ample confirmation of his belief that he has been robbed.   But there is still the puzzling fact of the door bolted on the inside.   As he walks down the passage he sees a light under the kitchen door.   Perhaps the burglar is still in the flat.   But the kitchen is empty.   On the table are the remains of a meal.   The window is wide open.   He remembers the parcels lift and now feels that the situation is explained.   Whatever the means of entry, the exit has been by way of the parcels lift.   The bolted front door was doubtless to give the burglar time to escape should the owner of the flat return too soon.[1]

[1] Stebbing, L. S., *A Modern Introduction to Logic*, pp. 233–234, The Thomas Y. Crowell Company, New York, 1930.   Reproduced here with the kind permission of the publishers.

Would the scientist treat this example in a different way? Essentially, no. Both the scientist and the common-sense thinker would attempt to collect and organize the facts in such a way as would provide an explanation.

The differences between common-sense thinking and the scientific approach become more obvious when a specific, easily observed, everyday phenomenon occurs and an explanation is demanded. Let us take as an example the apparent fact that memory for an event usually fades as time goes on. Chances are the layman has seldom thought about this ordinary happening. If his attention is directed to the phenomenon and he is asked to explain the reason for it, he might say, "It's just common sense that if you don't use the material you have learned, it disappears because of disuse." In his opinion he has cleverly answered your question and wonders why you could not have figured it out for yourself. But you, as a scientist, are not satisfied with this common-sense answer to what appears to him to be a simple, obvious answer to a commonplace question. So you decide to check and see if disuse alone can cause a fading of memory. Perhaps, as much of a surprise to both of you, you discover that it is not disuse alone that causes the memory fading, but rather it is mostly the so-called retroactive inhibition effect of learning during the interval between the original learning and the recall. A quick look in any good psychology-of-learning text would have told you the same thing. The experiment has not only shown that "common-sense" thinking can be wrong, but has demonstrated that the scientific approach can take a usual occurrence, find a verifiable answer for it, and, further, can suggest other hypotheses and solutions. Common-sense thinking alone seldom is able to do this.

The usual differences between the two approaches are these: the common-sense thinker is satisfied with an explanation that merely satisfies his immediate curiosity, while the scientist attempts to systematize the facts so that he may go beyond the obvious explanation. The layman feels the need for providing an explanation for only unusual happenings. The scientist feels the need of explaining any event, unusual or ordinary. Thus we see how the scientist differs from the common-sense thinker in both the way and degree to which he organizes the explanation and the type of events to which his curiosity extends. In addition, the scientist, because of his training in dealing with problems, introduces other elements when he deals with problem solution through the process of experimentation.

Woodworth (14) states:

An experimenter is said to control the conditions in which an event occurs.

He has several advantages over an observer who simply follows the course of events without exercising control.

(a) The experimenter makes the event happen at a certain place and time and so is fully prepared to make an accurate observation.

(b) Controlled conditions become known conditions, the experimenter can set up his experiment a second time and repeat the observation. . . .

(c) The experimenter can systematically vary the conditions and note the concomitant variation in the results. . . .[1]

The layman is not expected to offer any more than common-sense answers. The scientist is. Much of the damage done to psychology as a profession, and to those who come seeking psychological help, is done by the self-styled "psychologist" who may be only a layman with a common-sense knowledge of psychology. The scientific psychologist should demand the best thinking possible from himself and colleagues and should make use of only those explanations arrived at by a sound scientific approach.

Logic and Science

Two major overlapping logical systems have been set down for use as guiding rules for the scientist. These systems are known as (a) inductive and (b) deductive logic. See Bugelski (4, p. 46), Black (3, pp. 13, 291), and Andrews (1, p. 2).

Inductive logic assumes that the researcher begins his investigation by observing certain, separate instances of the occurrence of whatever phenomenon he is investigating. He observes measures and records these occurrences. Then, by examining the bundle of concrete data collected, he establishes some characteristic for these separate instances. As a result of his examination, he then makes a statement, or proposition, concerning the characteristic of the group from which the separate instances represented a sample. This is the inductive method.

Deductive logic has as its starting point a statement or proposition. From this premise an attempt is made to arrive at a specific, concrete truth by a process of reasoning. This concrete truth is called a deduction. A deduction is, thus, an inference that is believed to be valid and conclusive. Deductions are always preceded by "logical" reasons which appear to support the conclusion.

Inductive logic is often followed by deductive logic in the scientific process in that although inductive logic starts with the observation of phenomena, it ends with proof that the evidence justifies the conclusion. In this manner, inductive logic overlaps with deductive logic. The

[1] Woodworth, R. S., *Experimental Psychology*, p. 2, Henry Holt and Company, Inc., New York, 1938. Reproduced here with the kind permission of the publishers.

scientific methods of experimental inquiry are most heavily indebted to the inductive method. Validation of the results of experimentation owes its debt to deductive logic.

The following chart, Fig. 1.2, illustrates the relationship of the two systems of logic.

Cresswell (7) uses the following syllogism when attempting to represent logical inference symbolically.

Hypothesis: If A is B, then C is D.

Experimentation: Observation or experimentation shows that C is D.

Deduction: If there is no alternative explanation, A is probably B.

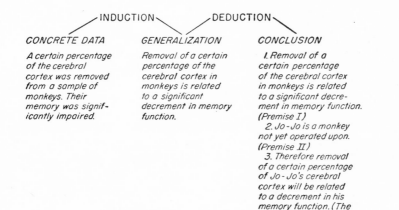

INDUCTION   DEDUCTION

CONCRETE DATA | GENERALIZATION | CONCLUSION

A certain percentage of the cerebral cortex was removed from a sample of monkeys. Their memory was significantly impaired.

Removal of a certain percentage of the cerebral cortex in monkeys is related to a significant decrement in memory function.

1. Removal of a certain percentage of the cerebral cortex in monkeys is related to a significant decrement in memory function. (Premise I)
2. Jo-Jo is a monkey not yet operated upon. (Premise II)
3. Therefore removal of a certain percentage of Jo-Jo's cerebral cortex will be related to a decrement in his memory function. (The Deduction).

Fig. 1.2.   The relationship of inductive and deductive logic.

This syllogism could be applied to Torricelli's work leading to the invention of the barometer. If it were true that air has weight (A is B), then a column of mercury should be higher at sea level than on top of a mountain (C is D). It was demonstrated that a column of mercury stood higher at sea level (C is D), thus air probably has weight (A is B).

Many scientific psychologists refuse to accept the psychoanalytic theory because it makes use of, and, indeed, is built upon certain nontestable hypotheses. The libido, id, ego, superego, etc., are postulates that have come into being in order to help explain human behavior. Because such concepts cannot be dealt with by rigid experimentation, they have been relegated, by some, to the area of nontestable hypotheses which we have labeled "mystical explanations."

Mystical explanations are so easy to invent and are so often logically self-consistent that it takes a firm believer in the scientific method approach to point out the fallacies. If the basic postulates are not capable of being proved or disproved, then any system of logical explanation built on them may be either right or wrong.   If the premises are false, then all that follows is wrong, since the logical deductions would of necessity be consistent with a false premise.   On the other hand, the basic premises assumed may be right, and in that case the system evolved would be a true system.

The psychoanalysts say that their basic postulates are sound because the system "works."   What they mean by this is that their deductions, when applied, work in the specific instances noted, and that the cures by psychoanalysis follow a logically expected sequence consistent with the system.   That the system probably works is denied by few who have witnessed its application, but what worries the scientific psychologist is how it works, in that other explanations of the cures by psychoanalysis are possible wherein the postulates of psychoanalysis need not even be mentioned.   Such are the difficulties of understanding a system built on nontestable hypotheses.

Most psychologists have chosen as their approach to the study of human behavior some system which is akin to behaviorism.   This means studying the human being as an organism that has the capabilities of receiving stimuli, integrating these stimuli, and responding accordingly.   In such a system of behavior explanation, one need not hypothesize forces other than those he can measure and manipulate.   Such a system has its beginning in the observation of an organism's reactions to its environment and heredity.   Such observations yield verifiable data from which premises may be made.   The scientific psychologist may then deduce from these premises certain valid truths.   An example of an explanation of the principles of behavior as deduced from behavioristic data is to be found in Hull's work (9).

The psychoanalytic theory may be as true an explanation of human behavior as any other, but its system of explanation is more doubted by the scientific psychologist than systems that make less use of nontestable hypotheses.

Scientific Steps from Observation to Generalization

If we agree that the correct approach to the solution of a problem is by progressing through the inductive-deductive path, then our itinerary is well marked for us.   Most researchers follow the four following steps in doing a piece of scientific research aimed at arriving at facts.   Northrop (11, p. 34) presents a related discussion.

Observation.   The researcher, during his contact with his field of study, is constantly alert through the process of observation for the detection of apparent relationships among factors.   When such relationships are suspected, he prepares to go through the process necessary to account for these relationships. He will wish to connect any fact observed with a total situation so as to bring the isolated fact into a meaningful light.

Classification. A researcher does not jump into a research project without selecting some frame of reference from which to view his data. He may decide to discover the reason for a particular type of behavior in human beings but he still must further decide which frame of reference he will use. If he is a psychologist, he most likely will view his subjects, and thus classify his data, in a different fashion than would a physiologist, a biochemist, or an endocrinologist. During the classificatory stage, the scientist will guess at the cause of the relationships and make what is known as a hypothesis. A hypothesis is in itself a form of classification of the impression made as the result of observation.

A biologist may literally classify a number of specimens he has collected in terms of traits they possess in common with existing categories, and thus gain scientific knowledge of the specimens through this process of classification. See Northrop (11) and Cohen and Nagel (6, p. 223).

Verification. Having observed the problem and having made it meaningful in terms of a particular discipline, the researcher proceeds to design an experiment to test the validity of certain answers he has suggested. During the experimental stage leading to verification the researcher controls the conditions in which the phenomenon occurs. He varies only that factor or those factors whose influence he wishes to measure as related to other conditions. Data are thus gathered that will serve as the basis for derivation of propositions arrived at by the process of induction.

Generalization. On the basis of having established that certain factors are responsible for the phenomenon observed, the experimenter states certain general inferences, principles, theories, or laws. He then deduces from these propositions certain statements relating them to specific occurrences of the phenomenon.

These four steps are utilized by science and are the basic elements in the logical progression in man's attempt to establish an orderly and systematic knowledge of natural phenomena by scientific means. The most important step is verification. The most dangerously difficult step is generalization.

Thus psychology proceeds along a difficult road full of pitfalls and armed only with a method that will, if faithfully followed, safely and efficiently carry it through to the maximum amount of reliable knowledge in the area of scientific psychology.

Pure and Applied Science

If a scientist is engaged in attempting to establish certain scientific laws as a result of the investigation of basic relationships between phenomena, then he may be said to be doing pure scientific research.   A synonym for pure research is fundamental research.   The reason for doing pure research is to gather facts for the simple reason that facts are worth gathering.   Whether the facts are of immediate use in solving an existing problem or whether they may not be needed for a hundred years is of no concern to the pure researcher.   He knows that all things in nature are related and that any new fact discovered will fit into the general scheme.

The "pure" researcher adds to our stock pile of information.   He most often works on his own, unsupported, and follows his own inclination in the choice of research problems.   Ebbinghaus was doing pure research in psychology when he gathered data on which to build his laws of learning. He was not meeting a current problem of his time, for his work assumed importance only after introspective psychology changed to applied psychology.

The "applied" scientist conducts experiments during which time he applies some basic law or laws of science to ascertain what will happen in a particular case of the law's application.   He attempts to answer a problem which is at the time in need of an answer.   Chapanis, Garner, and Morgan (5, p. 10) point out the two kinds of application of fundamental science, *applied research* and *design*.   Applied research has to do with the techniques of science as they are used in gathering information in specific instances.   The techniques of science in this case are used to answer a specific current problem.   The use of applied science in design means the use of information gathered in the past (perhaps by the pure scientist) in the development or evaluation of new devices.   The applied scientist most often is a member of an organization attempting to meet problems in a particular area, is supported by the organization, and may or may not have freedom in the choice of his research problems.   Clinical psychologists at work today experimenting with and evaluating the shock therapies, military psychologists experimenting with propaganda techniques, and industrial psychologists testing new personnel selection batteries are examples of applied scientists working in the field of psychology.

Problems Specific to Scientific Psychology

To do acceptable research in psychology places more demands on the experimenter than if he were experimenting in any of the other fields of science.   If he is conducting an experiment in chemistry, he may walk about his laboratory and pick up or put down the materials with which he is working.   He can hold in his hand the elements of carbon, magnesium, or copper.   He can collect hydrogen in a bottle and watch it ignite when he brings a flame near it.   He can be sure the concentration of his acids and purity of his salts are the same from bottle to bottle. The physicist can measure accurately the factors involved in his experiment. Heat, light, electricity, and mechanics all are capable of being highly controlled. The physicist can duplicate the conditions of his experiment just as accurately as can the chemist, for such variables as temperature and pressure, which might vary from experiment to experiment, or even during a single experiment, can be kept constant at any desired value. But not so for the psychological experimenter. He must deal with living organisms who have as their most common characteristic the accumulation of different experiences. No two individuals are alike, nor is any individual the same a moment after it has been established what he is like. The human being just will not stand still psychologically. Behavior is extremely variable.

The experimental psychologist does not deal with things such as chemicals or hot and cold metals; instead he deals most often with intangibles in the form of inferred "things," such as learning, personality, intelligence, and motivation. These intangibles are sometimes called *intervening variables*. An example will clarify this latter term.

A psychologist may decide to do a maze learning experiment wherein he will attempt to motivate his rats by depriving them of food for 24 hours. After 24 hours food deprivation the behavior of the rats is altered. They are now highly active and will race through the maze to get to food. Their food-seeking behavior has been observed and has been found to follow the removal of their normal food supply. Hunger as an intervening variable is, therefore, inferred from this situation, and the behavior of the animal is said to be due to hunger motivation. Actually no one could see hunger in rats, but only guess, quite logically, that hunger was the major factor motivating the animals. Hull's (9, p. 21) discussion of intervening variables should be consulted.

In this manner, the psychologist goes about experimenting with these unseen variables and treating them as if they were as obvious as the period at the end of this sentence. How can the psychologist deal with such intangibles? For instance, can he measure intelligence when neither he nor anyone else has ever seen it? The answer is simple. We seldom measure things as such in any of the sciences; we only measure their effects. Thus, is the problem of the physicist in measuring the effects of electricity much different from the problem of the psychologist in measuring the effects of intelligence? No one has ever seen electricity but most of us have noted its effects. Measuring instruments for electricity utilize the heating effect or the magnetic effect of electricity on metals or wire coils. These effects are then measured and the amount and kind of electricity present are inferred from these observations. The psychologist knows that the effects of intelligence are observed through the behavior of the individual. The individual who behaves in a way judged to be more intelligent is taken to be in possession of more of this inferred "thing" intelligence than is someone else who behaves "less intelligently." We can see, therefore, that psychology, while it most often deals with vague and intangible subject matter, can still gather its data and draw its inferences in a method used by the other sciences.

Although you may now believe that psychology is, and should be, recognized as a science and that the problems faced in psychology are also found in other sciences, I must stop you to point out that the latter is not entirely true. In the other sciences, a scientist observes and records the phenomena of nature about him. It is the picture of a human being, or a "mind" if you choose, observing nonmental or material events. But in the case of the psychologist, there is the picture of a human being or mind studying another human being or mind. Thus, the subject matter of psychology is made of the same stuff as the investigator.

Where does this strange situation leave us? The main effect of a human being studying another human being is to introduce the probability for more errors to creep into the investigation. Less errors are probable when a human being studies, for example, a piece of iron. Why? First, the investigator in the latter situation will make some errors because he is human. Regardless of the true size, or weight, or composition of the piece of iron, the observer may never more than approximate a knowledge of its characteristics. He can read a scale just so accurately and no more. Second, the measuring instrument itself contains more or less error in measuring that which it says it measures. These are the main sources of error. But the psychologist observing, measuring, and recording the behavior of a human being makes not only the usual errors of measurement but also makes errors because his subject is changing more rapidly than is the piece of iron. The piece of iron does not get hungry, tired, angry, more pleasant, offended, ill, sleepy, bored, or a thousand other things which the human being may. Each of these factors named has some effect on the individual's behavior and thus introduces more chance for error to enter the observation.

There is a type of error in observation which results from the characteristics of the observer. When one human being observes the behavior of another, the attitudes of the observer in regard to bias, prejudice, projection, etc., may introduce errors into the observation.

Another large source of error in dealing with human beings is made when one neglects to equate them in terms of past experience. Since each individual has had a different series of experiences and since present behavior is altered in light of past and present experiences, the experimentalist in psychology may never make the assumption that two individuals can be as much alike as two pieces of iron. Both iron and human beings have past and present experiences, but because the human is so vastly complicated and is constantly reacting to a multiplicity of changing conditions, all nonliving, unconscious things appear relatively stable.

The psychological researcher who wishes to operate from a scientific approach has chosen a rough row to hoe. He should look at himself as being a scientist, first, and a psychologist, second. Actually, he is a scientist who has simply chosen the behavior of organisms as his topic for research.

BIBLIOGRAPHY

1. Andrews, T. G.: *Methods of Psychology*, John Wiley & Sons, Inc., New York, 1948.
2. Bartley, S. Howard: *Beginning Experimental Psychology*, McGraw-Hill Book Company, Inc., New York, 1950.
3. Black, Max: *Critical Thinking*, 2d ed., Prentice-Hall, Inc., New York, 1952.
4. Bugelski, B. R.: *A First Course in Experimental Psychology*, Henry Holt and Company, Inc., New York, 1951.
5. Chapanis, A., *et al: Applied Experimental Psychology*, John Wiley & Sons, Inc., New York, 1949.
6. Cohen, M. R., and E. Nagel: *An Introduction to Logic and Scientific Method*, Harcourt, Brace and Company, Inc., New York, 1934.
7. Cresswell, J. R.: West Virginia University. Personal communication.
8. Cruze, Wendell W.: *General Psychology for College Students*, Prentice-Hall, Inc., New York, 1951.
9. Hull, C. L.: *Principles of Behavior*, Appleton-Century-Crofts, Inc., New York, 1943.
10. Munn, N. L.: Psychology: *The Fundamentals of Adjustment*, 2d ed., Houghton Mifflin Company, Boston, 1951.
11. Northrop, S. F. C.: *The Logic of the Sciences and the Humanities*, The Macmillan Company, New York, 1947.
12. Ruch, Floyd L.: *Psychology and Life*, 3d ed., Scott, Foresman & Company, Chicago, 1948.
13. Stebbing, L. S.: *A Modern Introduction to Logic*, The Thomas Y. Crowell Company, New York, 1930.
14. Woodworth, R. S.: *Experimental Psychology*, Henry Holt and Company, Inc., New York, 1938.
15. Zilboorg, G., and G. H. Henry: *A History of Medical Psychology*, W. W. Norton & Company, New York, 1941.

CHAPTER 2

CAUSAL SEQUENCES AND THE MEANING OF EXPLANATION

The untrained person is most naïve in his concept of what is meant by cause and effect. He speaks glibly of this being the cause of that. He assumes for the most part, and quite correctly, from a scientific point of view, that all events have a cause. But he is prone to assume that there is only one cause for an event. In addition, he sometimes jumps to conclusions. For example, many a man has been hanged for murder just because he was the only known person present when the victim died, and his accusers assumed that he caused the death. You push a light switch button and when the light goes on you make the assumption that you caused the light to glow. How can one be sure that anything causes any other thing to occur? This is an important question for everyday living, but it becomes the essential, vital question in experimentation.

Drawing Causal Sequences

If one performs an action directed toward altering a situation and a change does take place in the situation, then the layman often assumes that the act of altering is the cause and the alteration of the situation is the effect. But the scientist is only too eager to point out that while you may have given an apparent demonstration of a cause-and-effect sequence, it has not been proved that what was done caused the effect. Science no longer speaks of cause and effect as such; instead, a different concept of cause and effect has arisen and is simply called *invariant relationship*. In the above instance, for example, the most the scientist could say is that there appeared to be a relationship between the act you just performed and the change in the situation. You must be careful in the use of the words *act* and *result*, or *antecedent* and *consequence* for, although they imply nothing, some persons infer cause and effect from the use of these words.

Now suppose you repeat the act again and the same change appears in the situation. Suppose you repeat the act a thousand times and always the same change appears. You would be more and more confident that you had caused the effect to appear. The relationship of the act and the result would appear to be an invariant relationship. Yet you would not

16

have proved without a doubt that your act caused the effect.   For example, suppose you had flicked a light switch on a thousand times and each time the bulb lit.   You might be willing to wager that the light switch you had been flicking turned on the light.   It might be both costly and embarrassing to you if the person with whom you had bet pointed out that he had been secretly turning the light on by means of a concealed switch each time you threw your switch on, and, furthermore, the switch you had been using was not even connected in the light circuit!

If one can be so easily fooled, and we all are fooled in a like manner many times each day in ordinary pursuits, it is obvious that those who would attempt to infer cause-and-effect relationships about complicated psychological processes must be sophisticated in the handling of inferences.   The reader should see Cohen and Nagel (2, p. 245) for a further discussion of invariant relationships.

Principle of Determinism

One who would seek for answers to the problems put forth by the universe must have a certain faith.   He must believe in, or have faith in, two ideas.   First, he must believe that all events have a cause.   Second, he must believe that he is capable of finding these causes.   All scientists performing research believe thus and act accordingly.   A name has been given to the first belief mentioned above.   It is called the *principle of determinism*.   It is possible to believe in the principle of determinism without agreeing with the belief that man can know the causes of events.   However, if one does not also believe that man can find the causes of events, then he cannot call himself a scientist.   When one carries his belief in the principle of determinism into the field of psychology and makes the statement that all psychological events have a cause, he is affirming *psychic determinism*.   Many persons will agree as to the cause of so-called material events but will pull up short when one states that the motives of an individual can be investigated by testing certain hypotheses.   The nonscientific person would rather go to some outside force, nontestable, and attribute the desires of human beings to its influence.   Or he might say desires are caused by something equally vague, such as human nature.

Principle of Multiple Causation

An event may have not one, but a number of causes.   This is the *principle of multiple causation*.   Somehow, we like to simplify things to a ridiculous extreme by constantly asking the question, "What was the one thing that caused this to happen?"   Such a question can never be answered.   A simple example should demonstrate this.   Suppose an automobile slid on the wet pavement, going round a curve, and crashed into a tree, killing the driver. The newspaper account revealed that the driver had left his home immediately following a quarrel with his wife, had stopped at a tavern for a few drinks, and had driven rapidly away in his dilapidated car. What caused the death of the driver? A few possible causes are: emotion, alcohol, speed, poor traction due to wet pavement, faulty brakes, steering, etc., loss of blood, broken neck, deterioration of brain cells due to lack of oxygen, etc.

Take any event that you can think of and now tell without doubt what is the one cause of it. You cannot.

Referring again to the light switch example used previously and supposing the switch had been connected, tell what caused the light to glow? Was it the switch, or the electricity, or heat, or what?

Particularly do we run into difficulty in establishing cause-and-effect relationships when we attempt to deal with problems in the social sciences. When we think of the many causes of such things as divorce, crime, war, prejudice and suicide, to mention only a few, we must indeed be instilled with a faith in finding causes if we would venture into the business of determining relationships in these areas.

In the discussion of multiple causation two important related topics should be mentioned: *necessary* and *sufficient* conditions. Ruby (8, p. 381) defines a necessary condition as "an event or circumstance which must be present in order to get a certain result or effect, but which is not sufficient in itself to 'produce' the result." Suppose an automobile was parked on a steep hill and a child playing within the automobile released the emergency brake. The car coasted down the hill and crashed through a billboard. Did the release of the brake cause the accident? One might say that had the front wheels of the car been turned toward the curb the car would not have moved even if its brakes were released. The fact that the wheels were not turned toward the curb was a necessary condition for the accident to have taken place, but not a sufficient condition in itself for causing the accident. Ruby defines a sufficient condition as "one which can, by itself, produce the result, or effect, but which need not be present for the effect to occur." An example of a sufficient condition would be the following. A child is raised in a home where he is constantly prevented from and scolded for expressing himself. He grows into adulthood and demonstrates the characteristics of a repressed individual. This type of environment during childhood is perhaps a sufficient condition to produce a "repressed" adult, but the characteristics demonstrated by this adult could have been produced by other causes. Thus the sufficient cause might not have been the cause at all. To deal intelligently with cause and effect as relationships necessitates that whatever we say is the cause of an event must not only be a necessary but also a sufficient condition for causing the event. A quick glance through the chapter on causal analysis by Larrabee (5, p. 271) would supplement this discussion.

Bases for the Assumption of Causal Sequence

It should be fairly obvious that the relationship of cause and effect is difficult if not impossible to prove. Several impressions arise when one subjects to close scrutiny that which he usually assumes cause and effect to be.

First, he usually assumes that the cause must precede the effect. However, many times effects appear to precede the causes and thus an important relationship may be missed. If a door starts to open before you push on it, you do not assume you opened the door. Yet you might have caused the door to open if you had unknowingly broken a light beam that interrupted a photoelectric circuit that released a spring that opened the door before you touched the door. In this case the effect would have appeared to have preceded the cause.

Second, one assumes a necessary connection between the cause and the effect. If a light comes on while you are not touching the switch, but merely rubbing your forehead, there is no apparent connection between the act and the light coming on. However, a friend, having seen you rub your forehead, assumed that your eyes were strained, and turned on the light. In that case the necessary connection was present but not apparent enough for you to draw a cause-and-effect relationship. As such, the cause of the event might easily have been overlooked.

Third, it soon becomes apparent under close observation that practically the only condition always present when you make a causal connection is *contiguity*. By this is meant two things occurring in a direct temporal sequence. If the effect occurs directly following your act, and this happens regularly, then you do not hesitate to call it cause and effect, because the occurrence now fits the definition of an invariant relationship.

These three bases for the assumption of a causal sequence are part of Hume's famous doctrine of cause and effect. Boring (1, p. 191) presents a short discussion of Hume's point of view on this topic.

Sometimes the apparent precipitating factor occurs and a delay follows after which the effect occurs. This is referred to as *delayed effects*. An example would be death following the consumption of a poison. We infer a series of physiological causes and effects finally terminating in the effect called death. Because the taking of the poison and the effect called death occurred in a direct, though delayed, sequence, contiguity is assumed, although its strict definition is being strained.

We see, then, that contiguity is the most important condition we have that allows us to make inferences as to causal relationship.   Although we know now how dangerous it is to make such inferences, it is the best we can do, and we must use it in the practical situation.   We can and do in scientific work avoid the terms cause and effect wherever possible and sub-stitute the word relationship instead.   This allows the scientist to avoid the semantic difficulty involved.   When he says relationship, he merely means that two events are related in their quantity and temporal appear-ance, but not necessarily part of a causal sequence.   We shall later show how statistics will allow us to quantify the degree of relationship between two events and to make statements as to what level of confidence we have in the fact that they are related.

Explanation by Labeling

Some scientists in the past who have professed faith in the principle of determinism and thought they were dealing with testable hypotheses were only fooling themselves through a process of word magic.   The meaning of fooling oneself by word magic is the practice of explaining the cause of an event by simply saying it is due to some unknown cause to which one has assigned a name.

The use of the term instinct is an outstanding example of this self-deception.   Before scientists realized their error in the use of such a term, hundreds of causes of human and animal behaviorisms were attributed to the vague term instinct.

During the early 1900's it was a common and accepted practice to explain, particularly, social motives in terms of instincts.   Just how was the word instinct used?   Suppose you, as a student of behavior, asked the question, "What causes a particular phenomenon of behavior, A, to happen?"   Any number of famous social psychologists would have answered, phenomenon A is caused by instinct A.   They would have further said that instincts represent the original force that causes all activity in organisms and that without these instincts no behavior of organisms would take place.   Some of these social psychologists would have said that there are 13 major instincts, some more important than others.   McDougall (6) would have been typical of this group of social psychologists.

But actually, would you know any more about the cause of phenomenon A after someone said it was due to an instinct than you did before?   No. Such explanations are dangerous, for they only cover up our ignorance by giving a name to it.   When such a means of explaining events is carried far enough, one ends up with a knowledge of the causes of events that consists of only words that are in great need of explanation themselves.

If one accepts as a cause of behavior the mere statement that an instinct causes it and goes away satisfied that he now knows the cause, he is indeed to be pitied for he knows nothing more now than he did when he asked the question.

Morgan and Stellar (7, p. 402) point out that "at the present time there is no real need for the term instinct, except as a conventional rubric for referring to certain kinds of complex motivated behavior." They further remind us that "instincts are under the combined control of stimuli in the external world and subtle changes in the internal environment."

Because the word instinct became a dangerous term to use, some psychologists began to substitute the words motive and drive. If the words motive and drive are used to explain behavior in the same manner as was the word instinct, then these words are no better than the word instinct and just as meaningless. However, if the user defines his concept and shows that the behavior is due to certain existing conditions that his word stands for, then he breaks away from the use of the magic of words to explain events. Klineberg (4, p. 56) has written an excellent chapter on instinct theories and could well be consulted at this point.

Such word magic is on its way out in psychology, but psychology must beware, for such bad actors often play return engagements under different stage names.

Explanation by Stating Purpose

There are many laymen and, according to some, too many scientists who believe in what is known as teleology. Teleology is a system for explaining the causes of events in which phenomena are not thought of as being determined exclusively by mechanical causes. In other words, the cause of an event is not defined in terms of precipitating mechanistic principles by teleologists, but rather events are thought to occur because they are directed to the final accomplishment of some unified whole. Thus, the reason an event occurs is because it must occur to fulfill some purpose or to further some superimposed scheme. While it is true that much of the behavior of man can be looked upon as occurring to fulfill some purpose and to enable him to reach some end, many careful scientists will not allow themselves to believe that they are explaining behavior by citing the pattern into which such behavior falls. Those who adopt this type of purposive explanation may, and often have, ended up by stating sweeping laws which they believe to be universal. Actually, they may have led themselves into believing in a nontestable hypothesis as the cause of behavior. A top spinning on the floor might have to spin or else it would fall over. But some scientists feel there are better ways to explain the reason the top is spinning than to attribute the cause to some purpose the top is fulfilling.   If one answers the question, "Why does a chicken cross the road?" by saying, "To get to the other side," he is falling victim to teleological thinking.

Explanation by Familiarization

One group feels that scientific explanation as well as any type of explanation is aimed at only one goal, that is, to make the unfamiliar more familiar.   Thus, if one is attempting to explain the cause of any event, he must do so by beginning with those things already understood by the listener and proceed to the unknown.   By associating the known with the unknown, the unfamiliar becomes familiar.   Anything that is necessary to further the process of making the unfamiliar familiar is a necessary part of an explanation.

Explanation by Stating the Inferential Procedure

Another approach would be to say that whenever one has by some logical procedure of inference, such as the inductive-deductive method, arrived at a truth concerning an event, the scientific explanation of the event would involve not only the thing dealt with but also the logical steps leading to the inference.   Feigl (3) has elaborated on this topic and may be consulted for further information.

Explanation by Description

Some writers believe that there is no actual difference between description and explanation.   They would further state that the only way events are explained at all is through a process of description.   This may be so, for it does seem that science at present is at the descriptive level in its evolution.   The scientist is called upon not only to tell what causes what but how it is accomplished.   He is able to perform best when *describing* the events of nature.

To define an event in terms of an operation or a set of operations is perhaps the best description that can be given at the present time.   If you are asked what effect morphine has on the human being, it might be that the best answer you could give would be to describe the changes that take place following the administration of the opiate.   You could record what took place by describing not only your part in the process but also what happened to the subject.   You might even advance your idea as to how the changes in the subject's physiological condition came about.   But at the present time you could not go much further.   You would probably have made many errors in just telling what happened and how it happened.   Your description as to what happened would be no more valid or reliable than your most inaccurate and inconsistent tool of observation.

Your theory as to how the effects came about would be based upon the *correct* and the *incorrect* observations of what effects occurred.   In composing a theory of how the effects came about, you would be faced with the choice of a frame of reference from which you would draw your terminology.   Would you choose to tell how the physiological effects occurred, the psychological effects, or draw upon some other frame of reference?   If you chose only one point of view, you would not be revealing the entirety of the situation.   It would be improbable that you could cover all of the facts pertaining to what occurred and even less probable that you would be able to tell how each and every effect came about since you would not have complete knowledge of all the factors present.

The best possible definition of a phenomenon would contain a description of all the relevant factors and their relationship to the phenomenon. However, seldom is this high level of explanation required.   Instead, explanation starts with description of data and increases through a hierarchy of description until there is enough information revealed to account for the occurrence of the phenomenon to be explained.   The following example may help in the understanding of this hierarchy of explanation.

You may think that some of your professors have completely explained a phenomenon for you, but it is probable that their explanations were far from complete.   When faced with a question concerning the cause of a phenomenon, you attempt to relate to the questioner the events that immediately preceded the occurrence of the phenomenon and are apparently invariably related to the occurrence of the phenomenon.   But the questioner might be insistent and push you farther with the question, "Yes, but why did the preceding events occur?"   You then, in an attempt to further answer his question, relate the events that led up to the events that precipitated the event that became the subject of the question.   You could go on this way *ad infinitum* and never find out just why the event in question occurred.   However, in most explanations, it is seldom necessary to go much beyond a simple account of the facts that describe the setting in which the phenomenon occurred.   If one wishes to go to higher levels of explanation then, according to Feigl (3), he may rise through the level of empirical laws where functional relationships are stated, or on to first-order theories where sets of assumptions using higher-order constructs as the result of abstraction and inference are involved, or on to second-order theories where still higher constructs are used.

BIBLIOGRAPHY

1. Boring, E. G.: *A History of Experimental Psychology*, 2d ed., Appleton-Century-Crofts, Inc., New York, 1950.

2. Cohen, M. R., and E. Nagel: *An Introduction to Logic and Scientific Method*, Harcourt, Brace & Company, Inc., New York, 1934.
3. Feigl, Herbert: Symposium on Operationism, *Psychol. Rev.*, Vol. 52, No. 5, September, 1945.
4. Klineberg, Otto.: *Social Psychology*, Henry Holt and Company, Inc., New York, 1940.
5. Larrabee, Harold A.: *Reliable Knowledge*, Houghton Mifflin Company, Boston, 1945.
6. McDougall, W.: *Introduction to Social Psychology*, 1st ed., 1908.
7. Morgan, C. T., and E. Stellar: *Physiological Psychology*, 2d ed., McGraw-Hill Book Company, Inc., New York, 1950.
8. Ruby, Lionel: *Logic: An Introduction*, J. B. Lippincott Company, Philadelphia, 1950.

CHAPTER 3

ARMCHAIR EXPERIMENTATION

This chapter represents an attempt to defend the procedure of scientific experimentation against the practice of "armchair experimentation." By scientific experimentation is meant the actual work involved in directly dealing with the things about which one hypothesizes. Armchair experimentation refers to the habit of substituting reasoning alone for scientific experimentation in seeking the solution of a problem. It may seem that one is trying to knock down a "straw man" by arguing against armchair methods, but the beginning experimenter should know the reasons why he must "dirty his hands" to arrive at solutions to problems rather than by relying on his "gluteal omniscience" for solutions.

Armchair experimentation has been indulged in most heavily by philosophers whose knowledge of deduction has at times been outstanding. However, it is maintained here that deductive procedures without reference, for validation purposes, to the event under discussion is logic without logic.

Northrop (6, p. 19) points out that the philosopher makes no error when dealing with problems that merely involve deductions from true premises such as found in mathematics. For here the basic premises have been verified and preclude further verification. But the damage is done when the philosopher assumes certain premises to be true when they are not and then begins to build his card house on such false premises. There have been times when it would have been easy to check the basic premises but the philosopher either did not know how or did not want to take the time to verify his premises and deductions. It is to this laxity in some philosophers that the scientist objects.

The reasons armchair experimentation is dangerous are these. As indicated above, all deductive procedures begin with the acceptance of, usually, two premises as being true. If these two premises are true, then deductions can be made and eventually validated. However, if only reasoning is used minus the personal contact of the reasoner with the material being reasoned about, then error may enter the process. Error may enter in at least three ways: (a) the reasoner assumes propositions or premises which may or may not hold with the facts of the case, (b) the deductive process consists of thinking as the medium of the manipulation of symbols and as such is susceptible to all the errors involved in thinking and in using symbols, and (c) the final answer or deduction cannot be validated until an appeal is made to the facts to see whether the deduction holds.   Let us discuss these possible sources of error in some detail.

A person who decides to reason his way through to the solution of a problem must have several things at hand.   First, he must have a problem that is capable of being answered.   Second, he must have complete assurance that the information he will use as his basic premises is true in the particular context in which it is used.   But can he assume such things unless he or someone else actually checks the basic assumptions in regard to their truthfulness?   Certainly not.

Instead of appealing to facts, the reasoner often appeals to other quarters.   He may use one or more of three diverse and unprofitable methods which, while they are recognized by scientists as merely stumbling blocks on the road to knowledge, do plague all who attempt to arrive at facts.

Method of Authority

This method involves the statement that something is true because someone says it is true.   The someone who says it is true is usually some well-known authority in his field and should know what is true.   However, this appeal to authority only assumes but does not ensure that the authority has sufficient evidence to make the statement that something is true.   The average person depends on the authorities for much of his knowledge.   Thus if the authority is in error, so are those who cite him as an authority.   The great thinkers of the past have often chosen to be blind to fact and to follow some authority instead.   Aristotle and Galen were considered to be irreproachable authorities for hundreds of years after their deaths.   All that they had said was taken to be the absolute truth even when undeniable evidence was discovered that contradicted their views.   In attempting to find fact, the method of authority must not be used blindly as a means of deciding the validity of suggested premises.   The evidence back of the authority's statement must be *known* and *accepted* or the authority's statement should not be accepted at all.

Method of Tenacity

This means believing something is true simply because one has always believed it.   This method affects orderly thought because (a) continued belief in something does not make it true and (b) belief in one proposition for a long time may make one oblivious to any contradictory evidence. Anyone who would attempt to reason through to the solutions of problems would have to be free from the influence of this method or he would always be susceptible to the errors cited.

Method of Intuition

This method deals with the tendency of some thinkers to make statements which they feel to be true propositions simply because the statements are "self-evident." They feel that anyone who understands the proposition put forth must agree because the proposition is "undeniably and obviously true." At one time it was thought self-evident that man would never fly to the moon. It is considerably less self-evident today. Intuitions, therefore, are not necessarily true but must be tested as any hypotheses. To allow these self-evident truths to serve as basic premises in a deductive procedure is to court error. Northrop (6), Cohen and Nagel (2), and Ruby (7) give additional information relating to these practices.

Pseudo Science

The assumption of certain propositions as true when it is possible to appeal to the facts is the unexcusable error made by armchair experimentation. As an example of pseudo science built upon false premises, let us look for a moment at phrenology and how it managed to thrive for a hundred years.

Gall (1758–1828) was an anatomist of some note. However, he allowed his early observations concerning bumps on the skull as related to mental characteristics in human beings to overcome any objectivity he might have possessed as a scientist. He based his thinking on three *untrue* premises. First, he assumed that the mind of an individual is not unitary but is broken up into a number of faculties, each possessing or controlling a particular function as demonstrated by the individual. Second, he assumed that the brain had various enlargements that influenced the conformation of the skull over the location of the enlargement. Third, he believed that the greater the possession of a trait, the greater the enlargement of the brain at the place where the particular trait was localized. Thus the logical conclusion would be that one could by studying the distribution and relative size of the protuberances on a person's head make a valid assessment of his mental traits. But we now know that the mind does not consist of units, nor does the outer surface of the skull conform to the shape of the outer surface of the brain, nor do particular faculties of the mind reside in different localized areas such that an enlargement of an area is correlated with a greater possession of a given trait. Had Gall, by actual experimentation, utilized the process of scientific investigation, he would have found no real basis for phrenology.

Boring (1, p. 50) points out, after a similar discussion of phrenology, that today we would have been able to reject phrenology by the use of correlation techniques. Although the mathematics of correlation were not available to Gall, Boring indicates that physiologists at that time could have made personal observations and checks and safeguards but that such rigors depended upon the investigator rather than the sanctions of science. Thus observation plus verification before generalization could have taken Gall out of the armchair class of experimentation and into that of scientific experimentation. It is interesting to note that had Gall been more rigorous, there would have been no pseudo science of phrenology, and, consequently, Gall would probably not have been remembered.

Laws of Thought

When one reasons, one thinks. The action of the thought processes involved may be described by several laws. Philosophers have for a long time denoted certain fundamental principles in reasoning and called them the *laws of thought*. Many philosophers in the past have held these laws to be logic itself and central to sound thinking. Whatever exceptions we can find to these laws we can offer as evidence against their use in the solution of problems by reasoning. If we can throw doubt on the validity of such "mental gymnastics" then we strengthen the position of experimental laboratory science as being a better approach to the discovery of facts. Let us take a look at these laws of thought.

The Principle of Identity. If something is X it is X. This means a cow is a cow. You may agree, but wait! The main objection to this principle is not in its statement but in its frequent misapplication. You, as X, for instance, may be well today but ill tomorrow. Thus, X today is not X tomorrow. A cow at this instant is not the same cow it was an hour ago, for not only has the cow changed physiologically during that time, your attitude toward it has also changed. This is the position taken by Korzybski (4) and Hayakawa (3) and some of the other members of a school of thought called general semantics. They would agree that since reasoning involves the assumption that there is a certain permanence of things, then the fact that all things are undergoing change at a faster or slower rate dilutes the validity of reasoning.

However, those who believe in the law of identity, and contrary to the general semanticists' attitude, point out that it is possible to communicate by words only because there is a certain identity in our meanings. Also they believe that even if there is a change, it must be in relation to something that is constant, and this constancy is the meaning with which we deal. They would say, then, that the symbols used in reasoning are valid building blocks.

In order to make use of this law of thought properly, one must always give a time and place reference. An objection to this law then would be that too often such specific designations are omitted through a lack of knowledge, or carelessness, and thus may throw error into an otherwise logical progression of thought. If one reports that it is a clear day, he must be specific, for it may be raining only a hundred miles away. If one were to say it is a clear day in the city of Pittsburgh (unhappy choice) on April 1, 1952, at 12 noon, he would be specifying the time and place in such a way as would make his statement true for all time and place. In describing happenings, stating laws, or in any type of communication or reasoning, it becomes essential that a complete statement involving context is given so that the law of identity may apply.

The Principle of Contradiction. A thing cannot be both X and not X. For example, a man cannot be both tall and short at the same time. Those who object to this principle would do so by pointing out in the above example that a 5-foot man would be short in some tribes in Africa where the average height of males is considerably more, but the same 5-foot man would be considered tall by a band of pygmies. In a like manner, a certain table seen from directly above appears square (X) but when seen from one side appears rectangular (not X).

The objection to this law of thought is removed if the user again supplies a frame of reference involving time and place reference. Thus, the 5-foot man in a tribe where the average height is $5\frac{1}{2}$ feet will always be considered short as long as he remains in that particular frame of reference. The only remaining objection is whether in a complicated problem composed of many variables, it is probable that all such designations could be handled accurately.

The Principle of Excluded Middle. Anything must be either X or not X. For example, this is either a book or not a book.

To many persons, this is the most objectionable of the three principles. These critics would say that nowhere in nature do you find that things are either one way or another with a gap in between. One simply finds no dichotomies or mutually exclusive classes in nature. There is always the area of overlap. You may think that black and white are completely different, but you cannot find that nature has drawn a line between black and white. Instead of a point of demarcation, one finds a shading of black into white through the middle area of gray. How can you draw a line separating the two? You may think coal is black, but it becomes gray by comparison when held against a piece of black velvet. For the thinker arbitrarily to put the continuous order of nature into pigeonholes by excluding the middle is to cast aside much of his contact with things as they really exist. Many of the great problems argued in philosophy have come about only because of the acceptance of this law of thought. Instead of a two-valued orientation consisting of either-or they would suggest a multivalued orientation.

Ruby (7, p. 258) points out that the error made by some in criticising this principle is based upon the confusion between contrariety and contradiction. The law says that a book is either red or not red, it does not say that it is either red or reddish brown.

These laws are tools we all must use in our thinking. However, fewer errors will be made in their application if certain precautions are taken: (a) always designate time and place reference, and (b) remember that man has in many cases imposed artificial categories on nature and as such has introduced an error in drawing lines where they do not actually exist. For a more complete treatment of the laws of thought, the reader should consult Ruby (7) and Cohen and Nagel (2).

Errors in Using Symbols

The most common source of error is made when the thinker assigns symbols to the elements of the problem with which he is dealing. Thus he begins to use, perhaps, the letters A, B, and C as designations for the variables or factors. These letters are now used by him in his thinking as though each is defined by the characteristics of the factor for which it stands. But this cannot be true, for he does not know all about the characteristics of A, or B, or C. If he did, it would not be necessary for him to go through his reasoning process, for there would be no problem. Thus if he continues to use the symbols in the absence of the things for which they stand and continues to build inference after inference on such a structure, he may, and most often does, get farther from reality and finds in the end that he has been dealing only with words and not things. If he would, at each step in his thinking, check his logical result by referring to the real situation again, then he might safely proceed. He would find that symbols are more static than the things they represent and that due to the stability of symbols and the variability of the things for which they stand, his result from reasoning might differ grossly from his results by experimentation.

An example might help here. I once saw a man design a circuit for a radio. He carefully calculated the exact value each condenser, resistor, and other parts should have. On paper, it was perfect. But when he constructed the radio from the diagram, the radio refused to play. The reason it would not function was that he had assumed the parts corresponded exactly to the symbols used in the diagram. Yet the radio parts were not perfect and only approximated the characteristics they were supposed to have. The combined errors of all these small differences added up to an error so large that the radio needed much adjustment before it finally operated efficiently.

Any word may have many meanings, one of which may be applicable to the particular thing for which it stands at a precise moment. But the thing denoted is constantly changing in its relationship to other things and thus may require a different word if we are to keep track of it a moment later. Treating words, then, as accurate substitutes for things is dangerous to sound thinking if one does not constantly keep in touch with the reality of the situation. The point is this, a symbol is only analogous to the thing for which it stands. For a more complete discussion of semantics, see Larrabee (5).

If one wishes to deal with facts, he must restrict himself to dealing with whatever experiences he may have as the result of observing facts directly. If he attempts to communicate these experiences to others, neither he nor they are dealing with facts—they are now dealing with *described* facts. And description, as has been pointed out, is full of error.

We see, therefore, the dangers involved in attempting to solve problems by the use of symbols rather than directly dealing with the elements of the problem. Real advances were never made in science until man left his armchair and entered the laboratory. Going into the laboratory does not mean the scientist leaves logic and reason behind. Scientific methods are based on logic. The reader should have the impression that logical progression of thought concerning a problem is useful only in that it may lead to testable hypotheses which can be accepted or rejected in light of experimental data. This is the safest way to build a sound science.

BIBLIOGRAPHY

1. Boring, E. G.: *A History of Experimental Psychology*, 2d ed., Appleton-Century-Crofts, Inc., New York, 1950.
2. Cohen, M. R., and E. Nagel: *An Introduction to Logic and Scientific Method*, Harcourt, Brace & Company, Inc., 1934.
3. Hayakawa, S. I.: *Language in Action*, Harcourt, Brace & Company, Inc., New York, 1941.
4. Korzybski, Alfred: *Science and Sanity*, 2d ed., The Institute of General Semantics, Lakeville, Conn., 1941.
5. Larrabee, H. A.: *Reliable Knowledge*, Houghton Mifflin Company, Boston, 1945.
6. Northrop, F. S. C.: *The Logic of the Sciences and the Humanities*, The Macmillan Company, New York, 1947.
7. Ruby, Lionel: *Logic: An Introduction*, J. B. Lippincott Company, Philadelphia, 1950.

CHAPTER 4

LOCATING AND SIMPLIFYING PROBLEMS

Every individual is constantly faced with problems. Most of his problems are at a simple object level and involve no more than the manipulation of certain things in his environment to produce desired results. An individual is faced with a problem if in attempting to put on his coat his wrist watch catches in the lining of the sleeve. The problem is how to disengage the watch from the cloth of the coat. This is a very simple example, but it is of the class of problems everyone encounters constantly. More serious problems exist in everyday life when we find that we are running out of money and yet must pay certain bills that add up to more than our bank account. A more demanding problem and one bringing in more psychological involvement is the problem of how to get and stay married and yet continue with our education.

In each of these examples, from the simple object type to the type involving psychological concomitants, there is one common factor, namely, a problem is a question proposed for solution. Generally speaking, a problem exists when there is no available answer to some question.

Finding a Problem

Where are problems found that are worthy of investigation by experimentation? Sometimes problems in psychology are given to the experimenter by someone else, as when the laboratory instructor informs the class that the problem for today's experiment will be this or that. The student is relieved of the burden of finding a problem in this situation. The instructor is, too, for the most part, because he will probably suggest a problem that has already been formulated back in the history of psychology, already has been answered, and is nearly worn out by being used before in countless thousands of such laboratory situations. In this situation, the student may never have the experience of discovering for himself a question in psychology that would serve as a problem.

As the student progresses under such a setup, he may find that even while hemmed in by the limits of traditional problems and prefabricated experiments he may run into an honest-to-goodness problem. It might happen in this manner. During the performance of a typical laboratory maze learning experiment using the class as subjects, the student might suddenly think, what would the results of this experiment be if rats were used instead of human beings?   What if in doing the experiment using rats as subjects, I discovered a difference in results?   To what could I attribute the difference?   These questions in the student's mind have, besides demonstrating that the student is thinking about his experiment, caused the formation of the basis for a new problem in psychological research.   The student has perhaps for the first time in his life formulated a problem in the area of psychological experimentation.

The instructor, when asked about the plausibility of such an experiment, might say, "Oh, that has been done, and it has been found that sometimes rats can solve mazes better than college sophomores."   The student is not encouraged.

But suppose the instructor says instead, "Why don't you design an experiment to investigate this problem and I'll see if we can put it to a test."   Let us suppose the student does design the experiment, conducts the experiment, and finds a large difference between his rats and human beings as to maze learning ability, the difference being in favor of the rats.   The student may then ask what caused this.   In attempting to answer this problem, he is certain to create many other problems.   For instance, is the rat superior to the human being only when adult rats are used, only when extreme motivation of the rat is used, only when visual cues are excluded, etc.?

The student in the above example can now tell you where problems for research originate and how to recognize them.   He now knows that he can recognize problems in any area only when he is thoroughly acquainted with that area.   He will further tell you that the quickest way to be acutely aware of problems existing in a given area of science is to become familiar with the area to the point where it is possible to see the information that is needed to progress further and that it is totally or partially lacking.

Problems in the science of psychology range over a vast amount of human knowledge.   It might be said that any problem in any of the sciences involves a problem in psychology.   Is it not true that if any scientist is making an observation, his own psychology enters into his perception?   All phenomena appeal only to the experience of the observer. These "sense data" are then molded into whatever shape the psychology of the observer dictates.   This puts the psychologist right in the middle of all science, or anywhere sense data are collected.

See Northrop (4), Benjamin (2), and Cohen and Nagel (3) for discussions related to the location of problems.

But more specifically, just what are typical and legitimate areas for psychological investigation and just what are the problems dealt with within these areas?   The easiest place to look for such information would be the tables of contents of the *Psychological Abstracts*, or the tables of contents of experimental psychology texts by such authors or editors as Andrews (1), Stevens (5), and Woodworth (6).   By analyzing the contents of these sources, one would find psychology to be arbitrarily divided into 14 major divisions.   The following outline of such an analysis will aid the student in categorizing and defining the problem areas of psychology.

Animal behavior
Childhood and adolescence
Electrical activity
Experimental esthetics
General (test construction, statistics, theory, systems, new methodology, apparatus, other)
Intelligence and other aptitudes
Learning
Maturity and old age
Personality (including diagnosis and treatment)
Personnel selection and placement
Reading, work habits, and study skills
Receptive processes (example—vision)
Response processes (example—feelings)
Social interaction

As can be seen, the psychological researcher has considerable latitude in the choice of a problem for research.

It is not enough, however, just to discover problems and proceed to attempt to answer them by experimentation.   Most of the problems that the beginner thinks he has formulated himself for the first time in history have already been not only formulated previously but perhaps exhaustively studied in the laboratories of the science and acceptably answered. Knowing the field of psychology also means knowing its history.   By history is meant not only the names and dates of the happenings of psychology, but also the results of experimentation by past researchers on the problems that have faced psychologists.

The first step in evaluating a problem, therefore, is to seek information concerning the history of your problem.   Go to standard text and reference books that discuss the area in which your problem rests.   Often their bibliographies will direct you to more pertinent information to be found in the journals.

The more accessible journals of psychology and related sciences are listed below for the purpose of giving the student a quick glance at the scope of the journal literature of his and related fields. The asterisks preceding certain titles indicate those journals most often used as references by the author.

American Journal of Physiology
*American Journal of Psychology
*American Journal of Psychotherapy
*American Psychologist
*Archives of Psychology
Brain
Child Development
Child Development and Bibliography
Child Development Monographs
Child Study
Child Welfare
*Comparative Psychology Monographs
Crippled Child
Diseases of the Nervous System
Endocrinology
*Genetic Psychology Monographs
Genetics
*Group Psychotherapy
Hereditas Genetiskt Arkiv
Heredity
Human Relations
Industrial Arts and Vocational Education
Institute of International Education Bulletin
International Index to Periodicals
International Journal of Opinion and Attitude Research
Journal Lancet
*Journal of Abnormal and Social Psychology
Journal of Adult Education
Journal of Aesthetics and Art Criticism
Journal of Animal Behavior
Journal of Animal Science
Journal of Applied Anthropology
Journal of Applied Physiology
*Journal of Applied Psychology
Journal of Aviation Medicine
Journal of Clinical Endocrinology

Journal of Clinical Investigation
*Journal of Clinical Psychology
*Journal of Clinical Psychopathology and Psychotherapy
*Journal of Comparative and Physiological Psychology
*Journal of Consulting Psychology
Journal of Criminal Science
Journal of Cutaneous Diseases Including Syphilis
Journal of Ecology
Journal of Education
Journal of Educational Psychology
Journal of Educational Research
Journal of Educational Sociology
Journal of Experimental Biology
Journal of Exceptional Children
Journal of Experimental Education
Journal of Experimental Medicine
Journal of Experimental Psychology
Journal of Experimental Zoology
Journal of General Education
Journal of General Physiology
*Journal of General Psychology
*Journal of Genetic Psychology
Journal of Genetics
Journal of Heredity
Journal of Higher Education
Journal of Juvenile Research
Journal of Laboratory and Clinical Medicine
Journal of Medical Research
Journal of Neurophysiology
Journal of Nervous and Mental Diseases
Journal of Organotherapy
Journal of Parapsychology
Journal of Pediatrics
*Journal of Personality
Journal of Personnel Research

Journal of Philosophical Studies
Journal of Philosophy
Journal of Physiology
Journal of Psychiatric Social Work
*Journal of Psychology
Journal of Social Casework
*Journal of Social Psychology
Journal of Speech and Hearing Disorders
Menninger Clinic, Bulletin
Mental Hygiene
Mind
Mind and Body
National Society for the Study of Education, Yearbook
Occupational Index
Occupational Medicine
Occupations
Pedagogical Seminary and Journal of Genetic Psychology
Pediatrics
Personnel

Personnel Journal
Personnel Psychology
Philosophy of Science
Prison Journal
Progressive Education
Psychiatry
Psychoanalysis and the Social Sciences
Psychoanalytic Quarterly
Psychoanalytic Review
*Psychological Abstracts
*Psychological Bulletin
Psychological Clinic; A Journal of Orthogenics
*Psychological Monographs: General and Applied
*Psychological Review
Psychosomatic Medicine
Public Opinion
Social Science Abstracts
Sociology and Social Research
Sociometry

Most university libraries subscribe to most of these journals. Journals desired by a student, but not available in his university's library, may be secured through the interlibrary loan service.

Occasionally, reference is made in bibliographies to unpublished theses. These, too, may be secured, through the interlibrary loan service, by having your university's librarian request the theses from the universities where they were submitted. Several copies of all theses, published or not, should be on file at the institution where the research was completed and accepted.

Every good researcher recognizes the library as being a close friend. He should know his local library thoroughly. He should know where in the stacks the literature relevant to his field is shelved, the procedure for securing journals, theses, and books through interlibrary loan, limitations and privileges in reference to photostating and microfilming facilities, film service, etc.

The *Psychological Abstracts* and, for experiments published before 1927, the *Psychological Index* will aid a student in quickly evaluating an article before going to the trouble of seeking out the journal containing the article in its original, complete form. Those journal articles most relevant to research should be sought out and read and discussed with someone else interested in the same problem. Two heads are certainly better than one in this case. What a student misses and confuses, a coresearcher or other interested party may know, and vice versa.

If a student reads a relevant article in a journal and would like to have a copy of the article, not the journal, he may write to the author and request a reprint of the article. In case of coauthorship, he should write the first-named author. The following information should be included in the request: name of authors, name of article, the name, volume, date, number, and pages of the journal. The author will send the offprints free of charge as a matter of professional courtesy. The success of this procedure for securing offprints depends on how current the literature is and whether the author has any reprints left.

Manipulate the information given by the articles as much as possible by turning it over and over in your mind and verbalizing it in all possible lights. If you, yourself, write abstracts of the articles on filing cards, a valuable collection of information is soon gathered in one place. Such a historical survey is not only an efficient means of arriving at a clear-cut problem truly existing but it is indispensable to a sound foundation for the proposed research. A convenient form for abstracting articles is shown below. The headings may be typed or mimeographed on 8- by 10-inch filing cards.

Form for Abstracting Journal Articles

Reference: _____ _____

       Authors' Names   Abstractor

_____ _____

                               Date

_____

       Title of Article

_____ _____ _____ _____

   Name of Journal   Date   Volume   Pages

Problem:

Subjects:

Procedure:

Results and Conclusions:

In the preceding chapters, an attempt has been made to arm the beginning researcher with those concepts of thinking necessary to evaluate the way in which facts can be gathered. If the presentation is correct to this point, then we see that the end product of thinking about a problem and attempting to arrive at its answer rests in the act of performing and evaluating an experiment aimed at testing certain suggested answers to the problem. This procedure is the experimental method, only one of the scientific methods. Later on in this book the method of *naturalistic observation* and the *statistical method* will be briefly discussed.

Analysis of the Problem

The application of the experimental method starts at the point where any inquiry starts, that is, with the problem itself. It is only through a process of analyzing the problem with which he is faced that the researcher may choose the method with which he will deal with the problem. There are many who believe that the experimental method is the only method safe to use in the search for fact. However, Northrop (4, p. 20) points out that the problem decides the method. Often only the methods of formal logic are needed, as in mathematical deductions. Sometimes a problem such as might be found in the field of ethics is of such a nature as to demand a new method. The experimental method might not suffice, for some questions in ethics are not answerable by the search for empirical truth. For example, the experimental method does not necessarily apply when one seeks the answer to "ought" questions. New methods must be devised to discover what ought to happen, as in the case of "What ought the world do about the atomic bomb?" On the other hand, the experimental method applies when one wishes to answer the question, "What is happening?" Since such a distinction exists there are many who would exclude the word ought from the scientist's vocabulary, and say that "what is the case" is a better substitute. Thus these researchers would limit the area of scientific research to those problems wherein the experimental methods (or the empirical methods of observation and experiment) are applicable.

The analysis of the problem takes, or at least it should take, as much time as all the rest of the thinking concerning the research project. The problem is the first link in the chain of thoughts necessary for the successful planning of an experiment. After the precise problem has been decided upon, the other steps of the experimental method should follow in a standard order. Below is an outline of the steps the researcher goes through in his thinking and acting as he develops a design for his research.

Steps in Developing a Research Design

1. What is my problem?
2. What is my hypothesis?
3. What is my independent variable(s)? (Defined in Chap. 6)
4. What is my dependent variable(s)? (Defined in Chap. 6)
5. How is the dependent variable to be measured?

6. What controls are necessary?
7. What procedure will be followed in conducting the experiment?
   a. What apparatus will I need?
   b. How, exactly, and in what sequence, do I plan to conduct the actual experiment?
   c. How will I analyze the results?
8. Will I be able to use the results of this experiment to prove or disprove my hypothesis?   Have I made any mistakes?

These eight steps are commonly called the *research design,* and are completely thought through before the experimenter steps into his laboratory for the purpose of conducting his experiment.   Each of these steps is discussed at some length later on in this book.   Several of the steps will serve as the subject matter for separate chapters.   Let us now return to the first step, the problem and its analysis.

After the history of the general problem has been completely learned, you are ready to make the problem more specific.   History may have given you information in regard to the best type of apparatus to use, the best type and number of subjects, the least involved method of approach, variables relevant to the problem which may have to be included or excluded, the most efficient statistical tools, the least expensive procedure, the length of time estimated for the collection of data, common mistakes easy to make, correct interpretations of this type of data, criticisms of others' experiment in that area, and much more.   All this information, cheaply gathered, allows you to select the precise statement of the problem you had only stated generally before.   Little by little the problem should have reduced itself to a more meaningful question.

Take this example of the evolution of a problem from a general form to a clear, objective, concise question: a teacher of psychology in college noticed that certain students appeared less at ease than others, and yet the most stable were often only average in learning new things.   The psychologist thought of this question:

1. Could it be that average learners are less nervous because they are average?

Then he thought to himself, "By average learners, I really mean those having average intelligence."   This yielded the following question:

2. Are students with average intelligence less nervous than others? "But by nervous," he said to himself, "I mean that they have certain signs of abnormal or unusual psychological behavior."

3. Do students possessing average intelligence have fewer symptoms of abnormal behavior than those having very high or very low intelligence?

"But with which intelligence group am I going to compare those having normal intelligence?   Suppose I take just those students who have I.Q.'s between 90 and 110 and compare them, with respect to symptoms of abnormality, to students having I.Q.'s above 120.   I'll do another study later in which I will compare the amount of unfavorable psychological symptoms present in a group having I.Q.'s below 90 to a group of individuals having I.Q.'s between 90 and 110."

4. Will students having I.Q.'s between 80 and 110 have fewer signs of unfavorable psychological symptoms than students having I.Q.'s above 120?

"Of course," says the psychologist, "you can't use any old test for I.Q. and get reliable results, so I had better phrase my question again. Also I had better include the name of the test I am going to use to measure unfavorable psychological signs."

5. Will students having total I.Q. scores on the Wechsler Bellevue Adult Intelligence Scale within the range of 90–110 have lower percentile scores on the Minnesota Multiphasic Personality Inventory than students having total I.Q. scores in excess of 120?

And in final form:

6. Will college students at State University who have total I.Q. scores on the Wechsler-Bellevue Adult Intelligence Scale within the range 90–110 have lower percentile ranks on the subscores of the Minnesota Multiphasic Personality Inventory than a like group of students having total I.Q. scores in excess of 120?

In a similar manner most problems can be reduced to a specific measureable form.   As can be seen, considerable information was provided by the psychologist in the reduction of his observation to the form of a question.   With sufficient practice, the experimenter can quickly go from an observation that a problem exists to a statement containing the important elements of the situation.

In the above example, the original ideas concerning the problem changed from a vague impression that a problem existed to a complete statement of the problem in terms of a set of operations.   This is the correct procedure for the initial stage of inquiry, i.e., the problem.   However, it is sometimes necessary to go past the surface problem and on to a basic problem or problems whose answer would unequivocally answer the existing problem by testing the assumptions which gave rise to it.   Sometimes through such an analytic approach to a problem, it is found that an experiment is eventually performed not on the problem that first occurred but upon a basic problem obvious only after the phenomenon has been reduced to its simplest form by the process of analysis (4, p. 23).

A mother, with severe tooth decay, once made the remark to the author, "If a woman wants to have good teeth, she should not have children."

Put in problem form this statement becomes: Is the bearing of children significantly related to the incidence of tooth decay in women? If an experiment were performed, it is probable that, on the basis of the data collected, the answer would be yes. However, the problem is analyzed further, it is discovered that it is not the bearing of children that is probably related to the incidence of tooth decay but the amount of calcium present in the mother's body. The assumption back of the woman's question really dealt with calcium deficiency and not childbirth. Therefore the writer asked the woman, "Did you supplement your diet during pregnancy by adding calcium?" She replied in the negative, and admitted she had made a doubtful statement.

Thus both childbirth and calcium deficiency are related to the incidence of tooth decay in mothers, but under analysis we discover that tooth decay is more probable in calcium-deficient mothers than in calcium-sufficient mothers during pregnancy. We then decide that the problem deals with calcium deficiency and not childbirth. Our analysis of the problematic situation has led us nearer the truth.

In the earlier discussion concerning phrenology, it was noted that two different levels of experiment could have been performed. The first, to answer the problem, "Can the protuberances on the skull be used as a valid means of diagnosing personality?" This problem could be answered by a simple correlational study. The second, to answer the problem, "What is the reason or reasons phrenology is not valid as a means of diagnosing personality?" This problem could be answered by putting to a test the basic assumptions upon which phrenology was built. Once these assumptions are invalidated, it has not shown that phrenology does not work, but only that if phrenology does work, it must depend upon other assumptions for its support. The reason it works or does not work would never be found by observing the practice of phrenology and gathering data on its validity. Only additional proof that it works or does not work would be found. Later on it will be shown that problems may exist at two levels: (a) factorially, or the "what happens" type, and (b) functionally, or the "how it happens" type. The functional-type experiment is the one that offers explanations for phenomena, but this type can only be performed after the problem has been analyzed to the point where its basic assumptions can be tested.

Many, if not most, of the great discoveries of science came about through accidents. Of course, the word *accident* is hardly applicable here, for it was no accident that the experimenter was in his laboratory working in a particular area and observing when the phenomenon occurred. But what is meant by this is that the experimenter was not investigating a particular problem or seeking a particular result when it occurred. Often such happenings are overlooked by all but the genius. However, a rule that will allow the experimenter to capitalize on such an accident is: To observe, record, and investigate all unusual, unplanned, and nonconforming happenings in the laboratory. It may be that the happening that was unplanned and as yet unexplained is a signpost pointing toward a new discovery. The conditioned reflex was discovered in just this manner.

Because of the scope of psychology, the experimentalist of today finds he is unable to keep abreast of all that is going on. Therefore, either he is satisfied with only a shallow knowledge of all areas of research or he faces the only alternative—specialization. Good researchers usually have made the second choice.

In certain areas, the researcher finds that from necessity he is forced to make use of the lower animals as subjects. Not only are the lower animals, the rat for instance, more available as subjects but they can be used in ways human beings cannot be used. But mainly the use of lower animals is desired because they behave in a more simplified manner than the human being. Basic processes can be studied in the lower animals without the distracting influence of a culture entering into the experiment. Thus it is seen that the problem may be simplified if it is sought where it exists in its simplest form.

BIBLIOGRAPHY

1. Andrews, T. G. (ed.): *Methods of Psychology*, John Wiley & Sons, Inc., New York, 1948.
2. Benjamin, A. C.: *An Introduction to the Philosophy of Science*, The Macmillan Company, New York, 1937.
3. Cohen, M. R., and E. Nagel: *An Introduction to Logic and Scientific Method*, Harcourt, Brace and Company, Inc., New York, 1934.
4. Northrop, F. S. C.: *The Logic of the Sciences and the Humanities*, The Macmillan Company, New York, 1947.
5. Stevens, S. S. (ed.): *Handbook of Experimental Psychology*, John Wiley & Sons, Inc., New York, 1951.
6. Woodworth, R. S.: *Experimental Psychology*, Henry Holt and Company, Inc., New York, 1938.

PART B

DESIGN AND CONDUCT OF EXPERIMENTS

CHAPTER 5

FORMATION OF HYPOTHESES

An event occurs and you observe it. If you know very little concerning the area of knowledge within which the phenomenon exists, you may be able only in a general way to speculate about the cause of the event or its relationship to other relevant factors.

After basic speculations, which are only scattered thoughts about a problem and an occasional guess as to the cause of the phenomenon or its relationship to other factors relevant to it, you may seize upon one or more possible answers to the problem. But until these answers are put to an experimental test, that is, until an experiment is performed to test the possibility and establish the probability of the answer or answers, your hypothesis is still only a hunch.

Bacon and others of his ilk believed that hypotheses should be suggested as soon as the existence of a problem is discovered. It is true that one usually does this, but one does not then immediately follow with an experiment to test each of these hurriedly produced hypotheses. Instead, hypotheses should come along after one has completely analyzed the problem. The problem's the thing wherein one catches the reflection of hypotheses doomed to failure as the result of evaluation by experimentation. When the problem is completely analyzed and carefully defined, then the hypothesis, or hypotheses, becomes obvious, and occurs in the right place as the second step in the development of the research design.

Definition of Hypothesis

A hypothesis is defined as a suggested answer to a problem. But the acceptable hypothesis must be a suggested answer that meets certain important requirements (2, p. 207, 3, p. 197).

1. *A hypothesis must be an adequate answer to the specific problem that demanded an answer.* In other words, the hypothesis must fit the problem so as to provide one answer to the one problem stated. It is possible to have several hypotheses that may answer one problem, but each of these hypotheses must suggest an answer from a different point of view. Any one hypothesis must be clear-cut in its meaning and not contain

45

more than one possible answer. Compound, and thus complicated, hypotheses dealing with more than one suggested answer at one time yield complicated experiments and a resulting difficulty of interpretation.

2. *A hypothesis must be the simplest answer to the problem.* Hypotheses that are not clearly stated by containing only the essential elements of solution are inexcusable and troublesome. Since the experiment to follow your hypothesis is designed from the elements of the hypothesis, the simpler the hypothesis, the simpler is the experiment to test its validity.

3. *A hypothesis must be verifiable.* If the hypothesis is stated in such a way as to prohibit the testing of its value, it is worthless. Hypotheses such as "All men are mortal" cannot be tested because it would be necessary to wait for the death of all men to validate the hypothesis conclusively. However, hypotheses do not need to be directly testable. It is not necessary that the problem situation be one capable of being brought into the laboratory and manipulated. Astronomers have for centuries formed and tested good hypotheses concerning the planets in remote space. But their hypotheses were well formed and in line with the condition of a possibility of verification.

4. *A hypothesis must be stated in such a way as to allow it to be refuted.* If a hypothesis is stated in a manner allowing it to be proved by an experiment but not disproved, it loses the right to be called a good hypothesis. The hypothesis that men fight because they have aggressive instincts is not capable of being refuted. In every instance where fighting occurs, the presence of the aggressive instinct could be claimed, but the absence of the behavior in some men would not disprove the presence of a latent instinct.

In the development of a good hypothesis the student must observe the above rules. Forming acceptable hypotheses is not difficult if the problem giving rise to the hypothesis has been carefully stated and defined. The form of a hypothesis is that of a declarative statement containing a suggested answer to the problem, and which obeys the formal conditions of hypotheses. Following are two problems and their respective hypotheses.

PROBLEM 1. Does practice with the preferred hand improve the proficiency of the nonpreferred hand in the mirror drawing experiment?

HYPOTHESIS. Practice with the preferred hand significantly improves the proficiency of the nonpreferred hand in the mirror drawing experiment.

PROBLEM 2. Are male rats more active than the same strain of female rats during a 6-day period spent in an activity cage?

HYPOTHESIS. Male rats are not significantly more active than the same strain of female rats during a 6-day period spent in an activity cage.

Definition of Null Hypothesis

We can see from the two examples given above that in the first case the hypothesis was stated affirmatively and in the second case negatively. Hypotheses that will be tested by experiments with the results finally evaluated statistically are in their best form if stated negatively. Stating the hypothesis negatively may help to reduce the bias of an experimenter who is ego-involved in his attempt to prove his hypothesis. When a hypothesis is so stated it is called a *null* hypothesis. The word null means zero in German. Null hypotheses are, therefore, zero hypotheses. Let us see what is meant by that.

Let us take the null hypothesis which follows as an example. The average intelligence of a large group of men is not significantly different from the average intelligence of a large group of women. Suppose you then conducted an experiment to test this statement and discovered that a difference in the two averages actually did exist. However, you noticed in your data that some of the women were better than some of the men, but that the average for the men was a little above the average for the women. You might then be in doubt as to whether you had conclusively disproved your hypothesis, particularly since the averages were close together. In stating your hypothesis as a null hypothesis, you said in effect that no difference exists between men and women in respect to intelligence. Implicit in this statement is the idea that no difference exists between the scores of men and women in respect to intelligence *other than what could be due to chance fluctuation alone*. It is obvious that the averages you calculated were not necessarily correct and the chances are if you conducted the experiment again you would get at least slightly different averages than you did the first time. Now, due to a number of uncontrolled factors whose influence we call chance there would be many possible averages you could secure. In fact, even if it were absolutely true that men and women do not differ one iota in intelligence, you might, in securing averages of the intelligences of men and women, find that some differences were indicated by your experimental results. Such a difference would not, in this case, indicate that a difference in intelligence existed but only that through some chance factor, such as inaccuracy of your measuring instrument, your results indicated a difference while the true difference was zero.

The greater the difference between the two averages, the less probable it is that the true difference is zero. If it were possible to calculate just how large a difference might be due to chance even if the true difference were zero, then it would be known when the averages were so close together that the difference might be due to chance entirely. Likewise, if the experimenter could calculate in any experiment, wherein his results are in the form of two averages, whether his averages are too far apart for the difference to be easily accounted for in terms of chance fluctuation, then he would have an excellent way of deciding whether to accept the null hypothesis or not. The experimenter can, fortunately, do this as will be shown in the chapter on statistical techniques.

If the experimenter finds that the difference between his averages is so small that it might easily be due only to chance, then he may accept the null hypothesis and say that a true difference does not exist. If the difference between his averages is so large that it is only remotely probable that it is due to chance, then he may reject his null hypothesis and say that a true difference does exist.

The experimenter who uses the null hypothesis form provides himself with the opportunity to accept or reject his hypothesis in terms of the probability that the difference between his groups is due to chance alone. In the chapters on statistical techniques the reader will find additional advantages to be gained from using the null hypothesis.

One other point is especially important. The acceptance or rejection of a null hypothesis is no assurance that the alternative hypothesis can be accepted as true. It may very well be that the experiment was not an adequate test of the hypothesis and thus an error was made in accepting or rejecting it on the basis of such evidence.

Origin of Hypotheses

Hypotheses, in their broadest sense, offer more than mere declarative statements suggesting an answer to a problem. As a problem is reduced from its original unclear and ambiguous form to a specific question phrased in terms of a set of operations, the formation of hypotheses is already taking place. By the time the problem is reduced to an acceptable form and meaning it could easily be converted into a hypothesis by making the question into a declarative statement. In the process of simplification of the problem, then, somewhere along the line, the hypothesis was formed. Just where did this formation take place? Let us take a problem and see when the hypothesis first appears.

Suppose you are a clinical psychologist and have just met your patient. She is a twenty-year-old girl who was "promoted" on age through school to the ninth grade, can hardly read even simple material, has difficulty in pronouncing her words, and has a mother who finally came to the conclusion that she should seek help for her daughter. Your problems in this situation are three in number. The first, what is wrong with the girl? The second, how did it come about? The third, what can be done about it? *Whatever action you now take to answer any of these problems is a hypothesis.* Suppose you decide to administer an intelligence test to the girl. You are suggesting by that act that the girl's difficulty is related to her intelligence. You will, on the basis of the evidence provided by the results of the test, accept or reject the hypothesis that her intellectual status is a sufficient and necessary cause for her behavior. Suppose you find that the girl's I.Q. meets the mental deficiency classification. You have answered problem one, at least in part. Problem two now faces you. How did the mental deficiency come about? You now look closely at the girl and notice that one of her front teeth is directly on the mid-line, the left side of her face is slightly deformed, and there is a depression on the left side of her head over the temporal lobe. Your hypothesis was made the moment you started looking for organic brain damage. What you now see only confirms the hypothesis you had in mind as soon as you learned that the patient was mentally deficient. You ask the mother at what age the patient first walked and talked, when the mother first noticed the patient to be "different" from other children, and if the child had been an instrument baby? Yes, the child had been an instrument baby, and it's head had been severely damaged by the forceps, the child was late to talk, late to walk, and from very early in childhood had appeared to be "different." Further examination by a physician indicated definite brain damage of long standing. Problem two is solved. Problem three, what can be done about it, is quickly solved. You recommend that the patient be placed in a special school where she will be trained for a vocation with which she can cope. Your hypothesis appeared as soon as you suggested a special school. Past experience forced you to hypothesize that the condition is permanent, formal schooling of no use, and that specialized vocational training for a routine job is as much as could be done.

Now let us summarize. When did the hypotheses appear, where did they come from, and what use did they serve?

Hypotheses first appear when a definite set toward solving a problem is taken. The first act a person goes through, after a problem has been presented, directed toward a solution of the problem is a hypothesis. A hypothesis is, therefore, interposed between a problem and its solution as Fig. 5.1 indicates.

Hypotheses come from experience. Those men who have the ability to produce new and fertile hypotheses are the men who have the best grasp of the problems of the field and a knowledge of the general form of possible solutions for such problems. It is true that many of the "great hypothesizers" have not been able to tell how or from where their hypotheses came. But an outstanding hypothesis in the field of physics, for example, seldom if ever occurs to a man who has not had a background of experience in the field of physics. Pure "general intelligence" itself is

not enough to produce outstanding hypotheses.   Highly intelligent law-
yers seldom develop hypotheses in the field of nuclear physics, and vice
versa, for the simple reason that they lack the background necessary for
producing hypotheses in the other's field.

Munn's (4, p. 246) discussion of creative thinking is relevant to a discussion of hypothesis formation.   He points out that creative thinking
develops in a manner similar to trial-and-error learning and proceeds
through four stages: *preparation*, where the person gathers his background

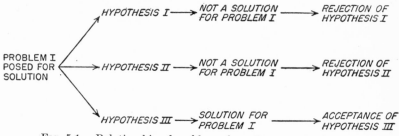

FIG. 5.1.   Relationship of problems, hypotheses, and solutions.

and training; *incubation*, the conscious or unconscious (some say) con-
tinuance of associational activities; *inspiration*, when the material suddenly seems to organize itself; and *verification* or *revision*, where one
evaluates and revises the idea.

Students who are faced with the need for "doing a piece of research"
often complain that they cannot find a problem "on which to experiment."   What they really mean is they have no answers to suggest.
Problems are easy to find but good, testable hypotheses with some chance
of acceptance are hard to find.

Discovery has to do with hypotheses, not data.   Benjamin (1, p. 173)
is particularly clear on this point.   Since all researchers aim at scientific
discovery, their hypotheses are "outstretched arms" reaching for the
truth.   The solutions to all problems already exist.   The researcher must
simply offer suggested answers and then accept or reject these answers in
light of the facts.

Hypotheses have their beginnings in two places, facts and theory.
There were facts first, and then there were hypotheses.   From the observation of facts, man began to classify and put together piece by piece the
web of scientific explanation.   As more and more facts were accumulated
and classified, the patterns of natural laws began to take shape, and at
last man could predict to some extent the occurrences of nature about
him.   He began to know that *this plus this leads to this*.   At this stage he
had a theory.   Now he was prepared to do more than catalogue facts.

He was now ready to go beyond facts. Was it not Huxley who said, "Those who refuse to go beyond fact rarely get as far as fact"? Man was now going beyond fact to the next stage called theory. His theories and laws were composed of statements describing the relationship existing between the facts he had been observing. Now, armed with theory, he could go beyond the fact gathering stage and could start to make higher-order hypotheses such as, *if this leads to this and that leads to that, then they must lead to such and such.* Looking there, he either found that the fact supported what he had theorized or that he had made a wrong prediction and consequently a poor theory. If he were right, then a new fact was discovered. Wherever these new hypotheses lead the scientist, he must keep his feet on the ground and realize that he started with fact and must end with fact. There is no better way to test whether the theory that started in fact now allows the researcher to predict new facts than to put the theory to a test by calling it a hypothesis and appealing to fact again to see if the facts support the theory. Some researchers have had so much faith in their theories that when the facts failed to support the theory they felt compelled to throw out the facts. This is, of course, the cardinal sin of scientific endeavor.

BIBLIOGRAPHY

1. Benjamin, A. C.: *An Introduction to the Philosophy of Science,* The Macmillan Company, New York, 1937.
2. Cohen, M. R., and E. Nagel: *An Introduction to Logic and Scientific Method,* Harcourt, Brace and Company, Inc., New York, 1934.
3. Larrabee, H. A.: *Reliable Knowledge,* Houghton Mifflin Company, Boston, 1945.
4. Munn, N. L.: *Psychology: The Fundamentals of Adjustment,* 2d ed., Houghton Mifflin Company, Boston, 1951.

CHAPTER 6

INDEPENDENT AND DEPENDENT VARIABLES

After the statement of the problem under investigation and the formulation of the hypothesis, the researcher is now prepared to design an experiment for the specific purpose of testing whether his hypothesis is to be accepted or rejected as an answer to his problem.

If the problem was clearly stated and the resulting hypothesis formulated to answer the problem *specifically*, then much of the work of designing the experiment is completed. The hypothesis, if well conceived, contains two all important elements: (*a*) an independent variable and (*b*) a dependent variable.

An *independent variable* is that factor manipulated by the experimenter in his attempt to ascertain its relationship to an observed phenomenon.

A *dependent variable* is that factor which appears, disappears, or varies as the experimenter introduces, removes, or varies the independent variable.

Munn (2, p. 29), Andrews (1, p. 7), and Woodworth (3, p. 2) offer further definitions of independent and dependent variables.

In psychology, we speak of stimuli and responses. We say that a response is due to a stimulus or a stimulating situation. In the absence of a stimulus no response can occur. An organism is considered dead when it is no longer capable of making responses to stimuli. The interplay of stimuli and responses in the human being is vastly complicated due to the numerous response mechanisms it contains. Since these response systems are the means by which the behavior of the individual is demonstrated, we see that much of what is called psychology today involves the study of the responses of the individual to stimuli. In most psychological experiments, therefore, the independent variable is the stimulus variable and the dependent variable is the response variable.

A few examples of hypotheses with their independent and dependent variables indicated are given below.

HYPOTHESIS 1. A blow delivered to the patellar tendon of the bended knee of an individual will cause the leg to straighten.

Independent Variable. The blow delivered to the patellar tendon of the bended knee of an individual.

Dependent Variable. The straightening of the leg of the individual.

HYPOTHESIS 2. The higher the intensity of a 1,000-cycle note, the faster an individual can react to its onset by removing his hand from a push button.

Independent Variable. The various intensities of the 1,000-cycle note presented to the subject.

Dependent Variable. The length of time required by the individual to remove his hand from a push button after he hears the onset of the sound.

HYPOTHESIS 3. Individuals whose parents were feeble-minded have lower intelligence than do individuals whose parents were not feeble-minded.

Independent Variable. The presence or absence of feeble-mindedness in the parents.

Dependent Variable. The amount of intelligence possessed by the individuals whose parents were feeble-minded as compared to the intelligence of those whose parents were not feeble-minded.

In these simple and not completely defined hypotheses we see that the independent variable is presented as a proposed antecedent to the dependent variable, which is the assumed consequence. An inference of cause and effect between the independent and dependent variable is the object sought by the experimenter. The experimental evidence of a relationship between the independent and dependent variable is taken as supporting the inference.

Very often the student will have difficulty in ascertaining just which is the independent variable and which is the dependent variable. There is a little device which seems appropriate for presentation here because it seems to serve as an eye opener for many students. In the following diagram (Fig. 6.1) the reader sees a sector of a circle. At the point of the drawing are the letters D.V., which stand for dependent variable. At the upper left part of the drawing are the letters I.V.$_1$, standing for the first condition of the independent variable. At the upper right part of the drawing are the letters I.V.$_2$ standing for the second condition of the independent variable. Note that the arc drawn between the two conditions of the independent variable is drawn as a curved double-headed arrow and indicates movement between condition one and condition two. Also note that the lines connecting each of the two conditions of the independent variable, respectively, to the dependent variable are also arrows and they are pointed from the independent variable toward the dependent variable. Any given hypothesis can be symbolized and incorporated into this diagram. When this is done, the hypothesis can be instantly analyzed and simplified by the use of this diagram into its related component parts, the independent and dependent variables. In this manner, the experiment to be performed is immediately made clear because once the independent and dependent variables are selected, and the relationship between them made clear, the experiment has reduced to a point where its intent is obvious to all.

It would perhaps be well here to select for careful discussion a few different hypotheses on the basis of their demonstration of the general broad types of hypotheses one encounters in the usual type of experimental research.   Each of these hypotheses will then be put on the diagram in the correct fashion to bring out and clarify the relationship between the independent and the dependent variables.

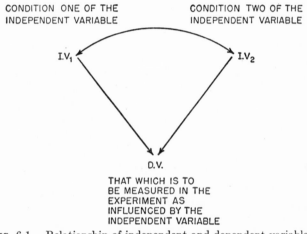

CONDITION ONE OF THE
INDEPENDENT VARIABLE

CONDITION TWO OF THE
INDEPENDENT VARIABLE

I.V₁

I.V₂

D.V.

THAT WHICH IS TO
BE MEASURED IN THE
EXPERIMENT AS
INFLUENCED BY THE
INDEPENDENT VARIABLE

FIG. 6.1.   Relationship of independent and dependent variables.

PROBLEM 1.   Is the reaction time to a visual stimulus faster than the reaction time to an auditory stimulus?

HYPOTHESIS.   The reaction time to a visual stimulus is significantly faster than the reaction time to an auditory stimulus.

The first question to ask in the quest for variables is, "What is going to be measured in this experiment?"   We see that we are interested in three things: light, sound, and the length of time it takes to react to each of these.   Our experiment is one which will yield an indication of the speed of reaction under each of the two conditions of light stimulation and sound stimulation.   It is clear that we are going to measure reaction time. Since this, then, is the behavior that is going to be measured under each of the two conditions of stimulation, it must depend on the two types of stimulation, and thus if it varies under the two conditions, its variance will depend on the difference between the influence of the two variables. Reaction time is our dependent variable and is, as we see, recorded on the diagram at the appropriate place in Fig. 6.2. The next step is to go back to the hypothesis and see what two conditions were mentioned as being related, or suspected of being related, to the dependent variable in the form of antecedent and consequence. We see that the two conditions of light and sound are all that are left and are the independent variables of the experiment. The variation of each of these two conditions independently is hypothesized to be related to the variations in the dependent variable. We therefore record on our diagram, as the first condition of the independent variable, light stimulation, and, as the second condition of the independent variable, the condition of sound stimulation. This process is given in what may seem to be a backward order, since the dependent variable was located first. There is nothing magical about locating and defining

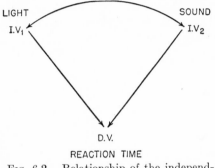

Fig. 6.2. Relationship of the independent to the dependent variable in a hypothesis comparing two stimuli as to their respective effects on a response.

the dependent variable before the independent variable. It just seems that once the dependent variable is isolated, the task of finding the independent variables is much simpler. Besides, it is usually easy to locate in any hypothesis the thing that is to be measured. Since the thing to be measured is the dependent variable, it can be identified and gotten out of the way, thus revealing the independent variables more easily.

In the above problem, we saw that the two conditions of the independent variable involved two classes of stimuli, light and sound. The diagram would have worked equally well if we had been dealing with the type of hypothesis where we have various conditions of the same class of stimulus. In this type of problem setting one is interested in what effect various intensities of a particular stimulus will have on some dependent variable. The following exemplifies this type.

Problem 2. Will the greater the intensity of the light used as the stimulus in the reaction-time experiment be related to a greater speed of reaction time?

Hypothesis. Increases in the intensity of the light used in the reaction-time experiment will be significantly related to faster reaction to the light.

Here it is obvious that we are again going to measure the reaction time and as such it becomes our dependent variable. Our independent variable will be each of the various intensities of light used in the experiment.

The following diagram (Fig. 6.3) shows this type of relationship between the independent and the dependent variables.

A third type of situation may arise where the experiment has to do with a problem in which the independent variable is in the form of the presence and the absence of some stimulus or stimulating situation. The following example will demonstrate this.

PROBLEM 3.   Will students who complete a how-to-study course make higher honor-point averages than students who have never taken such a course?

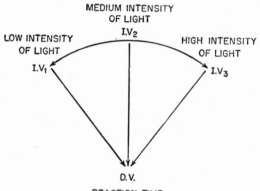

FIG. 6.3.   Relationship of the independent to the dependent variable in a hypothesis comparing different intensities of a stimulus as to their respective effects on a response.

HYPOTHESIS.   Students who have completed a how-to-study course will make significantly higher honor-point averages than students who have never taken such a course.

The thing to be measured here is the honor-point average.   The honor-point averages of the two groups thus become the dependent variable. The condition upon which the honor points may depend is whether or not the students completed a how-to-study course.   These conditions become the independent variables.   Figure 6.4 shows this relationship.

The most clear-cut experiments are those that contain only one independent and one dependent variable.   However, there is nothing unscientific in measuring and recording the effects of one independent variable on several dependent variables.   The following hypothesis with its variables will demonstrate this.

HYPOTHESIS.   When a person becomes startled as the result of a loud noise, his arterial pulse rate increases, he perspires, and the pupils of his eyes dilate.

Independent Variable.   The loud noise producing the condition of being startled in the person.

Dependent Variable.   Increase in arterial pulse rate, perspiration, and the diameter of the pupils of the individual's eyes as the result of the startle occasioned by the loud noise.

Each of these physiological dependent variables can be measured simultaneously and independently.   In this way the experimenter can gather more data than if he limited himself to the measurement of only one dependent variable.

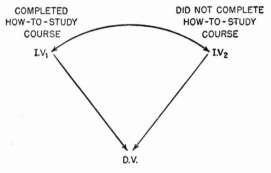

FIG. 6.4.   Relationship of the independent to the dependent variable in a hypothesis comparing the presence and absence of a stimulus as to its effect on a response.

Although it has been said that the ideal condition is to have only one independent variable, it does not necessarily follow that it is impossible to perform successfully an experiment containing two or more independent variables.   Recent developments in the area of statistics have made available to the experimenter certain statistical techniques, particularly those dealing with the analysis of variance, partial correlations, and multiple-factor analysis, which permit him to analyze and relate changes in the dependent variables to the contribution of each of many independent variables acting simultaneously.

BIBLIOGRAPHY

1. Andrews, T. G. (ed.): *Methods of Psychology*, John Wiley & Sons, Inc., New York, 1948.
2. Munn, N. L.: *Psychology: The Fundamentals of Adjustment*, 2d ed., Houghton Mifflin Company, Boston, 1951.
3. Woodworth, R. S.: *Experimental Psychology*, Henry Holt and Company, Inc., New York, 1938.

CHAPTER 7

CONTROL OF THE EXPERIMENT

No experiment is better than its poorest control. This statement is the major issue involved in the evaluation of any experimental attempt to arrive at factual knowledge. In this chapter will be discussed the meaning of "control" and how the control of a situation is accomplished.

When an experimenter wishes to apply scientific methodology to the solution of a problem, he most often turns to his laboratory as a place for conducting the experimentation. He does this so that he may not only have at hand the tools and techniques for carrying on his experimentation or so that he may be fully prepared to observe and record his data as it appears, but he goes to the laboratory so that he may be able to set up a stable environment in which the phenomena under observation can occur. In addition, he wishes to be sure that the phenomena he is studying is "pure" in the sense that he wants to make certain that only the phenomenon he wishes to observe is present and that it is allowed to vary only in response to the stimuli he presents to it. He deliberately removes the phenomenon from its place of natural occurrence in the world outside the laboratory and brings it into what some have said is an artificial environment. These critics claim the phenomenon is thus changed. This latter, however, is not true, for the simple process of bringing a phenomenon into the laboratory does not necessarily change the phenomenon. If one were to say that it does, then this would be equivalent to believing that changing the place of a phenomenon is the same as changing the phenomenon itself. See Benjamin (2, p. 107). What is usually meant is that when one changes the location of a phenomenon one most often changes the environment in which it occurs. This does not necessarily happen, for the scientist attempts to change the location of the phenomenon without changing its environment. Whether this can be done or not is dependent upon the ability of the scientist. The attempt to produce a phenomenon in a pure condition by regulating its environment is called "controlling the situation" or "controlling the experiment."

To control a situation is to have it so much under command as to be able to enumerate the factors present and to manipulate them at will. Seldom is such a position attained in an experiment. One must be satisfied with a degree of control over the *known* relevant factors. However, the experimentalist should constantly, both before and during the experiment, and especially before, attempt to lengthen the list of known relevant variables.

The following (Fig. 7.1) may help to show the part played by controls in an observation. In any experiment we attempt to relate the presence or variation of an independent variable to changes in the dependent variable. It has previously been implied that if we wish to determine most

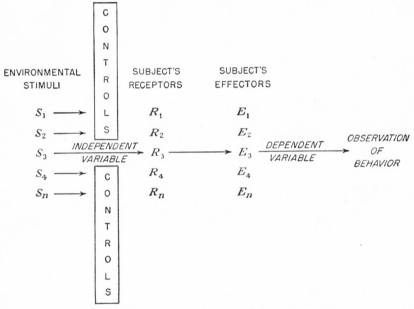

Fig. 7.1. The part played by controls in an experiment.

precisely the influence of an independent variable we must have only one such variable present. This is reasonable in that if more than one variable were present when the dependable variable changed in value, the researcher would have difficulty determining which factor was really related to the change or if all were necessary for the change. How often we hear someone make a statement such as, "Tom and Pete were here, and I don't like him." To make sense from this statement the listener must counter with the question, "Which one don't you like, Tom or Pete?" The issue involved is clear: the antecedent for a consequence must be established and the reference made unequivocally if meaning is to be obtained.

The relevant variables must be ascertained in any experiment. There's the rub. The meaning of relevant variables was previously mentioned but not explored; so let us now look at methods of determining relevant variables in an experiment.

The first step in approaching a problem is to find in the literature those studies pertinent to the area in which the problem to be investigated rests. Usually an investigator searches in the literature for previous studies dealing with the same dependent variable to be investigated in the present study. When such studies are located, their results will provide information concerning the relationship between the independent variable used in each and its relationship to the dependent variable. These previous studies have, in effect, determined the relevance of certain variables which must be considered for control in an experiment. The investigator will probably be considering the manipulation of some independent variable not previously investigated and will want to control all known relevant factors related to a change in the dependent variable.

The Control Group

The procedure of control is usually accomplished through the use of a second group of subjects called a *control group* (see Fig. 7.2). The

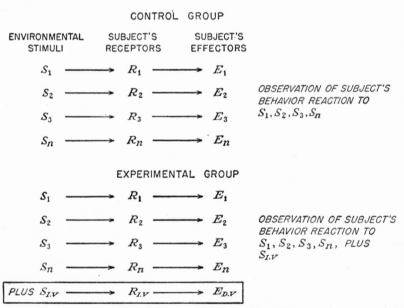

FIG. 7.2. The parts played by the control and experimental groups in an experiment.

behavior of the control group is compared with the behavior of the experimental group. The major difference between an experimental group and a control group is that the independent variable is introduced to the former but not to the latter. Thus the control group's result reveals the behavior of the dependent variable in the absence of the independent variable. The experimental group's results show the behavior of the dependent variable in the presence of the independent variable. If a control group is not used, and only the experimental group received the independent variable, an investigator can never be sure but what the same change in the dependent variable would have occurred in the absence of the independent variable.

An example of the use of a control group in a psychological experiment is seen in the following. Suppose an investigator believes that he has found a drug or chemical which if administered to feeble-minded subjects will raise their intelligence quotients. In order to test the effectiveness of his drug, he would make it the independent variable in an experiment, and the intelligence quotient of his group of subjects the dependent variable. If he were simply to administer the drug to, let us say, one hundred subjects and then again measure their I.Q.'s, how might he interpret his data if he found a significant increase in the I.Q.'s?

The investigator could not say that the increase in I.Q. was caused by the drug he administered. Why not? Because he would not know whether the I.Q.'s of the subjects would have raised even if he had not given them the drug. It is possible that the subjects were more highly motivated on the second administration of the test than they were on the first administration. Further, the entire group might have received a better diet, been exposed to a more favorable environment, and been given closer and perhaps better medical attention because they were under observation, or perhaps there were certain transfer effects or carry-over from the first to the second administration of the tests. Any one of these conditions, and many more, might have been responsible for the apparent increase in I.Q.

In order to find out just what changes were due to the influence of the drug alone, the careful experimenter would include in his study a control group. This control group would be treated in exactly the same manner as the experimental group with one important exception, that being, instead of receiving the drug, this group would be given a harmless, non-effective chemical such as common table salt. Such a device is called a *placebo*. However, the subjects would not know whether they were members of the experimental group or the control group. Very likely, the safest procedure would be to administer the drug and the placebo to the two groups without the subjects realizing that they were serving in an experiment. The drug and the placebo could be administered in capsule form before each meal and the subjects told, if necessary, that they were being given vitamins. Now, if the experimenter had put his subjects into two groups of fifty each and treated each of them the same, with the exception of the fact that one group received the drug and the other received the placebo, then he could, after the second administration of the test, note if there were any increase of the experimental group's I.Q.'s over the control's.   If such a difference occurred, and if it were significant, then he would have more reason to say that the increase was due to the effect of the drug than if he had not used a control group for comparison.

Andrews (1, p. 10), Underwood (6), Munn (5, p. 30), and Larrabee (4, p. 333) present discussions of controls and the control group.

Equating the Control and the Experimental Groups

We have indicated that it is necessary before the introduction of the independent variable to have the control and experimental groups equal in respect to their possession of variables relevant to the dependent variable being measured.   This means that if an investigator has reason to believe or even suspect that a particular difference in his two groups would either directly or indirectly influence the response of his two groups to the independent variable imposed upon them, then he is bound to see that his two groups are equated with respect to that relevant variable.   This is not an easy task, for not only is it difficult to know the relevant variables, but it is often even more difficult to see that their effects are equal in the two groups.   Three methods are commonly employed by the experimenter in his attempt to equate his groups.

Matched-pairs Technique.   In this method, the subjects are examined one by one and are selected for the study and assigned to their respective groups on the basis of their equal possession of the relevant factors.   One, therefore, begins to match the two groups by deciding upon what factors the groups will be matched, and proceeds to select only qualified subjects. It is obvious that "many will come but few will be chosen," and this raises one of the objections to the matched-pairs technique.   Finding subjects is often a serious problem in research.   Sometimes the criterion is so stringent that only a relatively few subjects will be acceptable.   In such instances the group of available subjects from which the final two groups will be selected must be quite large if one is to have a fair-sized sample in the final groups.   However, if many subjects are available from which one may pick and choose, and if the most relevant variables are known and can be measured accurately, then this method of equating the groups is a handy and useful device.

Matched-group Technique.   In this method the experimenter does not attempt to match each individual with each other individual, but rather tries to make certain that the average possession and extent of distribution of the important characteristics of the groups, with respect to the relevant variables, is the same for each group. He might tentatively assign half of his subjects to the experimental group and half to the control group and then proceed to find the central tendency and the variability of the two groups. If it were found that there were no significant differences between these statistical measures, then it might be assumed that the groups were fairly well equated. If differences were found, then exchanging subjects between the two groups would aid in equating them. It is necessary, as indicated above, that both the average possession of a trait and the distribution of that trait around the average be the same for the two groups. Suppose the experimenter assumed that his two groups of subjects were equal in intelligence because they each had an average I.Q. of 100. Further examination of the distributions of I.Q.'s might show 60 per cent of the subjects in one group have I.Q.'s below 100, and 60 per cent of the subjects in the second group have I.Q.'s above 100. These groups could not be considered equated in I.Q. until there were no significant differences in the distribution of I.Q.'s as well as in the average I.Q.'s. Calculation of statistical measures of variability of the two groups (discussed in the chapters on statistics) serves as a means of comparing the variability of two groups.

Randomized Group Technique. If an experimenter finds that he is unable to match his two groups, either because he is unable to decide upon the most important factors upon which to equate them or because he cannot measure or perhaps even discover the relevant factors, then it is suggested that he make use of the process of randomization in equating his groups. This technique, however, also demands a large number of cases, for an experimenter must make his assignment of the subjects to the groups upon a chance basis, and in order to give chance differences an opportunity to nullify each other, he must use many subjects. It can be shown that as the number of subjects selected randomly increases, the two groups become more similar.

For a more complete discussion of the techniques of equating experimental and control groups the reader is referred to Jahoda, Deutch, and Cook (3).

A control group is not essential, however, in performing an experiment wherein various intensities of the independent variable are given to the experimental group. In this instance, the experimenter is interested in the concomitance of variation between the independent and dependent variables and not in the presence or absence of the independent variable as related to the occurrence of changes in the dependent variable. Relevant variables must still be controlled, nevertheless, even if a second group for control is not used.

Techniques for Controlling Experiments

Once the relevant variables are known, their effects must be eliminated from the experiment. There are several ways to do this.

Method of Removal. If possible, the relevant variables should be removed from the experimental situation. If, for example, it is known that light and noise influence the dependent variable under investigation, then the experimenter should remove these conditions through the use of a lightproof and sound-deadened room.

Method of Constancy of Conditions. As is often the case, the effects of certain known relevant variables cannot be completely or even partly eliminated. For instance, age is a known relevant variable which affects the behavior of most dependent variables. Since it is obvious all subjects must have age, elimination of this variable is impossible. Control over the variable in such instances is secured by the means of keeping the variable constant for all the subjects used in the experiment. In this manner, if all the subjects were of the same age, the effect of age on the experimental group balances its effect on the control group.

When using a control group, it is not always absolutely essential to know which relevant variables should be removed. The control and experimental groups may be equated before the experiment in such a way that they represent random samples of the same population. By this procedure, one has two groups with the best chance of being equal in all respects. In such a selection of the two groups, there will be a constancy of conditions between them that will extend to factors beyond the experimenter's ability to know, and thus remove, or even designate.

Screening Method. Variables may be controlled by what is known as *screening them out.* Suppose in an experiment the measurements of the dependent variable might be influenced by some uncontrollable sound which occurs unexpectedly, if not erratically. An example would be the ringing of a buzzer to announce the end of class periods. Such an auditory disturbance might easily occur at a crucial point in the experiment and upset the results. The influence of the sound could be eliminated by producing a sound in the laboratory loud enough to screen out the buzzer sound if it occurred. If the deliberately produced sound were constant, it would perhaps have an effect on the results, but the effect would be known and apparently equal for all subjects.

Counterbalancing Method. In many experiments it is necessary to control for an apparent progressive change in the subject's response as he continues to serve in the experiment. Practice effects and fatigue effects are so often present in psychological experiments that they are referred to as *constant errors.* These constant errors must be controlled in any good experiment or their effects will obscure the changes in the dependent variable which is being investigated as related to an independent variable other than practice and fatigue.   The simplest way to control such constant errors is to use the process known as *counterbalancing*.   Suppose that an experiment is being performed wherein two light stimuli, red and green, are being presented to the subject and the object of the experiment is to measure for comparison the reaction time of the subject to each color of light.   If the experimenter presented the lights in the sequence red-red-green-green, the combined effects of practice and fatigue of dealing with the red stimulus would be present when the subject was finally presented with the green stimulus.   The effect would probably be seen in the subject's response to the green stimulus, and thus give different

| SUCCESSIVE TRIALS | A | B | B | A |
| EFFECT ON RESPONSE | 1 | 2 | 3 | 4 |

TOTAL EFFECT OF CONDITION A   1+4 =5
TOTAL EFFECT OF CONDITION B   2+3 =5   > SAME

| SUCCESSIVE TRIALS | A | A | B | B |
| EFFECT ON RESPONSE | 1 | 2 | 3 | 4 |

TOTAL EFFECT OF CONDITION A   1+2 =3
TOTAL EFFECT OF CONDITION B   3+4 =7   > DIFFERENT

FIG. 7.3.   Comparison of the sequences *abba* and *aabb* to show how the effects of constant errors on the response can be better equalized by an *abba* sequence.

results than if the sequence green-green-red-red had been used.   In this latter case, the results of the subject's reaction time would contain the error occasioned by practice and fatigue from dealing with green.   The counterbalanced order of presentation solves this problem by making use of an *abba* sequence of presentation of the stimuli.   Thus the red and green stimuli should be presented in the sequence red-green-green-red or green-red-red-green.   By using the *abba* sequence the changes in the dependent variable attributed to constant errors are spread equally over all conditions.

Underwood (6, p. 30) indicates that the assumption behind the use of the *abba* sequence is the idea that "the progressive change in response which may take place as experimentation proceeds is a straight line function."   This means that if the stimulus variable under study, and no other stimulus variable, equally influences the response on each trial, then the effect of the stimulus on the response should be such that the total effects of the systematic errors would be the same throughout the experiment.

In Fig. 7.3 it is seen that when the sequence *abba* is used and the accumulative effect on the response following each presentation of each stimulating condition is considered to increase by one on each trial, then it becomes obvious that the total effects of conditions a and b can be equalized only by the *abba* sequence of presentation. Underwood (6, p. 31) presents this idea in graphical form and deals with the average influence of each block of trials instead of the total effect. His is probably a more accurate presentation, but of necessity it is a little more complex.

Method of Systematic Randomization. When more than five conditions are to be counterbalanced, the procedure becomes difficult to handle,

PRESENTATION OF CONDITIONS
A B C D

SUBJECT	TRIAL I	TRIAL II	TRIAL III	TRIAL IV
I	A	D	B	C
2	C	B	D	A
3	B	A	C	D
4	D	C	A	B

FIG. 7.4. Systematic randomization table for four conditions, four subjects, and four trials.

particularly if all subjects are to be tested under all conditions. It is suggested that in such instances the method of *systematic randomization* be used. The name of this method appears to involve a contradiction, for how could something be systematic and at the same time random? The following discussion should help to clarify this matter.

If an experiment required the use of more than five conditions, and each subject was to be exposed to all the conditions in a sequence, it is obvious that the issue involved is one of deciding what order of presentation should be used for each subject so that practice and fatigue effects may be the same for all conditions investigated. If nonsystematic randomization were used, that is, chance alone decided which subject would receive the conditions in which order, the experimenter would need a large number of subjects before he could be sure that each condition occurred equally often at each stage of practice. However, if a system were imposed so as to ensure randomization, *i.e.*, each condition preceded and followed each other condition about equally, but not necessarily that every possible combination was used, then the experimenter could be certain that randomization was effected even when dealing with a few subjects. Figure 7.4 illustrates this method.

These methods of controlling psychological experiments do not comprise the entire list but are rather the most commonly used devices.

It is through the application of controls that experiments become capable of being duplicated. Any good experiment must be repeatable and still yield the same results. This is possible only if the experimenter has carefully controlled all relevant factors and reported his controls in detail.

BIBLIOGRAPHY

1. Andrews, T. G. (ed.): *Methods of Psychology*, John Wiley & Sons, Inc., New York, 1948.
2. Benjamin, A. C.: *An Introduction to the Philosophy of Science*, The Macmillan Company, New York, 1937.
3. Jahoda, Marie, *et al: Research Methods in Social Research: Part One: Basic Processes*, The Dryden Press, Inc., New York, 1951.
4. Larrabee, Harold A.: *Reliable Knowledge*, Houghton Mifflin Company, Boston, 1945.
5. Munn, N. L.: *Psychology: The Fundamentals of Adjustment*, 2d ed., Houghton Mifflin Company, Boston, 1951.
6. Underwood, Benton J.: *Experimental Psychology: An Introduction*, Appleton-Century-Crofts, Inc., New York, 1949.

CHAPTER 8

PROCEDURE FOR EXPERIMENTATION

In this chapter there will be discussed several methods of procedure which have been utilized in the past by psychologists and which may be considered standard procedures for the types of experiments where they apply. It is wise for the beginner to use a standard and well-defined procedure in his experiment wherever possible. By so doing, he is less likely to go astray than if he set about designing new methods of procedure himself.

Since the psychologist is interested in the investigation of all possible relationships of stimulus variables to response variables, he must on some occasions use procedures which allow him to collect data under obscure conditions. Sometimes he simply cannot use an apparatus to measure the behavior of an individual, but must deal instead with such intangibles as judgments by the subject. The question in such instances becomes centered around the selection of a procedure which when used will yield reliable data.

Methods of Expression and Impression

If we measure the internal and external changes in the behavior of the individual by means of observation, often aided by detecting apparatus, we would be using the *method of expression*.

An apparatus called a *lie detector* exemplifies this. In such an application of the method of expression, the experimenter utilizes various devices that will record the subject's physiological changes. We know that when an individual experiences an emotion certain physiological changes take place in his body. Lying is an emotion-provoking experience for most individuals. Thus if we are prepared to measure the change that takes place in a subject's respiratory rate, his psychogalvanic skin response, and his blood pressure when there is a possibility that he may lie in response to a question, and compare these changes in his physiological functioning to his normal emotional level when he is answering "harmless" questions, we may relate his emotionality to lying.

Much of the psychology of an individual is covert, that is, the person is experiencing responses to stimuli but gives no apparent overt behavior response.   An unspoken judgment is such an experience.   To make such experiences overt, the subject is instructed to state his impression of the stimulus or stimulating situation.   Thus we are employing a procedure called the *method of impression.*

Woodworth (8) treats the subject of methods of expression and impression in detail.

Regardless of which of the two previous methods is used (and they are not essentially different), one main objective is sought: the experimentalist is attempting to quantify qualitative behavior as a result of stimulation.   This means only that he wishes to convert the behavior observed into numbers so that he can more readily deal with it.   The researcher deals with these numbers, which are actually symbolic representations of the amount of a quality present, and attempts to reduce these numbers to meaningful concepts expressed in terms of trends, relationships, and the like.   While certain errors are made in going from qualities to quantities, it is even more probable that errors will be made when the experimenter attempts to return from quantities to qualities and make his newly calculated statistical ratios meaningful in terms of qualities again.

Psychophysical Methods

Several procedures falling mainly under the classification of methods of impression are known as the *psychophysical methods.*   These psychophysical methods are procedures by which the experimenter may quantify relations between a stimulus and the sensation or experiences that follows. The best single reference for this topic is Guilford's *Psychometric Methods* (4).

Stevens (5) has listed seven categories into which the problems of psychophysics fall.   These categories are absolute thresholds, differential thresholds, equality, order, equality of intervals, equality of ratios, and stimulus ratings.   In the discussion that follows, each of these problems will be treated with the exception of the problem of the equality of ratios. Certain of the problems are dealt with by psychophysical methods bearing the name of the particular problem.   The name of the method will be presented as a heading.   The method will then be discussed as to its characteristics and applicability to the problems of psychophysics.

Method of Limits (or Method of Serial Exploration, or Method of Just Noticeable Difference, or Method of Least Noticeable Difference, or Method of Minimal Change)

The procedure involved in this psychophysical method consists of the experimenter gradually lowering the intensity or value of a stimulus until it is no longer perceived by the subject, or by increasing or decreasing the value between two stimuli until it becomes just noticeably different (JND), or by increasing the value of a stimulus until it is no longer perceived.

As can be seen from the above synonyms for the method of limits, the use to which the method is put decides the name by which one identifies it. However, the basic idea of establishing limits is contained in all variations of the method of limits. Usually the method is used to ascertain the threshold of a subject's sensitivity.

At a given moment, a stimulus must achieve a certain intensity in order to be perceived. This value of the stimulus is known as the *absolute threshold* or *stimulus threshold*. It is a point on the physical continuum of the stimulus. The difference in stimulus value between the zero value of the stimulus and the absolute threshold is called the *absolute limen*. Because sense organs operate efficiently only within certain ranges of stimulus intensity, there is an upper limit above which some stimuli, sounds, for example, are not perceived by the individual. This upper threshold is called the *terminal threshold* or *terminal stimulus*. One other type of threshold is used frequently. It is called the *difference threshold*, and is established by varying a stimulus from the intensity of an identical constant stimulus and increasing the difference until the subject reports that he perceives a difference. It is a point on the physical continuum at some distance from the standard stimulus. The distance from the standard stimulus to the difference threshold is called the *difference limen*. Figure 8.1 shows the relationship of the thresholds and limens to one another.

Thresholds are stated in terms of units of whatever type of stimulus used. For instance, a subject's absolute threshold for pitch might be 20 cycles per second. The absolute threshold is considered an inverse measure of sensitivity, meaning that the lower the threshold, the more sensitive is the subject. This means that the nearer the subject's absolute threshold is to zero value of the stimulus, the more acute is his sensitivity to the stimulus. The statistical calculation of the subject's response deviations from the standard stimulus in determining the difference threshold yields a measure of variability called the standard deviation[1] which becomes an inverse measurement of the subject's sensitivity. Apparently, the smaller the difference limen, the more sensitive is the subject to changes in the value of the stimulus.

One of the questions the experimentalist in psychophysics encounters is, "Just how intense a stimulus must be presented to a subject to evoke a response on his part?"

[1] See the chapters dealing with statistics for a discussion of the standard deviation.

First of all, it should be realized that any threshold or any limen is not a static thing, but rather tends to vary within a subject throughout even a short examination period, and, of course, often varies greatly from subject to subject. Because this is so, the thresholds have become statistical entities and are defined here in statistical language as follows: a limen is that value of the stimulus which the subject can discriminate 75 per cent of the time. Thus, your difference limen for sound intensity would be that intensity of sound that you could correctly notice as being

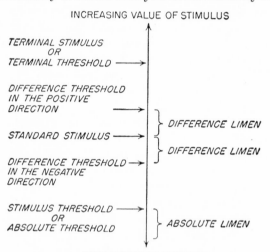

INCREASING VALUE OF STIMULUS

TERMINAL STIMULUS
OR
TERMINAL THRESHOLD ———→

DIFFERENCE THRESHOLD
IN THE POSITIVE
DIRECTION ———→

DIFFERENCE LIMEN

STANDARD STIMULUS ———→

DIFFERENCE LIMEN

DIFFERENCE THRESHOLD ———→
IN THE NEGATIVE
DIRECTION

STIMULUS THRESHOLD ———→
OR
ABSOLUTE THRESHOLD

ABSOLUTE LIMEN

ZERO VALUE OF STIMULUS

FIG. 8.1. The relationship of thresholds and limens on the stimulus continuum.

different from a standard intensity of sound on 75 per cent[1] of the comparison trials. Your absolute threshold would be that minimum physical value of sound that you could just notice at least 75 per cent of the times it was presented. The usual method used in ascertaining absolute and difference thresholds is the method of limits.

The determination of the absolute threshold of a stimulus is most accurately performed by using an ascending and a descending series of presentations. The experimenter gradually increases, in an ascending series of presentations, the stimulus value from a point well below the possible threshold of the subject to a point where the subject reports perception of the stimulus. Then the experimenter explores the series in a descending fashion by lowering the stimulus from a point well above the

[1] Some have used 50 per cent as the proportion of discriminations necessary for the subject to demonstrate that he can identify a difference. Since the subject could be right 50 per cent of the time by merely guessing, the 75 per cent level is used in the discussion here. At best, the proportion of correct discrimination demanded is an arbitrary distinction.

perception point to a point where the subject reports no perception of the stimulus. The mid-point between these two determined points is taken as the stimulus threshold. It is wise for the experimenter to approach these thresholds in a systematic manner with "catch" stimuli thrown in. That is, he should avoid presenting the series by a routine predictable raising or lowering of the stimulus. If he does not do this, the subject may make what are known as *errors of anticipation* by reporting the next value because he expects a change and not because a change is apparent. The subject may also make *errors of habituation* which are caused by his having developed the habit of reporting, for instance, the absence of the stimulus and continuing to report so even when the stimulus becomes apparent. The latter type of error is more commonly encountered. Underwood's (7) discussion of this topic would be of help here.

Let us apply the method of limits to the determination of the two-point threshold.

The two-point threshold is an often determined entity used by psychologists primarily to demonstrate the difference in cutaneous sensitivity in one part of the body as compared to another part. The problem involved in the two-point threshold determination is one of finding out just how far apart the two points of a piece of apparatus called an aesthesiometer must be for the subject to report that he feels two points instead of one. An ordinary set of carpenter's calipers and a small millimeter ruler serve well as the apparatus in this experiment.

The procedure is as follows: The experimenter applies to the subject's upper arm, for example, the two points of the aesthesiometer when they are very close together, perhaps only 10 millimeters apart. The subject should have been blindfolded and the procedure explained to him only so far as to make sure that he understands that he is to report whether one or two points are stimulating him. One must be careful in applying the aesthesiometer so that it is always turned in the same direction. Changing its direction from trial to trial would have an effect on the subject's response and exist as an uncontrolled variable. The trials are conducted by increasing the distance between the two points for stimulation in a systematic order. The trials are continued with increasing separations between the two points until the subject reports two points. A wise precaution would be adding a few more trials, using a little wider distance between the points, so that one is sure that the subject's threshold has been reached during the ascending series. The descending series of trials is conducted in a similar manner starting, however, with the points very far apart, say, 100 millimeters, and decreasing the distance throughout the trials until the subject reports one point. The ascending and descending series should be repeated a number of times.

The calculation of the two-point threshold of the subject from these data involves finding the average of all the thresholds discovered as the result of the ascending and descending series. Figure 8.2 shows a possible set of hypothetical data that might be expected in such a threshold determination when only one ascending and one descending trial is given.

ASCENDING SERIES	SEPARATION IN MILLI- METERS	DESCENDING SERIES	
TWO POINTS REPORTED 100% OF THE TIME → +	100		
+	95		
+	90		
+	85	−	
+	80	−	
+	75	−	
+	70	+	ABSOLUTE THRESHOLD FOR TWO POINT DETERMINATION
+	65	+ ←	
+	60	+	
−	55	+	
−	50	+	
−	45	+	
	40	+	
	35	+	
	30	+	
	25	+	
	20	+	
	15	+	
	10	+ ←	ONE POINT REPORTED 100% OF THE TIME

FIG. 8.2. Data sample expected for one ascending and one descending trial in the determination of two-point thresholds.

The calculation of the terminal threshold presents the problem of ascertaining the upper limit of the range of the subject's sensitivity to the presentation of a stimulus. The difference threshold allows the experimenter to answer the problem of just how much change must take place in a stimulus before the subject will be able to report accurately a change. Both of these problems of threshold determination are met by observing the general procedure of the Method of Limits.

Method of Average Error (or Method of Reproduction, or the Equation Method)

In some types of experimentation it becomes necessary to deal with the problem of the equality of two stimuli. The problem might be phrased as follows: if one presents two different stimuli to the subject, how similar in value must they be for him to report that they are equal in his judgment? This type of problem may be handled by the psychophysical method known as the method of average error.

Broadly speaking, this method is used when the experimenter desires the subject to reproduce a stimulus accurately. The stimulus presented is constant, and the subject manipulates a variable stimulus until he feels the two are subjectively equal. A record is kept of each attempt of the subject in terms of the amount of error (variable error) between the subjective estimate of the stimulus and the known stimulus value. The average of these variable errors is established and this value taken as a measure of the systematic error involved in the subject's judgment that the two stimuli were subjectively equal. If the subject tended to vary considerably in the errors he made, then he is considered to have less precision of response. In this way, it is believed that the sensitivity of the subject is determined by his consistency and variable error. The constant error is stated in terms of the mean, and the sensitivity of the subject is stated in terms of the variability, or standard deviation,[1] of his errors. The nearer his mean to the standard stimulus value, the less his constant error. The smaller the variability of his responses, the greater is his sensitivity.

An example of this method would be demonstrated when the experimenter presents to the subject, by means of an oscillator, a tone of 1,000 cycles. The subject would be allowed to manipulate a second tone by means of another oscillator until he judged the two tones to be equal. From a comparison of the readings of the dials on the two oscillators, each time the subject reported the two tones to be equal, an average variable error could be calculated.

A further example of the application of the method of average error with the presentation of some sample data expected follows.

The problem in our particular instance is to discover how accurately a subject can match the diameter of a circle of light projected on a screen. Two projectors would be required. The first of these would project a circle of light constant at three inches in diameter. The second projector would be adapted in such a way that the subject could by a mechanism adjust the circle of light it projected from 1 to 5 inches in diameter. Both projectors would be turned on, and the subject instructed to vary his projector in the manner necessary to make the circle projected by it equal in size to the 3-inch circle produced by the set focus projector. The subject might be given 50 trials, and after each trial the experimenter would meas-

---

[1] See the chapters dealing with statistics for a discussion of the standard deviation.

ure the size of the circle adjusted by the subject. Such data may be represented as shown in Fig. 8.3.

M_s in Fig. 8.3 is the point denoting the average size of the circle reproduced by the subject. The diameter of the presented stimulus circle is the distance from A to B. The subject's average variable error is computed by adding up all his errors in estimating diameters and dividing by the number of estimations he made. His constant error is the difference between the value of his average variable error and the true size of the presented circle. In this case his constant error is equal to the

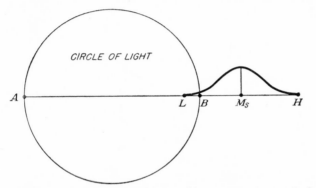

FIG. 8.3. Hypothetical data expected when a subject attempts to reproduce a circle.

distance A to M_s minus the distance A to B. The sensitivity of the subject can be calculated by determining the variability of his estimates. Roughly, the greater the width of the curve L to H, the greater the subject's variability.

The Constant Methods (or Method of Right and Wrong Cases, or Constant Stimuli Method, or Method of Constant Stimulus Differences)

This is the name applied to the method of establishing absolute and difference thresholds when the subject is requested at each trial to report the presence or absence of a constant stimulus which has been presented to him or to compare two stimuli, one constant and one variable. This method is used for determinations of equality of two stimuli, the equality of certain intervals, and in the locating of thresholds.

In the usual application of this method the subject is confronted with the task of reporting to the experimenter whether one stimulus of a pair presented to him is (a) stronger or weaker or (b) stronger, equal to, or weaker than the other stimulus of the pair. In the first instance, it is common practice to call the situation a two-category judgment, and, in the latter instance, a three-category judgment.   Let us talk for a moment about the two-category type of judgment.

This might be a typical application of the method.   A standard weight of 50 grams is chosen for comparison and is included in a set of weights having the values 30, 32, 34 grams, etc., up to and including 70 grams. The subject is to compare the standard weight with each of the other weights.   The weights are presented to him in an irregular order, and he reports, in each case, whether the second is heavier or lighter than the first.   The upper threshold for the subject in determining a perceptible difference in weight is given by the weight above 50 grams, which was

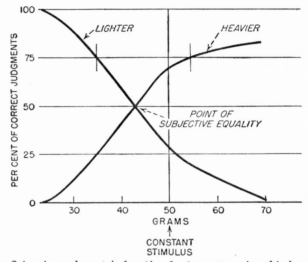

FIG. 8.4.   A psychometric function for two categories of judgment.

called "heavier" 75 per cent of the time.   The lower threshold is determined by that weight below 50 grams, which the subject called "lighter" 75 per cent of the time.   As can be seen, the average of these two threshold values represents the subject's difference limen.   To determine this average most easily, the graph shown in Fig. 8.4, which represents some hypothetical data, is used.   A graph of this type is called *the psychometric function for two categories of judgment*.   It is to be noted that the steeper the climb of the curves, the greater the subject's sensitivity.

The determination of the difference limen under a system of three-category judgment is the same as for the two-category method except that the subject reports whether the second of the two weights is heavier, lighter, or equal to the first.   The plotting of such data is shown in Fig. 8.5.   Again the data are hypothetical.

The addition of the third category of judgment requires that a third curve be added to the psychometric function for two categories, and is shown as the bell-shaped curve at the bottom of the graph. This bell-shaped curve represents the distribution of responses when the subject reported the two weights to be of equal value. The difference limen is considered by some to be one-half the difference between the upper and the lower thresholds.

Thurstone, writing in Andrews' book (1), indicates that whether one uses two or three categories of judgment depends upon the purpose of the experimenter. If the experimenter is studying sensory discrimination

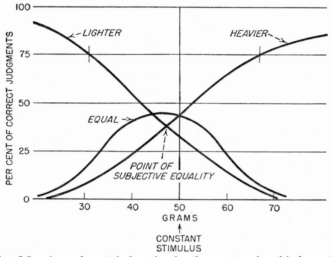

FIG. 8.5. A psychometric function for three categories of judgment.

and attempting to find a limen, then he should use the two-category method. If he is studying the experience of equality, then he should use the three-category method.

Method of Single Stimuli (or Method of Absolute Judgment)

This method differs from the previous ones in that in using it no direct comparison is made between the stimulus being judged and another stimulus. Instead, the subject is presented with a series of single stimuli and asked to describe each. The standard the subject uses is his own and usually approximates the average of the series presented to him. This method would be involved in the following situation. The subject is presented with a number of blocks of wood and is asked to judge the actual weight of each block. This is different from the method of constant stimuli, where he would be asked which of two blocks is the heavier. The subject has built up a standard and uses it for comparison with the stimuli presented.

Still another example of this method would be when the subject is asked to rate the stimulus on some scale and assign a value to it.   The scale might consist of heavier and lighter or, instead of a two-category response, it might be one of three categories, such as heavy, medium, and light.   In case the two-category type of response is to be dealt with, then the data are treated by finding the mean, or average, and the variability, or standard deviation,[1] of the distance between the two types of responses.   When three categories are used, then the data are treated by finding the mean and standard deviation of the two extreme categories, and the width of the middle class.   This latter yields the difference limen which is one-half the distance between the lower and upper thresholds.   In other words, these data are treated the same as were the data for the method of constant stimuli.   Occasionally, when this method is used as in an opinion survey, where a question is asked such as "Are you in favor of, or against, high taxes at this time," the data may be treated by simply finding the per cent of the persons interviewed who respond "in favor of" or "against" in answer to the question.   Sometimes many categories are used, as when the subject must rate some stimulus as follows:

1	2	3	4	5	6	7
Exceptionally strong	Very strong	Strong	Average	Weak	Very weak	Exceptionally weak

In treating the data from many subjects who used this scale for rating purposes, numbers 1 to 7 inclusive assigned to the seven categories could then take the place of the descriptive categories during the calculation of the data.   The mean scale value, or perhaps better, the median, would serve to inform the experimenter of the judgment tendency of the subjects.

Method of Paired Comparison

Here, each stimulus of the series is compared with every other stimulus. The subject must judge which of two stimuli being compared at the time has a greater amount of whatever characteristic is being considered. Since each stimulus must be compared with each other stimulus, including itself, there are, considering n stimuli in the series, n^2 separate comparisons.   Eliminating the comparisons of each stimulus with itself, there are $n(n-1)/2$ comparisons needed if each stimulus is to be compared with every other stimulus (ignoring order).   The method becomes laborious when more than a few stimuli are to be compared.   For instance, if 20 stimuli were used and it were desired that each stimulus be compared with

---

[1] Discussed in the chapters on statistics.

every other stimulus, but not with itself, then 20(19)/2 or 190 comparisons would have to be made.

This method is used when the experimenter is interested in learning the relative preference of the subject for the various stimuli presented. An example of the application of this method would be as follows. A manufacturer of cosmetics is about to place on the market a new type of face powder. He is faced with the problem of deciding which of three different trade names to use for his new product. The three names he has considered using are Smooth-On, Talcumsea, and Forbidden Tryst. He presents these three names for his face powder to a large sample of women who represent the population to whom he eventually wishes to sell the product. With only three stimuli to be compared, his task is relatively simple. Letting A, B, and C stand for Smooth-On, Talcumsea, and Forbidden Tryst, respectively, his presentations of the stimuli will involve each woman comparing A with B, A with C, and C with B. His results might look very much as follows:

75 per cent of the women preferred A to B
25 per cent of the women preferred B to A
15 per cent of the women preferred A to C
85 per cent of the women preferred C to A
95 per cent of the women preferred C to B
5 per cent of the women preferred B to C

The choice is obvious. The women prefer C, Forbidden Tryst.

Method of Rank Order

A group of stimuli is presented to the subject, and he is instructed to rank them in order from the highest to the lowest in terms of some characteristic the stimuli have in common. If more than one subject assigns ranks to the series, then the average rank for each stimulus is computed.

The following question is inherent in the use of this method. If the subject is presented with several stimuli that are not related to each other by any one specific characteristic and is instructed to put them in rank order on the basis of some standard not included in the physical aspects of the stimuli themselves, what characteristics of the stimuli will he draw upon to fulfill his task? The answer to this question may be very difficult to discover, as in the case of a subject making esthetic preferences in ranking abstract art works.

The method of rank order yields results that are similar to those resulting from the application of the method of paired comparisons. In addition, the method of rank order is most often preferred when the number of stimuli is large. The method of rank order is perhaps slightly inferior to the method of paired comparisons on another account, however, because in the former method, the subject may not take into consideration the merits of all the stimuli, since he is not forced to do so. The method of rank order is not usually used if the stimuli to be compared are of such a nature that they cannot be almost simultaneously perceived by the subject. For instance, if one were to ask the subject to compare several tones as to loudness, the subject would have difficulty in ranking them unless he were able to compare each tone with each other tone at the same time, in which case it would seem preferable to use the method of paired comparisons.

An example of this very simple psychophysical method is easy to find. Suppose you have the job of hiring a new professor in a university department. Perhaps there have been five applicants for the position and each applicant was interviewed and his credentials studied by each of ten staff members of the department. You would apply the method of rank order to this situation by having each of the five applicants ranked by the ten staff members. You would instruct the staff members to assign a different rank to each of the applicants, and in such a manner that the applicant most preferred received the rank of one, the one next preferred the rank of two, etc., until the one least preferred received the rank of five. The average rank for each applicant should be found. You would hire, according to the dictate of this method, the applicant receiving the lowest mean rank. Sample hypothetical data follow:

Applicant	Staff members										Mean rank
	1	2	3	4	5	6	7	8	9	10	
A	4	5	4	2	3	5	5	4	3	4	3.9
B	3	4	1	5	5	1	2	1	5	5	3.2
C	1	2	2	1	1	2	4	3	2	1	1.9
D	2	1	3	3	2	3	1	2	1	3	2.1
E	5	3	5	4	4	5	3	5	4	2	4.0

Applicant C is ranked first.

Method of Equal Appearing Intervals (or Method of Mean Gradation)

Two different stimuli are presented, and the subject is requested to adjust a third stimulus until it appears to bisect the "sense distance" between the two. Again, this method is being used if the subject is given a group of various stimulus objects representing a wide range of characteristics to be dealt with and is instructed to sort the objects, according to some characteristic, into a definite number of piles or categories which appear equally spaced to him. If more than one subject is used, then the mean scale position is calculated for each stimulus and compared with the real categories involved as determined by actual measurement where possible.

Ordinarily, this is not possible, since it is, as was previously pointed out, very difficult for the judges to define the aspects of the stimuli that allowed them to make their decisions. An example of the application of this method in a practical situation is presented below.

A young instructor who had just received an appointment in the psychology department of a university found that one of his duties was to grade laboratory reports turned in by the students in the laboratory sections of general psychology. Since he did not have much experience in grading such reports, he decided to use the method of equally appearing intervals to help build up a standard for grading the papers.

The problem involved assigning five different letter grades to the papers, A, B, C, D, and F. Thus the instructor had 5 categories with which to work. He secured 50 laboratory reports that had been turned in the previous year by students enrolled in the course, and, after removing all identifying marks, and previously assigned grades, he gave the papers, in turn, to each of the other 5 laboratory instructors. He requested that they sort the papers into 5 piles equally spaced so that pile 1 represented the best work and pile 5 the poorest.

Each of the instructors complied with the instructions (under protest), and a record was kept of the interval into which each paper was sorted by each instructor. The data then appeared as follows: for each paper there were five judgments as to which interval it should occupy. A mean scale value was calculated for each paper. Also a standard deviation was calculated, but proved meaningless, due to the small number of cases. However, it did, perhaps, roughly show the amount of variability of opinion among the judges concerning the interval any given paper should occupy. This variability determined whether the paper was a poor fit for any one interval or one upon which most of the judges agreed.

The instructor then threw away all papers on which there was too much disagreement and placed the remaining papers in five piles according to their mean scale value. He named these piles by his letter grades, and studied the contents of each pile until he began to form the concept, or perhaps a general impression, of what were the essential components of a paper that caused it to be graded in terms of one letter instead of another.

General Use of the Psychophysical Methods

One may look at psychophysics as Boring (2, p. 294) claims James did, and agree with James that "the proper psychological outcome was just *nothing.*" Yet on the other hand one may look at the uses to which the psychophysical methods have been put and say, "Does this add up to nothing?" What have the psychophysical methods allowed us to do? Binet used the method of constant stimuli as the means of arranging his items on an age scale in his test of intelligence. Whenever the Seashore Measures of Musical Talent is administered to a subject, it represents an experiment in the use of the same method. The lower limits of sensory sensitivity of man and animals were determined by the method of average error in some cases. All thresholds in sensory discrimination, whether absolute, terminal, or differential, were determined by either this method or the method of limits. The method of paired comparisons has come into great use in the field of advertising psychology and in the field of business where it is important to know how your products compare with your competitors' in the eyes and appetites of the consumer. Cattell (3) used the method of rank order in his famous studies where he dealt with the scientific merit ranking of famous scientists, including astronomers and psychologists. In other instances, the ranking method has been of great value in attempts to find how much prejudice a certain group feels against other groups. This method has proved to be a quickly applied and easily understood psychophysical method for all types of situations. Its use has varied from rating employees to appraising public opinion in respect to the moving pictures put out by the film industry. Thurstone and Chave (6) used the method of equally appearing intervals in their now famous studies of attitude.

It is impossible to think of measuring the preferences and opinions of human beings in ways exclusive of the psychophysical methods and still keep some semblance of scientific methodology in the attempt. An improvement upon the methods of psychophysics would be to find the neurophysiological correlates of judgment. This refinement is at the moment, unfortunately, only in the speculative stage.

Throughout this discussion of the psychophysical methods, there have been statements of the same tenor as the following: if the subject is presented with two stimuli that are of the same class but differing in some characteristic and is instructed to divide the sense distance between the two stimuli into two, or perhaps even more, equal units, what stimuli serve to inform him that the point or points he has chosen is equal distance between the two extremes of the stimuli? If the stimulus is one that can be measured in terms of some physical characteristic, then well and good, for we might say that he makes use of that characteristic as his stimulus for decision making. However, we do not know this, and are constantly cautioned by those who are skilled in interpreting the results of a psychophysical experiment not to forget that the stimulus has meaning only in terms of the response it sets up in the subject. Thus these methods do not by themselves answer questions such as that posed above but only allow us to quantify a subject's response in a given situation.

Factorial and Functional Approaches as Methods of Procedure

In Chaps. 4 and 6 reference was made to two levels of attack in any experimental situation. The first of these levels, the *factorial* approach, involves an attempt on the part of the experimenter to discover what condition or factor will cooperate with what other condition or factor to produce some desired result. To do this, only two values of the independent variable are used. These values are the presence compared to the absence of the independent variable as seen in the following example and in Fig. 6.4.

Form taken by factorial approach:

	Phase I	Phase II	Phase III
Experimental group	Both groups equated in terms of all known relevant factors	Independent variable introduced	Dependent variable measured for each group so that the effect of the presence compared to the absence of the independent variable is demonstrated
Control group		Independent variable *not* introduced	

The factorial design is used most often in early, exploratory experiments. Such attempts yield results that tell you *what* conditions produce what results but do not tell you *how* these conditions are related.

The *functional* approach is usually undertaken after one knows, through the outcome of an experiment performed under a factorial approach, that a certain condition produces a certain other condition. The functional approach involves choosing many, or at least several, different values of the independent variable as is shown in the following example and also in Fig. 6.3.

Form taken by functional approach:

	Phase I	Phase II	Phase III
Experimental groups	All groups equated in terms of all known relevant factors	A different value of the independent variable is introduced to each experimental group	Dependent variable measured for each group. Relationship sought between different and specific values of independent variable and corresponding changes in performance of dependent variables

The results of an experiment performed under this approach yields information as to *how* variations in the independent variable are *related* to changes, if any, in the dependent variable.

In the next few pages, we see the application of the factorial and/or functional approaches to typical experimental situations in the three broad subdivisions of the general area of learning: learning experiments, retention experiments, and transfer of training experiments.

Factorial and Functional Approaches in Learning Experiments

Learning is commonly defined as the change that takes place in an organism's performance of a task as it continues to practice the task.

Many factors are responsible for changes and differences in what we call learning in the individual. Some of these factors are part of the equipment possessed by the learner: motivation, age, sex, past experience, etc. Some of these factors are located in the method used in learning the material: logical memorizing compared with rote, amount of practice permitted, kind of practice, and distribution of practice, etc. Others of these factors are generated by the nature of the tasks to be learned: meaningfulness, amount, affective tone, etc. An experiment in learning involves the manipulation of at least one of the above factors. Both factorial and functional designs may be used in their ordinary sense when dealing with such problems.

Below is the factorial approach used in learning experiments wherein some variable is introduced and its influence on *learning ability* is calculated.

	Phase I	Phase II	Phase III
Experimental group	Both groups equated in terms of some learning task similar to the one used in phase III	Independent variable introduced	Presented with second learning task (learning measured as dependent variable)
Control group		Independent variable not introduced	Presented with second learning task (learning measured as dependent variable)

The difference in the learning time, trials, and/or errors between the two groups in phase III yields an indication of the effect of the independent variable on the learning ability of the experimental group.

A use of the functional approach in the same *learning ability* situation is as follows:

	Phase I	Phase II	Phase III
Experimental groups	All groups equated in terms of all known relevant variables	A different value of the independent variable is introduced to each experimental group	All groups presented with the task to be learned; performance on this task is the dependent variable for each group

Factorial and Functional Approaches in Retention Experiments

Retention is the persistency of a response, or the modification of a response, which may be produced some time after the learning episode. Retention depends upon all the factors discussed under Learning. A typical factorial approach to a *retention* experiment follows:

	Phase I	Phase II	Phase III	Phase IV
Experimental group	Both groups equated in terms of all relevant factors	Learns material A to criterion	Independent variable introduced	Retested on material A
Control group		Learns material A to criterion	Independent variable not introduced	Retested on material A

In phase III, the independent variable introduced to the experimental group may be any activity or stimulus whose effect on retention is being investigated. The control group either rests or is given some task to perform that has been demonstrated to have no effect on retention. The amount of retention of material A as a function of the interpolated activity in phase III is indicated by the difference between the two groups in respect to their respective performances on Test A in phase IV.

A functional approach to a *retention* experiment follows:

	Phase I	Phase II	Phase III
Experimental groups	All groups equated in terms of performance on material A	A different value of the independent variable is introduced to each experimental group	Retested on material A. Performance on this retest is the dependent variable for each group

Factorial and Functional Approaches in Transfer of Training Experiments

Transfer of training occurs when the retention of a response previously learned has an effect on the learning of a new response. Thus transfer may facilitate (positive transfer), inhibit (negative transfer), or not determine (zero transfer) the acquisition of new material.

A *transfer of training* experiment procedure under a factorial approach follows:

	Phase I	Phase II	Phase III
Experimental group	Both groups are tested on performance of task A and equated	Training on task B	Test on task A
Control group		Nonlearning activity	Test on task A

The influence of learning B on the performance of task A is equal to the difference between the performance of the two groups in phase III. If the control group's results are subtracted from the experimental group's result in phase III and the correct sign ($+$ or $-$) is retained, the kind of transfer is ascertained.

Savings Method

One other method worthy of note used by investigators of memory phenomena is the *savings method*. This method differs from the others discussed in that it is a method for calculating the savings involved in relearning, to the same criterion of mastery, previously learned but apparently forgotten material. The following formula proves adequate:

$$\text{Per cent of savings} = \frac{\text{original learning} - \text{relearning}}{\text{original learning}}$$

If the measurement of performance is in terms of trials, errors, or time, then the per cent of savings is in terms of the trials, errors, or time, respectively. An example would be: the subject originally learned to solve a maze in six trials. Four weeks later he relearned the maze, needing only three trials to reach the criterion. He learned under the same conditions each time. His per cent of savings in relearning the maze was $(6 - 3)/6 = 50$ per cent. See Woodworth (8, p. 9).

Notes on Procedure

In general, procedures are important because they set the stage for the experiment. It is under the heading of procedure that the experimenter describes the progression of acts to be performed by him during the collection of the data. The procedure differs from the controls in that controls dictate the procedure.

Simple variations of the procedures used in the psychophysical methods and methods for dealing with learning, retention, and transfer, previously discussed, will suffice to serve in most experiments the beginner will be undertaking. The tabular form of presentation of procedure using headings of phase I, phase II, etc., is useful but should always be supplemented by a more completely written description of the procedure. A good procedure prospectus would cover such items as (a) the common name for the procedure used if it is standardized, i.e., method of average error, etc.; (b) a complete description of the acts to be performed by the experimenter, i.e., a description of the equating procedure for the control and experimental groups, the method of introducing the independent variable to the experimental group and the treatment of the control group which is not presented with the independent variable, and the method of recording results; (c) discussion of the particular statistical technique to be used in dealing with the data; (d) a discussion of possible interpretations of the results which may be produced during the execution of the experiment, i.e., if the data support the hypothesis, what conclusions are justified in light of the procedure, or, if the data do not support the hypothesis what are the limits imposed on the interpretation of these data by the procedure used?

Once the experimenter has progressed from the problem stage through the series of steps involving the formation of a hypothesis, determination of independent and dependent variables, and the selection of controls to the description of the procedure, he must then stop and look back upon this *research design* he has evolved. All these steps mentioned are dealt with and exactly formulated before the researcher ever enters his laboratory to collect data. If he stops and evaluates his procedure before he performs his experiment, he runs less risk of finding out too late that he forgot a control or had not anticipated a difficulty sure to arise in the collection of his data.

Researchers sometimes design experiments in such a way that it is virtually impossible to apply an ordinary statistical technique. Some statistical devices are usable only under certain conditions. The sophisticated experimenter solves this problem by the simple expedient of preventing it from occurring. He selects the statistical technique to be used, *first,* and then collects his data under a procedure which is most favorable for the use of the statistical technique.

BIBLIOGRAPHY

1. Andrews, T. G. (ed.): *Methods of Psychology,* John Wiley & Sons, Inc., New York, 1948.
2. Boring, Edwin G.: *A History of Experimental Psychology,* 2d ed., Appleton-Century-Crofts, Inc., New York, 1950.
3. Cattell, J. McK.: *Science,* 1906, **24,** 658–665, 699–707, 732–742.

4. Guilford, J. P.: *Psychometric Methods*, McGraw-Hill Book Company, Inc., New York, 1936.
5. Stevens, S. S. (ed.): *Handbook of Experimental Psychology*, John Wiley & Sons, Inc., New York, 1951.
6. Thurstone, L. L., and E. J. Chave: *The Measurement of Attitude: A Psychophysical Method and Some Experiments with a Scale for Measuring Attitude toward the Church*, University of Chicago Press, Chicago, 1929.
7. Underwood, Benton J.: *Experimental Psychology: An Introduction*, Appleton-Century-Crofts, Inc., New York, 1949.
8. Woodworth, R. S.: *Experimental Psychology*, Henry Holt and Company, Inc., New York, 1938.

CHAPTER 9

METHODS OF INFERENCE

Although this book aims at presenting only one of the scientific methods—the experimental method—let us take time out to look briefly at the other major methods available.

There are several well-known scientific methods available for the psychologist to use. The investigator may find he is forced to use one rather than another because of the nature of the problem he is undertaking. The major methods available to him are, in order of increasing importance, (a) naturalistic observation, (b) statistical methods, and (c) experimental method.

Naturalistic Observation

Naturalistic observation is used if the subject matter of the problem must be studied as it occurs naturally. If we wish to study the influence of competition in a society on its attitude toward war, it is obvious that the experiment should, and must, be conducted where the society exists and not in a "tiled wall" laboratory situation. In the same manner, it would be impossible to study the prediction of attitudes and their alteration in a mob by attempting to create a mob made up of volunteer subjects. Even if one were to experiment with the members of a mob by separately interviewing each member, we would not be able to uncover certain important aspects of the individual's personality that are only revealed when the individual is stimulated by being part of a mob. Such problems must, because of their very nature, be studied where we find them. However, although we may find it necessary to go outside the typical laboratory setup and study the phenomena where they exist naturally, and without instigation by the experimenter, we must still take with us any experimental procedures applicable and utilize such experimental methods as supplements to the method of naturalistic observation. In a broad sense, we would still be in a laboratory. Munn (9, p. 26) also presents a discussion of this method.

Statistical Methods

Statistical methods are mathematical devices of use in discovering certain relationships, trends, differences, and probable predictions from pre-

89

viously collected data or findings. Statistical methods aid the experimenter in uncovering facts that may not be immediately obvious in his mass of data. They aid him in deciding whether small differences between groups are large enough to be considered significant. They are basic to the development of norms of behavior by quantifying the tendency of a group, in respect to a certain trait, to cluster around a given point. Also, they help to quantify the variability of a group in respect to its possession of a given trait.

The statistical methods must be looked upon not as experimental methods but rather as tools of science which aid us in dealing with existing data. As was true in the method of naturalistic observation, the statistical methods serve their most useful purpose when used in conjunction with the experimental method. See Munn (9, p. 36) for additional information on this method.

Types of Experimental Designs

Grouped under this title are the basic experimental designs man has for ascertaining facts by experimentation. We have previously indicated the need for man to deal directly with the things he wishes to understand. The methods about to be presented are logical devices that will enable the experimenter to set up research designs and to draw inferences directly from his data. In each method discussed we will find flaws which create the possibility for error in deciding just what has been demonstrated through the use of the method. Following the presentation of each method will be a discussion of the validity of the method.

Francis Bacon (1561–1626) was one of the first men to write about logical devices that could be used to aid the researcher in his search for scientific knowledge. He did not feel that such rules would be many in number, difficult in application, or yield results capable of more than one interpretation.

John Stuart Mill (1806–1873) undertook with enthusiasm the task of polishing the general concepts of Bacon and presented the logical devices as short rules under the title "Methods of Experimental Inquiry." Mill found he needed just five methods to cover all the types of logical procedures required in establishing order among facts.[1] He stated these methods as five indicative canons. The canons were theoretically airtight, but so perfect that, in actuality, no experimenter could completely meet the requirements. The phraseology used in the statements has been difficult for the beginning student to comprehend quickly. For this reason, and for the further reason that Mill's statement is more of historical importance than it is of importance in teaching, the author wishes to use

[1] Mill, John Stuart, *A System of Logic*, Vol. 1.

only the names of the canons as labeled by Mill and to proceed to treat the canons as they are used in modern context. However, credit is here given to Mill for the heavy contribution of his writings to the material presented in this chapter.

If one were to go through the literature of science, and particularly that dealing with psychology, he would find only a few basic approaches used in experimentation. The particular research design in any one experiment might not be immediately obvious, but under close examination it would be discovered that an inductive procedure was involved which would (a) allow for the collection of data based upon a controlled observation, (b) the method of collecting the data allowed the experimenter at the end of the experiment to relate the performance of one variable to that of another variable, and (c) the experimenter usually manipulated only one variable at a time in the experiment. As one reads one experiment after another, each time abstracting the three points mentioned above, he would in time, through generalization, build up a concept of the experimental method. The various types of approach used by the investigators would begin to fall into at least five basic categories. These types of application of the experimental method could be named so that each name described the manner in which the experiment was designed and conducted. Let us discuss these five types of research designs for conducting an experiment.

Method of Difference

The investigator proceeds as follows:

1. He uses two groups of subjects equal in all respects.

2. He "does something" to only one of these groups. That is, he manipulates an independent variable in, or introduces an independent variable to, one of the two groups (experimental group) but does nothing to the other group (control group).

3. If a change takes place in some dependent variable he is measuring in the experimental group, but does not take place in the control group, then he attributes that change to the independent variable he manipulated in the experimental group.

The design is summed up by the following symbolic presentation:

$$JKC \rightarrow LME \qquad \text{(experimental group)}$$
$$JK \rightarrow LM \qquad \text{(control group)}$$

therefore, C is related to the occurrence of E.

The experimentalist in psychology may make use of this method in the following manner: he may choose two groups of subjects and equate the two groups as well as he can in respect to all relevant variables. By *relevant variables* is meant all the factors known to influence, to a measurable extent, the phenomenon to be studied. Therefore the experimenter carefully sees that each of his two groups is composed of individuals having characteristics as similar as possible. Perhaps he knows that the age, intelligence, and sex of the subjects are capable of influencing the phenomenon to be studied. In that case he would make sure that the subjects were all of the same age, that the I.Q.'s of the individuals were the same, and that they were all of the same sex. He would then proceed to do something to only one of the groups, and would then measure the difference that exists in the two groups following the manipulation of the one group. If a difference then existed between the two groups that did not exist before, he would be justified, according to the method of difference, in assuming that whatever he did to the one group was associated with the change that took place in that group.

The literature of the field of psychology is full of experiments performed under method of difference designs. Let us look at only one of these studies. Russell (10) used the method in an experiment aim at discovering the effects of mild anoxia on simple psychomotor and mental skills. In his study, 244 Army Air Corps Cadets were used as subjects and were divided into subgroups. These subgroups were equated in terms of their initial performance on finger dexterity, arm-hand coordination, and simple addition. These equating tests were administered under "ground" or normal oxygen supply conditions. One independent and three dependent variables were involved. The independent variable to which the experimental group was subjected was deprivation of oxygen occasioned by a high-altitude pressure chamber where the barometric pressure was reduced to simulate 18,000 feet altitude or anoxic (lack of normal amount of oxygen) conditions. The subjects were kept under the influence of the independent variable for 35 minutes during which time eight subsequent trials on the performance tasks were made. Thus performance on these tasks was the dependent variable. After the subjects had been "brought down" to ground-level atmospheric conditions again, the performance tasks were administered under the same conditions as during the initial equating trials. The control group was treated in exactly the same manner except that these subjects were not exposed to the anoxic conditions. The results indicated an immediate drop in performance on the tasks by the subjects under the influence of mild anoxia. More additional controls were instituted in this study than can be allotted space here. In addition, Russell drew further conclusions from his results. However, the study is presented here only to show the use of the method of difference as it may be correctly applied.

It is important to know the possible fallacies in the application of this and the other methods. Therefore, under the discussion of each method, there will be a section discussing the favorable and unfavorable points. It is hoped that the reader will not look upon the criticisms as an attempt to damn the methods but rather as a critical analysis of the pitfalls into which the experimenter may fall as he applies the methods.

Comments on the Method of Difference

Unfavorable: What assumptions have we stated that may be fallacious?

1. We specifically stated that the two groups of subjects are to be equal in all respects, *i.e.*, they must be equated. Is this ever possible in psychology or any other science? How can one be sure, or even assume, that two peas in a pod are alike in all details? In the experiment mentioned above, the assumption was made that the subjects all had the same age, among other things. But did they, for were they all born at the same instant? You may say, "Yes, but you said the two groups needed to be alike in only relevant variables and just how important is it that all the subjects be born at precisely the same instant?" The answer is twofold. First, the method demands that they be absolutely of the same age. If we are going to adhere strictly to the method, we must follow this condition. In addition, who am I to say arbitrarily what is a relevant variable and what is not? The only way I can establish relevance is by doing another experiment making use of this method. The method does not tell me what is relevant, and, thus, to discover relevant variables so that we can use the method we must use the method to discover relevant variables. This just does not sound right to me.

2. This method is *not a method of discovery*. That is, it does not discover previously unsuspected facts, because in the application of the method, it is necessary that the experimenter have a knowledge of all factors that he manipulates. He has to have knowledge of what might be the cause before he can apply the method. He chooses his independent variable because he believes that it may be related to the dependent variable and not for any other reason.

In the previous example cited, Russell believed that reduced oxygen supply might be responsible for a decrement in the performance of simple psychomotor tasks and mental skills. His hypothesis was based on unverified observations that he had previously noted. His experiment that followed was designed to put this hypothesis to a test for purposes of verification.

3. The method is *not a method of proof*. So long as the cause of an event may be due to a multiple factor which loses its effect upon analysis, or retains the effect in part if only one element is present, then the method does not prove that one thing causes another. To show that a partial set of circumstances is related to the occurrence of a phenomenon is not the

same as proving that C causes E.   You may discover what appears to be a factor related to the occurrence of a certain event only to find that when the factor alone is used as a cause the event does not appear.   An example would be the discovery that adding a certain amount of high-test gasoline to regular fuel in your car yields better performance.   You suggest the use of high-test gasoline to your friend only to find out that he does not report better performance.   You then realize that the performance of your car is due to many factors, only one of which is the type of gasoline used.   It is not just the gasoline that yields the performance of your car, or the setting of the air-gasoline mixture in your carburetor, or the size of your fuel pump, etc., but the interrelationship and combined operation of all these factors.   Your application of the method of difference in this situation only gave you a partial answer and did not conclusively prove anything.

Favorable: 1. The good of this method rests on the fact that it permits the use of a control group.   An observation of the occurrence of a phenomenon, when an experimenter introduces a variable with an eye toward establishing a relationship, is meaningless unless he is certain that the phenomenon would not have occurred without the variable.

2. Although the method is not a method of discovery, it does allow the experimenter to verify his hypothesis concerning the importance of his independent variable.

3. Although the method is not a method of proof, it does allow the experimenter to reduce the area of possible explanation of a relationship to a point where a given factor can be evaluated in terms of its contribution to the production of the phenomenon.

4. This method justifies its use in experimentation, if only for the fact that it can serve as a tool of elimination.   It can help an experimenter decide whether a given variable could not be the cause of a phenomenon when stated as follows: no variable can be the cause of a phenomenon if it is absent when the phenomenon occurs.

5. The method has "worked" consistently in countless experiments, and much of the knowledge of the world as gathered by scientists depended upon its application and validity as a method of experimental inquiry. There is no better approach to the investigation of problems, where this method applies, available to the scientist today.

We might note here that a statistical procedure known as the t test, discussed later in this book, is usually used in conjunction with this method.

Method of Agreement

The experimental situation in which this method applies would be set up as follows:

1. The investigator would observe *two or more* instances where the phenomenon occurs.

2. Each time he observed the occurrence of the phenomenon, he would note specific independent variables present and the occurrence of specific dependent variables.

3. He would continue to observe the occurrence of the phenomenon with different combinations of independent variables present until he ascertained that there was one and only one specific independent variable always present when a specific dependent variable occurred.

4. He would infer that the independent variable that alone was common to the occurrence of the specific dependent variable was the factor related to the occurrence of the dependent variable.

We could symbolize this method by

$$ABC \rightarrow FGE$$
$$BDC \rightarrow GHE$$
$$ADC \rightarrow FHE$$

Therefore C is related to E.

Let us see how the experimentalist might make use of this method. Suppose a psychologist were investigating the factors related to success in airplane pilot training. Case history records on 100 trainees, successful during training and later, revealed the fact that in all cases of successful pilots there was one outstanding factor in common throughout the entire group: each man had at one time either owned or operated a motorcycle. The psychologist might, if he were applying the method of agreement, state a relationship between the operation of motorcycles and success in piloting airplanes.

The use of the method of agreement has been made in many studies wherein it was extremely difficult to manipulate the presence or absence of an independent variable. Often such problems are encountered in dealing with the relative importance of heredity and environment on the developing individual. Sometimes we control hereditary factors by using identical twins, or litter mates, and placing the subjects in different environments; we then attribute the similarities in the developing individuals to hereditary influences. It is much more difficult to hold the environment constant so that it may serve as an independent variable. In cases such as these mentioned, the method of agreement comes to play as the type of design often best fitted.

Kuo (6) performed an experiment to determine whether heredity was responsible for the cat's response to the rat. His procedure was, in part, the providing of different groups of kittens with different experiences in relation to rats and then checking to see if all the groups of kittens reacted the same toward the rodents.   If they did, he would then suspect that the hereditary background was responsible.   If they reacted differently and in keeping with their respective experiences with the rodents, then he would expect the influence of the environmental contacts to have resulted in a learned response.   The three different experiences given one to each of the three groups of cats were (a) each cat was reared in isolation from cats and mice, (b) each cat lived with its mother and was exposed to the situation of seeing her kill rats, and (c) each of the cats was raised in a cage with a rat.   Data were gathered by giving cats from each group opportunities to kill rats from the time the cats were six to eight days old until they had either reached the age of four months or had killed a rat. Actually, the design was more complicated than reported here, but what is presented above is sufficient for our purpose.

The situation might be symbolized as follows if heredity is responsible for the typical response of cats to rats:

Isolation plus heredity → killing of rats
Saw killing plus heredity → killing of rats
Raised with rat plus heredity → killing of rats

Actually, Kuo found that the killing of rats depended upon the experience of the cat.   The cats that had seen their mothers kill rats killed the most rats.   The isolated group ranked second in rat killing.   The cats that had been raised with rats killed the least rodents.   The method of agreement allows us to say that the common factor of heredity was not related to the killing of rats to the extent that the environmental factors were.   Thus the results support the hypothesis that the rat-killing behavior of cats is primarily acquired through learning.

Comments on the Method of Agreement

Unfavorable: 1. The correct use of this method demands that the two or more occurrences of the phenomenon have only one circumstance in common.   In the first example of the application of this method which dealt with pilots, it is obvious that there were more common instances than just experiences with motorcycles.   Each of the pilot trainees had gone to high school, could speak and write English, wore a wrist watch, ate the same breakfast cereal each morning at mess, etc.   You would have just as much reason to say that the possession of hair on their heads (since none of the trainees was bald) caused their success as to attribute their success to any other common factor.   Of course, there is a similarity or relevance between motorcycles and airplanes in that both have motors, travel at high speeds, and may attract a more adventurous type of person. But the method of agreement did not give the psychologist this information. He already had an idea that such was true even before the experiment started. So the method itself only yielded evidence that was previously suspected anyway. This is the reason the method of agreement is not correctly called a method of discovery.

2. How many of the men who failed as pilots also had owned or operated motorcycles? The results of the experiment would be meaningless if just as many men who had had experience with motorcycles passed as failed. We see, therefore, that the method of agreement could use some of the characteristics of the method of difference if it is to aid in gathering facts. The next method to be discussed, the joint method, aids in overcoming this handicap to some extent.

3. The method of agreement may cause the experimenter to incorrectly identify some factor as a cause. This example, often quoted, will show what is meant here. Jim drank the following, and with the indicated results, on three successive Saturday nights:

1. Scotch and *soda*   → inebriated
2. Rye and *soda*   → inebriated
3. Bourbon and *soda* → inebriated

By applying the method of agreement we arrive at the startling conclusion that soda causes drunkenness. Of course, it is obvious in this example that alcohol was also a common factor. We can see that in a more complicated situation and one wherein we have little knowledge of all factors present, the wrong conclusion may be reached through the use of this method.

Favorable: 1. The method allows the experimenter to develop hypotheses as to what could be the cause of a given event and provides a means of verifying his hypotheses by a systematic methodological approach.

As the experimenter works in his laboratory, he may see a particular phenomenon occur for which he has no ready explanation. However, through keeping the method of agreement in mind he may watch for a common circumstance always present when the phenomenon occurs. If he discovers what he believes to be the common factor, then he may apply the method more rigorously in a more controlled experiment. Sometimes, after hypothesizing a certain factor to be responsible for the phenomenon, on the basis of the method of agreement, he turns to another method, such as the method of difference, for additional evidence that the factor is related to the phenomenon.

2. The definition of this method is similar to the definition of the goal of science, for they both aim at identifying a constant relationship between an independent and a dependent variable.

3. The method, although not a method of proof or discovery in the

positive sense, does serve as a method of proof when stated in a negative sense.   Thus, if a factor is not always present whenever a given phenomenon occurs, then that factor cannot be the only cause of the phenomenon.

Joint Methods of Difference and Agreement

This type of research design follows the procedure outlined below.

1. The experimenter tests to see if two or more instances of the occurrence of the phenomenon have only one factor in common.

2. He then tests to see if, in two or more instances where that common factor is absent, the phenomenon does not occur.

3. He concludes that since the only way the two situations differed was with regard to the presence and absence of one factor, then that factor is related to the occurrence of the phenomenon.   A symbolic presentation of this would be:

First Instance:

$$ABC \rightarrow JKE$$
$$DFC \rightarrow LME$$
$$GHC \rightarrow NOE$$

Second Instance:

$$PQ \rightarrow VW$$
$$RS \rightarrow XY$$
$$TU \rightarrow Za$$

therefore C is related to E.

An example of this method would be as follows: a psychologist is interested in discovering the cause of temper tantrums in children.   He secures many case histories of children having temper tantrums and many case histories of children who have never demonstrated this type of behavior. In the first instance, the investigator would search for conditions common to the case histories of all the children having temper tantrums.   In the second instance, he would find out how many of the factors present in the temper tantrum group are absent in the nontemper tantrum group.   It is doubtful whether he would be able to go much further in his interpretation than to say that a certain relationship appears to exist between the presence of certain factors in the lives of the temper tantrum group and the occurrence of the behavior and that the absence of these factors are related to an absence of the behavior.   On the other hand each group had many factors in common which have no relative importance in determining the frequency of temper tantrums in children.

Quite a few investigators have performed experiments involving the removal of various parts of the cerebral cortex of rats and other laboratory animals in an attempt to evaluate localized areas of the cortex in terms of their contribution to learning, retention, sensory discrimination, etc.

Some of these studies have followed a type of methodology that most closely approximates the characteristics of the joint method of difference and agreement. One of these studies by Smith (11) dealt with an attempt to locate the cortical area most closely associated with tactile discrimination in rats. The rats were given initial training in solving a Y-shaped, elevated-path apparatus. The rats were taught to select the arm of the Y which had been covered with sandpaper and avoid the pathway with a smooth surface. Surgery was then performed on the rats, and many lesions, involving most of the different parts of the cortex, were made. The animals were given postoperative training, the results of which were compared with the initial training results. Those animals who lost the habit after the operation were found to have a common site of lesion. These lesions were in the frontal and dorsal part of the brain. Smith then inferred that the tactile, or somaesthetic, function for the problem used in the study was localized in the frontal part of the rat's brain.

This type of design might be indicated for this problem as follows:

First Instance:

Animal A: Lesion$_1$ in frontal lobes → loss of tactile discrimination
Animal B: Lesion$_2$ in frontal lobes → loss of tactile discrimination
Animal C: Lesion$_3$ in frontal lobes → loss of tactile discrimination

Second Instance:

Animal D: Lesion$_1$ outside frontal lobes → no loss of tactile discrimination
Animal E: Lesion$_2$ outside frontal lobes → no loss of tactile discrimination
Animal F: Lesion$_3$ outside frontal lobes → no loss of tactile discrimination

Lesions in the frontal lobes are apparently more related to the loss of tactile discrimination than lesions outside the frontal lobes. The frontal lobes, then, are the most probable site of cortical localization of tactile discrimination.

Comments on the Joint Method of Difference and Agreement

Unfavorable: 1. It is doubtful whether two or more instances of a phenomenon can have only one circumstance in common. The experimenter can only attempt to accomplish this and hope he has overlooked no other common circumstance present.

2. The part of the statement which says "two or more instances where that common factor is absent" is misleading and in a sense meaningless. It would be very simple to find incidents not related to the phenomenon in which the phenomenon does not occur. What is really meant is that the negative instance or instances where the phenomenon does not occur must be so related to the phenomenon that there is a possibility for the phenomenon to occur.

Favorable: 1. This method overcomes the objection to the use of the method of agreement alone, for the joint method deals not only with those instances of the occurrence of the phenomenon when the factor thought to be related to it is present, but also when the factor is absent. This introduces a control group into the situation.

2. One of the greatest advantages of this method over the two previously cited is that here we are by definition working with several instances of the phenomenon and, as such, are doing a group study. Only through the study of many individuals can we arrive at a level where we may be confident of our results. If we knew all the factors involved, then we could speak in terms of certainty, but since we seldom attain this, we must be satisfied with results in terms of probability. Using a method which deals with several rather than only two instances is a step in the right direction.

3. The demand that the two instances differ with respect to only one factor is impossible to meet. It is only an ideal condition to be hoped for and not the practical situation with which the experimenter usually deals.

Method of Concomitant Variation

It is to be noted that the three previously discussed methods treat only of the presence or absence of a phenomenon. These methods aid in ascertaining whether a difference exists in a phenomenon due to the presence or absence of a factor. Such methods are used in experiments known as *factorial experiments*. Factorial experiments are usually of the exploratory type and tell you *what* occurs when you introduce a factor. After the experimenter has shown that the presence or absence of a factor is related to the presence or absence of the phenomenon, he is ready to launch into experiments aimed at discovering *how* variations in the amount of the factor are related to corresponding changes, if any, in the phenomenon. Such experiments are typed as *functional experiments*. The method of concomitant variation is basic to functional-type experiments.

The usual application of this method involves the following:

1. An independent variable is varied in some systematic manner.

2. A dependent variable is measured in the presence of this varying independent variable.

3. The experimenter records the variation of both the independent variable and the dependent variable.

4. If the dependent variable varies in any manner whenever the independent variable varies in some particular manner, then the experimenter concludes that the two variables are related.

This method expressed symbolically is

$$ab\ (1C) \rightarrow df\ (1E)$$
$$ab\ (2C) \rightarrow df\ (2E)$$
$$ab\ (3C) \rightarrow df\ (3E)$$
$$ab\ (4C) \rightarrow df\ (4E)$$
$$ab\ (5C) \rightarrow df\ (5E)$$

therefore C is related to E or is connected with it through some fact of causation.

A typical use of this method follows: an experimentalist was interested in discovering what relationship existed between the number of years of schooling completed by employees in an industrial concern and their efficiency ratings as judged by their immediate superiors. He discovered that there was a positive relationship between his two measures on each employee, indicating that the employees with the greatest number of years of schooling were rated highest in efficiency. The investigator advised the personnel office to hire the applicants having the most schooling. In this example we see the type of concomitant variation wherein as one factor is increased another increases with it. This type and others are presented below symbolically to show complete ramifications of the method. Only Types I and III are actually exclusive.

Type I:	$C \uparrow$ $E \uparrow$	
Type II:	$C \downarrow$ $E \downarrow$	(reverse of I)
Type III:	$C \uparrow$ $E \downarrow$	
Type IV:	$C \downarrow$ $E \uparrow$	(reverse of III)
Type V:	C ↕ E ↕	(combination of I and II)
Type VI:	C ↕ E ↕	(reverse of V)

Type III serves to describe the events in an experiment such as the investigation of the size of the pupil of the eye as compared to the amount of illumination to which the eye is exposed. Here we see that as the intensity of the light increases, the size of the pupil decreases.

Curtis (3), at Princeton University in 1943, attempted to establish the relationship between hypnotic susceptibility and intelligence by means of a method of concomitant variation design. The experiment resulted from an attempt to resolve conflicting evidence in the literature which reported to favor in one instance a positive relationship between susceptibility to hypnosis and intelligence (5) and in another instance to indicate no relationship (4). To establish the intellectual level of the 32 subjects, who ranged from a chronological age of sixteen to thirty-two, the Stanford-Binet Intelligence Scale was administered prior to the application of a hypnotic susceptibility scale. A control was instituted to prevent experimenter bias in the application of the hypnosis susceptibility scale. After the administration of the intelligence scale, each subject was scored in terms of the hypnosis susceptibility scale which gave a higher numerical score for those subjects who responded most to various levels of suggestion given. The suggestions varied from simple eyelid closure through increasing degrees of response to a posthypnotic suggestion of reinduction of hypnosis 5 minutes after the subject awoke from the original trance. The data collected consisted of paired scores on each subject, a hypnosis susceptibility score, and an intelligence quotient. The investigator found a significant positive relationship between the two sets of scores that could only remotely be attributed to chance. Thus, there appears to be a strong indication that the more intelligent individuals in the study were more susceptible to suggestions given under hypnosis.

Comments on the Method of Concomitant Variation

Unfavorable: 1. The statement might be made that age varies concomitantly with the number of words in a person's vocabulary due to the fact that such a relationship has been found to exist in an experiment performed under the conditions of the method of concomitant variation. But can age be the cause of anything? Age is like time, it is only a succession of events. Thus age, per se, can cause nothing to happen. The real cause is, instead, the events that have occurred during the passage of time called age. The experiment did not yield any useful evidence as to the cause of the acquisition of words as age increases. Plainly, this method did not ferret out in this case the cause of the phenomenon. It only allowed the experimenter to secure supporting evidence for a causal connection already suspected.

2. The investigator finds in an experiment, and most often does in psychological experiments, the condition wherein the relationship of one variable that varies concomitantly with another variable holds only over a particular range of intensity of the precipitating factor. For instance, he may find by applying this method to the problem of age compared with strength of grip that as a child grows into manhood there is a direct increase of strength of grip with age. But if he carries the experiment on into later life, he finds the age continuing to increase and the strength of grip reversing its direction and decreasing. Thus what holds true for one range of a continuum may not hold true for another.

3. In the example under (2), the experimentalist has just as much reason for concluding that strength of grip causes age as to conclude age is a cause of strength of grip. But the former statement is ridiculous. Yes, but how is this made known by the bare application of the method? The point is, the method does not tell which is the cause and which is the effect any more than do the rest of the canons. Additional information

is needed, therefore, to interpret the results of experiments performed under this and the other methods.

4. Discovering that two variables vary in a constant relationship with one another is no proof that they are related in a cause-and-effect relationship. One might easily find two variables whose variations are apparently related quantitatively but which are almost certainly not related in any cause and effect manner. For instance, if one discovered that the birth rate of Eskimos increased and decreased as the price of cotton in the southern part of the United States increased and decreased, he would doubt if the relationship were any more than a chance one, devoid of cause and effect implications. However, if he also observed that as the price of cotton increased, the number of lynchings of Negroes in the South decreased, and vice versa, then he might logically suspect a cause-and-effect relationship. One must make certain that there is a logical connection between two events that vary concomitantly before he may draw causal connections. However, most rigid experimentalists will deny that there are independent or dependent variables in correlated events—or even any basis for causal connections.

Favorable: 1. The method allows the experimenter to do easily the thing he wants most, *i.e.*, to establish relationships between variables. By repeating observations many times and using the method of concomitant variation intelligently in securing data, he would collect scientific information of considerable usefulness and reliability.

2. The method of concomitant variation suggests cause-and-effect relationships only when a sufficient degree of correspondence is present in the variations of the factors involved. If the factors vary without any more than a chance relationship with each other, then no cause-and-effect relationship is suspected.

3. This method is a method of proof when stated negatively: nothing can be the cause of a phenomenon which does not quantitatively vary when the phenomenon varies.

We should note here that the statistical technique known as *correlation* is most useful in dealing with data collected under the method of concomitant variation. The use of correlational techniques in relation to this method is discussed later on in this book.

Method of Residue

Briefly stated, this method involves the following steps:

1. The investigator first attempts to determine, through experimentation and deduction, that specific and identifiable dependent variables present in a phenomenon are due to the effects of specific and identifiable independent variables.

2. He continues to ascertain such information until the relationship

between only one dependent variable and one independent variable yet remains unknown in the situation.

3. He infers that this remaining dependent variable is related to the remaining independent variable.

Stated symbolically, if it is known that A causes B, D causes F, and G causes H in the paradigm $ADGC \rightarrow BFHE$, and that there is yet only C and E remaining, then the statement which follows can be made:

$$A \rightarrow B$$
$$D \rightarrow F \qquad \text{(known)}$$
$$G \rightarrow H$$
$$\overline{}$$
$$C \rightarrow E \qquad \text{(inferred)}$$

Therefore C is related to E.

Using a method of residue design through the technique of sensory elimination, Watson (13), in 1907, reported that his rats were not seriously handicapped in solving a maze habit, although he both successively and simultaneously removed various sensory cues by blinding, deafening, removing vibrissae, and anesthetizing the soles of the rats' feet. Apparently, the rats, in solving the maze, could only use the remaining senses, namely, kinesthetic (which provides cues from the muscles) and organic sensitivity—the residue. Such results, as typical of those secured through the use of the method of residue, give only negative evidence. The question still remains, "What are the processes which are responsible for the rats solving the maze?"

Lashley and Ball (8), dissatisfied with Watson's interpretation of his data, performed an experiment aimed at partially eliminating the kinesthetic sensitivity of the animals. If the rats could not run the maze as well after partial elimination of kinesthesis as before, then they believed that Watson's interpretation of the importance of kinesthesis would be correct. However, if the rats could learn the maze as well with partial destruction of kinesthesis as they could with no destruction, then Watson could be wrong. Lashley and Ball first trained their animals to solve a maze under the condition of an elimination of cues for vision, touch, smell, and hearing. Experimental animals had their kinesthetic senses impaired by surgery. Some operated animals, when later returned to the maze, solved the maze without making a significant amount of errors. Control animals continued to use kinesthetic cues to solve the maze.

What does this leave for the rat to use as cue material in solving a maze? The best thinking at present concerning this problem is that the rats form a "cognitive map" as Tolman (12) has explained such reactions. The rat may have developed a general pattern or "brain picture." A general movement orientation to the goal can be built up in the nervous system of the animal even when no sensory cues of direction are present. This, then, is the residue of the residue.

Comments on the Method of Residues

Unfavorable: 1. The question remains, however, "What if the animal still has another sense organ remaining besides the kinesthetic, this other remaining sense organ being unknown to the experimenter?" This method, then, as in the case of the others, requires that the experimenter have knowledge as to where to look for the cause. In addition, he must know that he has overlooked no factor that could be the cause.

2. The cause must be clear-cut and not part of a complex factor whose mutual interaction is responsible for this cause. If a phenomenon is caused by such a complex factor whose force as a causative agent disappears when one after another of its elements is eliminated, then the method of residue does not apply.

Favorable: 1. This method allows one by a process of elimination to approximate with greater and greater accuracy the area within which the cause of the phenomenon rests. Its greatest use is as a tool of elimination, where so stated it would become: those factors which may be removed from an experimental situation without eliminating the occurrence of a phenomenon cannot be the cause of the phenomenon.

Experimenters who base their designs on these five methods do so fully aware of the fallacies of the methods. Because they are forewarned, they are forearmed. Such methods allow the experimenter to establish relationships among variables. Such methods allow the experimenter to eliminate false hypotheses and thus narrow to a great extent the area wherein the truth lies. Such methods allow us to describe restricted conditions which will probably produce an effect time and time again. This is all the scientist can do in ascertaining cause and effect. Perhaps it is enough, for everything that we now know as a fact resulting from observation and experiment, whether true or false, was discovered by the use of one or another of these methods. Statistics will show us how to quantify our level of certainty through the use of probability theory. Statistics will help us to accept or reject information gathered through the use of these methods. The use of the correct statistical tools in addition to the use of the correct method of experimental inquiry is a "must" for satisfactory research.

Cohen and Nagel (2) and Larrabee (7) have direct discussions of the five inductive methods of experimental inquiry discussed above. Their treatments deal with the canons as originally stated by Mill. Andrews

(1) and Woodworth (14) offer discussions relevant to the application of several of these methods.

BIBLIOGRAPHY

1. Andrews, T. G. (ed.): *Methods of Psychology*, John Wiley & Sons, Inc., New York, 1948.
2. Cohen, M. R., and E. Nagel: *An Introduction to Logic and Scientific Method*, Harcourt, Brace and Company, Inc., New York, 1934.
3. Curtis, J. W.: A study of the relationship between hypnotic susceptibility and intelligence, *J. Exp. Psychol.*, 1943, **33**, 337–339.
4. Friedlander, J. W., and T. R. Sarbin: The depth of hypnosis, *J. Abnorm. Soc. Psychol.*, 1938, **33**, 453–475.
5. Hull, C. L.: *Hypnosis and Suggestibility*, Appleton-Century-Crofts, Inc., New York, 1933.
6. Kuo, Z. Y.: The genesis of the cat's response to the rat, *J. Comp. Psychol.*, 1930, **11**, 1–30.
7. Larrabee, Harold A.: *Reliable Knowledge*, Houghton Mifflin Company, Boston, 1945.
8. Lashley, K. S., and Josephine Ball: Spinal conduction and kinesthetic sensitivity in the maze habit, *J. Comp. Psychol.*, 1929, **9**, 71–101.
9. Munn, N. L.: *Psychology: The Fundamentals of Adjustment*, 2d ed., Houghton Mifflin Company, Boston, 1951.
10. Russell, Roger W.: The effects of mild anoxia on simple psychomotor and mental skills, *J. Exp. Psychol.*, 1948, **38**, 178–179.
11. Smith, Douglas E.: Cerebral localization in somesthetic discrimination in the rat, *J. Comp. Psychol.*, 1939, **28**, 161–185.
12. Tolman, E. C.: Cognitive maps in rats and men, *Psychol. Rev.*, 1948, **55**, 189–208.
13. Watson, J. B.: Kinaesthetic and organic sensations; their role in the reactions of the white rat to the maze, *Psychol. Rev. Monogr. Suppl.*, 1907, **8**, 1–100.
14. Woodworth, R. S.: *Experimental Psychology*, Henry Holt and Company, Inc., New York, 1938.

CHAPTER 10

APPARATUS

The development of apparatus for use in psychological experiments has been important to modern psychology. During the latter part of the last century and the first part of the present century a peak was reached in the invention of instruments for use in experiments. Many of these pieces of apparatus were developed, or at least constructed, in Germany and were finely made of the best materials, usually brass. The use of such apparatus in psychological experiments gave the early experimental laboratories the air of a physics laboratory with all its assurance of being a science. Psychologists who used such apparatus in their experiments were sometimes facetiously spoken of as "brass instrument psychologists." Sometimes this title was applied in the absence of good humor.

As psychology progressed along stimulus-response, or behavioristic, lines, more apparatus was developed to fill the existing needs. In general, such apparatus was designed to do two jobs: First, to present, systematically, controlled stimuli, and, second, to measure behavior accurately following the presentation of stimuli. Actually, the need for control of an experimental situation is the mother of most psychological apparatus inventions. If a light, sound, or other stimulus source is to be controlled, some type of apparatus must be used. Likewise, the measurement of the response of the subject to the stimulus can best be reliably measured by some objective means involving apparatus. But some apparatus used by psychologists are not brass instruments or of electrical or mechanical nature. Paper-and-pencil tests, such as an intelligence test, are also apparatus. One may look at the administration of an intelligence test as a situation where the subject's intelligence is the antecedent, his intelligence quotient is the consequence, the standardized procedure of administering the test is the means of controlling the situation, and the test itself is the apparatus.

A good piece of apparatus should have several important characteristics: (a) it should measure accurately and consistently within the range where the stimulus or response is produced, (b) it should not itself produce any effect that would obscure or alter the event being investigated, and (c) it should provide a means of collecting, automatically, if possible, an objective, permanent record (1).

During the course of an experiment, particularly if data are gathered over a long period of time, the apparatus used should be routinely checked for efficiency of operation by recalibrating it in terms of some criterion. This is particularly important when two supposedly identical pieces of apparatus are being used, one for the experimental group and one for the control group. It is obvious that changes in the performance of one of the pieces of apparatus could be the cause of a difference in the results between the two groups and mistakenly interpreted as a difference due to the independent variable under investigation.

List of Apparatus Used by Psychologists

A list of the apparatus most often used in psychological experiments (2) follows. The apparatus listed was chosen for inclusion here because each piece is mentioned in at least one or more good general or experimental textbooks. The best definition or picture in the world would not help fix in the student's mind a concept of the apparatus defined as well as would a brief personal contact with the apparatus. The student should attempt to examine each type of apparatus mentioned and, if possible, have its function demonstrated for him.

Activity cage. A cage which records the gross movement of its occupant by having each movement of the cage contact or vary a marking device.

Activity wheel. A cage built in the shape of a wheel and rotated by the activity of the animal as it climbs the inside of the outer rim.

Aesthesiometer. An instrument (often in the form of calipers) which has two rounded points capable of being varied at different distances from each other. It is used in the determination of the two-point threshold and other skin-sensitivity experiments (see Fig. 10.1).

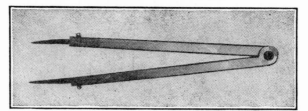

Fig. 10.1.   Aesthesiometer.   (*C. H. Stoelting Company, Chicago.*)

Ataxiameter. Measures the amount of "sway" of a person who is attempting to stand motionless.

Audiometer. Measures the intensity threshold and range of hearing of an individual.

Automatograph. Measures the undirected movements of an individual. The Jastrow automatograph records the movement of an individual's hand as it rests on a sheet of glass supported by three ball bearings.

Barany chair. A rotating chair on which an individual sits and is spun around in a vertical plane. Used to stimulate receptors of bodily motion.

Beat-frequency oscillator. An electronic apparatus which beats two frequencies together producing a third tone. Various controlled frequencies and intensities of sound are produced.

Bell Adjustment Inventory. Paper-and-pencil personal adjustment questionnaire which purports to measure adjustment in the areas of home, health, social, emotional, occupational, and total.

Chronoscope. An instrument for measuring duration of time, usually graduated into hundredths of a second or less, and equipped with a clutch mechanism so that time elapsed between a start and stop is measured and accumulated.

Color wheel. A disk having various colors as sectors and rotated at a high speed to produce color mixture (see Fig. 10.2).

Fig. 10.2.   Color wheel.   (*C. H. Stoelting Company, Chicago.*)

Conditioning unit. An apparatus used to present an unconditioned and a conditioned stimulus simultaneously so as to produce a conditioned response (see Fig. 10.3).

Depth-perception box. An elongated box containing two movable upright poles with strings attached to them. The subject attempts to align the poles so that they are each equal distant from him (see Fig. 10.4).

Dynamometer. An instrument containing a hand grip which when squeezed records the strength of grip of the individual (see Fig. 10.5).

Electrocardiograph. An electronic instrument used in recording the electrical activity of the heart muscles.

Electromyograph. An electronic instrument used in recording the frequency, intensity, and duration of the activity of a muscle.

Electrostimulator. A device used to deliver an electrical stimulus. Usually, it highly controls the frequency, intensity, and duration of the electrical stimulus delivered.

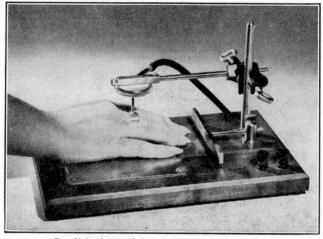

FIG. 10.3. Conditioning unit. (*C. H. Stoelting Company, Chicago.*)

FIG. 10.4. Depth-perception box. (*C. H. Stoelting Company, Chicago.*)

Episcotister. A rotating disk having open sectors. Used to regulate the intensity of light emanating from a source, and to present short exposures of visual material.

Ergograph. A device utilized in the study of change in muscular contraction under conditions of work and fatigue. Usually only the muscle group being investigated is free; all other related muscle groups are immobilized.

Eye-movement camera. An instrument which projects small beams of light on the subject's cornea. The light reflected is focused onto a moving strip of film. As the eyeball turns in a horizontal plane, as in reading, the searching movements of the scanning eyes are recorded.

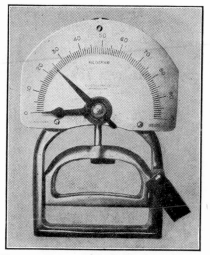

FIG. 10.5. Dynamometer. (*C. H. Stoelting Company, Chicago.*)

Eye perimeter. An instrument consisting of a quadrant which rotates on an axis. The subject fixates at the center of the quadrant's rotation. Various visual stimuli, usually colors, are moved along the quadrant as the subject attempts identification. In this manner the retinal field is mapped.

Galton bar. An apparatus used in demonstrations of psychophysics. The subject is to move a white strip in and out of a black tube by means of a lever until it is equal in length to a standard white strip of a previously set length extending from the other end of the black tube.

Galton whistle. An instrument used to produce high-frequency sounds. The user squeezes a small bulb attached to a tube whose length is varied by means of a screw piston. The screw is graduated and roughly indicates the frequency of the sound produced (see Fig. 10.6).

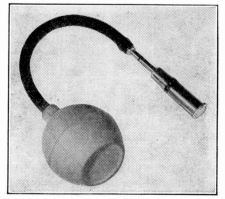

FIG. 10.6. Galton whistle. (*C. H. Stoelting Company, Chicago.*)

Healy puzzle box. A box with one side made of glass. The subject attempts to open the box by releasing a series of strings and rings inside.   His only tool is a buttonhook which is introduced into the box through a hole (see Fig. 10.7).

Impulse counter.   An electrical instrument which records on a mechanical revolution counter each discrete impulse delivered to it.   A prolonged stimulus will record only once in that the counter records how many impulses are delivered but ignores the duration of the impulses.   Each time an electric circuit is made and broken, one impulse is recorded on the counter.

FIG. 10.7.   Healy puzzle box.   (*C. H. Stoelting Company, Chicago.*)

Ishihara test.   A test for color-blindness.   It consists of a number of plates having a circular patch made up of color dots of various sizes, hues, and intensities.   Numbers are seen in the pattern of dots, and their identification reveals whether the subject is capable of discriminating among the hues (see Fig. 10.8 for a color-blindness test).

Koenig bars.   Steel bars of various lengths, suspended by strings, which yield sounds of various frequencies when struck with a hammer at their mid-points.

Kuder Preference Record.   A questionnaire used to determine the preference of an individual for various vocational areas.   Norms are provided for men and women in the areas of outdoor, mechanical, computational, scientific, persuasive, artistic, literary, musical, social sciences, and clerical.   A validity score is achieved for each person's answers.

Kwalwasser-Dykema.   A test of musical aptitude.   It consists of five phonograph records which are played for the subject.   The subject must make difference discriminations in the areas of quality, tonal memory, feelings and tonal movement, intensity, rhythm, time, pitch, melodic taste, rhythm imagery, and pitch imagery.

FIG. 10.8. Color-blindness test. (*C. H. Stoelting Company, Chicago.*)

Kymograph. Used to record changes in the intensity and frequency of a
response during a passage of time. It is a
revolving drum covered with graph paper (or
smoked) and has in contact with it a writing pen (or stylus) which moves at right
angles to the direction of rotation of the
drum. The pen is usually fastened to a
rubber tambour or an electromagnet to
which is delivered the response effect to be
recorded (see Fig. 10.9).

Memory drum. A motor-driven drum
used for the presentation of materials in
learning experiments. The material is typed
on a strip of paper which in turn is fastened
around the outside of the drum. As the
drum turns at a selected speed, the material
is seen through a slot in the case housing the
apparatus (see Fig. 10.10).

Mirror tracing board. An apparatus consisting of a small mirror, usually 6 by 8
inches, mounted on a flexible joint so that
it can reflect the image of a design fastened
on the board to which the mirror is attached. The subject attempts to trace

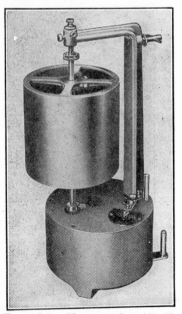

FIG. 10.9. Kymograph. (*C. H. Stoelting Company, Chicago.*)

FIG. 10.10.   Memory drum.   (*C. H. Stoelting Company, Chicago.*)

the design accurately on the board while viewing it in the mirror (see Fig. 10.11).

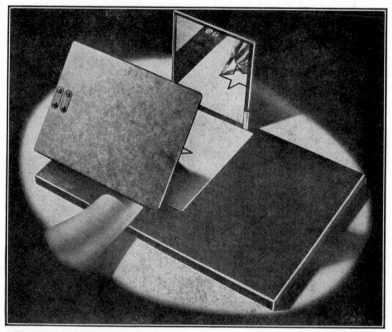

FIG. 10.11.   Mirror tracing board.   (*C. H. Stoelting Company, Chicago.*)

Müller-Lyer illusion.   Two lines of exactly the same length but appearing unequal because one line has arrowheads at its ends and the other has arrow tails at its ends.

Multiple-choice apparatus (Yerkes).   The subject is presented with a number of stimuli at once, such as lights or doors, and must "discover" certain arrangements, preset by the experimenter, in order to give a correct response. The "third light or door from the right" may be the right response or the "middle" light or door may be the key regardless of how many lights or doors are presented on various trials (see Fig. 10.12).

Multiple-T maze. A spatial maze whose pathways are composed of a number of T's combined into a continuous pattern.

Obstruction box (Columbia). Apparatus used to measure the strength of drives in animals. It consists of two cages separated by an electrified grid. The animal is placed in one cage and its reward (a mate, food, water, litter) placed

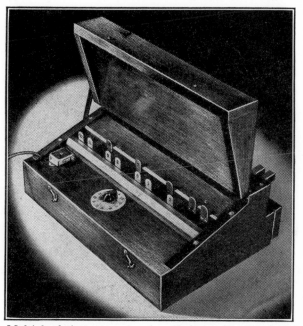

FIG. 10.12. Multiple-choice apparatus by Yerkes. (*C. H. Stoelting Company, Chicago.*)

in the other cage. The number of crossings of the animal in a 20-minute period is a reliable test of the strength of the animal's particular drive.

O'Conner Finger Dexterity Test. The test consists of a block containing 100 holes into each of which the subject must manually insert *three* small metal pins. The amount of time required to fill all holes is then converted into a percentile rank.

O'Conner Tweezer Dexterity Test. The test consists of a block containing 100 holes into each of which the subject must insert, by means of a pair of tweezers, *one* small metal pin. The amount of time required to fill all holes is then converted into a percentile rank (see Fig. 10.13).

Olfactometer. An instrument used in psychophysical investigations of the sense of smell. It consists, essentially, of two glass tubes curved to fit the nostrils, and which extend through a shield. The distal ends of the tubes are fitted into larger tubes lined with odorous substances and which can be extended to any desired length.

One-way vision screen.   Used to permit the experimenter to observe the subject without in turn being observed himself.   A one-way mirror may be used.   A second, and very simple, setup consists of the subject being placed in a closely woven, black screen cage.   Bright light inside the cage and darkness outside allow the experimenter to see in the cage but prevents the subject from seeing out.

Oscilloscope.   An electronic instrument having as its major component a cathode-ray tube.   Alternating voltages, such as those produced by sound activating a microphone, cause an electron stream to deviate proportionally and to

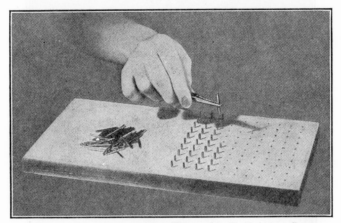

Fig. 10.13.   O'Conner Tweezer Dexterity Test.   (*C. H. Stoelting Company, Chicago.*)

trace a wave pattern on the end of the cathode-ray tube which appears to the observer as a screen.

Photometer.   An instrument used to measure the brilliance of light in terms of candlepower.

Plethysmograph.   Measures changes in size of parts of the body due to alteration of blood supply.   It consists of a closed cylinder filled with water into which is extended the member.   Changes in size of the part of the body enclosed causes a change in the level of the water which in turn varies a column of air in a tube extending from the cylinder to a tambour recording device.

Pneumograph.   Used to record the breathing rate of a subject.   It consists of a flexible and stretchable rubber tube closed at one end and having the other end connected by a hose to a tambour recording device.   The apparatus is fastened snugly around the subject's chest or diaphragm (see Fig. 10.14).

Polygraph.   A kymograph-type revolving drum which provides for the simultaneous recording of several physiological processes (see Fig. 10.15).

Problem box.   A problem situation for animals where the animal must learn to move levers or pull string, etc., to get in or out of a box in order to reach a reward.

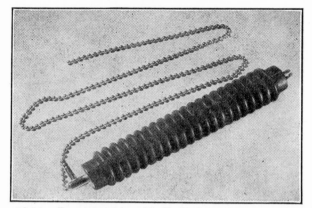

FIG. 10.14. Pneumograph. (*C. H. Stoelting Company, Chicago.*)

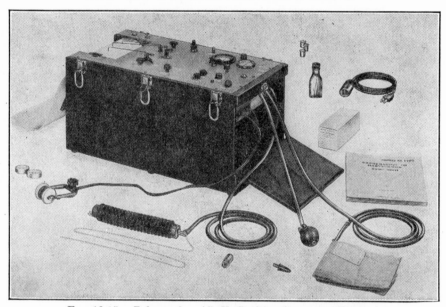

FIG. 10.15. Polygraph. (*C. H. Stoelting Company, Chicago.*)

Pseudophone. An instrument used to carry sounds, whose source is to the right of the individual, to the left ear, and vice versa. It consists of two receiving trumpets equipped with tubes bent to go around the individual's head and fit into his ears (see Fig. 10.16).

Psychogalvanometer. An instrument used in the measurement of the changes in skin resistance or changes in the electrical potential on the surface of the skin (see Fig. 10.17).

Pupillometer. An instrument used to measure the size of the pupil of the eye.

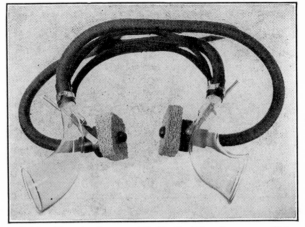

FIG. 10.16.   Pseudophone.   (*C. H. Stoelting Company, Chicago.*)

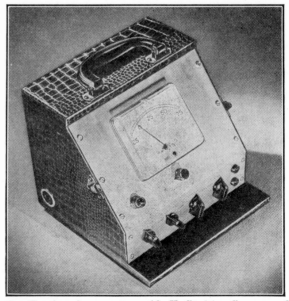

FIG. 10.17.   Psychogalvanometer.   (*C. H. Stoelting Company, Chicago.*)

It consists of a telescope type of arrangement equipped with adjustable cross hairs.

Pursuit meter. A revolving disk such as a phonograph turntable having a metal spot on its surface near the outer edge.   The subject attempts to keep a stylus in contact with the spot as the disk rotates.

Reaction-time apparatus. An apparatus consisting of two switches, a chronoscope, and a light or sound source in series.   The subject closes one of the

Fig. 10.18. Reaction-time apparatus. (*C. H. Stoelting Company, Chicago.*)

Fig. 10.19. Part of Revised Stanford-Binet Intelligence Test. (*C. H. Stoelting Company, Chicago.*)

switches when given a ready signal, and, at a staggered time interval following, the experimenter closes the second switch. The stimulus and chronoscope are thus turned on and time is recorded until the subject is able to react to the stimulus and opens the circuit stopping the chronoscope (see Fig. 10.18).

Revised Stanford-Binet. A test of general intellectual development achieved by an individual (see part of test in Fig. 10.19).

Rorschach Test. A personality test used in the diagnosis of personality. It consists of ten cards containing ink blots, five of the cards being black and white and five containing colors. The subject tells what he "sees" in the cards and in this way reveals his personality through the mechanism of projection.

Seashore measures of musical talent. By using phonograph records as the means of presentation, various musical capacities of the individual are measured. The materials present tests for tonal memory, pitch discrimination, intensity, time, rhythm, timbre, and consonance.

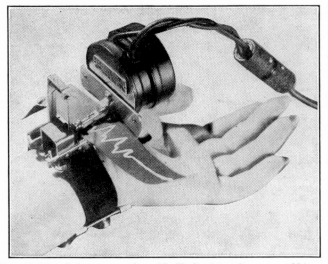

Fig. 10.20.   Sphygmograph.   (*C. H. Stoelting Company, Chicago.*)

Singerman color-mixture apparatus. Consists of a box inside of which is a light source that illuminates a milk-glass screen. Red, green, and blue filters may be adjusted to overlap. The overlapping of red and blue produces purple; green and red produces yellow; and green and blue produces blue-green.

Skinner box. A type of problem box where the animal is automatically delivered a pellet of food each time it presses a lever.

Sound perimeter. An apparatus used in sound-source localization experiments. It consists of a fixed chair upon which the subject sits, a movable sound source (usually a buzzer mounted on one end of a stick five feet long and a push button on the other end), and a large, circular azimuth indicator which can be moved in horizontal-vertical planes.

Spectrometer. An instrument used in the study of color. It is capable of analyzing white light into its separate wavelengths.

Sphygmograph. An instrument used in measuring the rate and force of the pulse. It consists of a device which is attached to the wrist. Each pulse beat causes a lever to move and activate a tambour attached to a polygraph (see Fig. 10.20).

Sphygmomanometer. An instrument used to measure arterial blood pressure. It consists of a rubber cuff which is inflated around the subject's upper arm and a mercury column used to indicate the pressure of the cuff at the point where the pulse ceases.

Stabilimeter. A cage or a bed so suspended or supported that it is moved by movements of its occupants. These movements of the cage are recorded by a pneumatic, electrical, or mechanical system.

Steadiness tester. Used to test the hand steadiness of subjects. It consists of a metal plate containing apertures of various diameters, a metal stylus, and

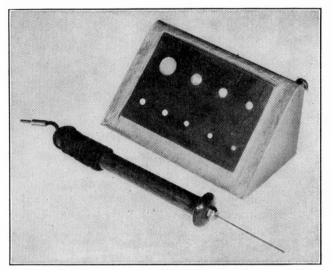

Fig. 10.21. Steadiness tester. (*C. H. Stoelting Company, Chicago.*)

a chronoscope or impulse counter. All are connected in series with a battery. Each time the stylus makes contact with the aperture plate the circuit is closed, causing the chronoscope or counter to record. The steadiness score is the accumulation of recorded contacts made (see Fig. 10.21).

Stereoscope. An optical instrument used in studies of depth perception. It consists of a pair of prisms so arranged that each displaces a picture presented to each eye. Thus two pictures taken from slightly different angles are combined and the illusion of depth is perceived in the picture (see Fig. 10.22).

Strong Vocational Interest Blank. An inventory which purports to measure the interest a subject has in various types of vocations. Scales are available for all the major professions and vocations.

Szondi Test. A personality test of the projective type. It consists of six sets of eight pictures. In each set are pictures of persons who were diagnosed as having mental disorders. The testee sorts the pictures into those he likes and dislikes. The results are profiled in terms of eight factors: homosexual, sadistic, epileptic, hysteric, catatonic, paranoid, depressive, and manic.

Tachistoscope. An instrument used to present any type of stimulus material for a brief duration (see Fig. 10.23).

Tautophone. Also known as a *verbal summator.* A phonograph recording of samples of a man's speech is played at a low intensity. The subject listens and

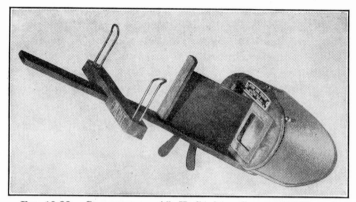

Fig. 10.22.   Stereoscope.   (*C. H. Stoelting Company, Chicago.*)

Fig. 10.23.   Tachistoscope.   (*C. H. Stoelting Company, Chicago.*)

attempts to tell what was said. In doing so it is felt that he will "project" into his interpretation his own feelings of guilt, etc.

Temporal maze. A maze used in studying a temporal succession of movements on the part of the subject without changes in the stimulating situation. It consists of two rectangular-shaped pathways having one side in common. The subject, starting up the middle pathway, must discover the key to a previously decided solution, such as twice to the right then twice to the left.

Thematic Apperception Test. A personality test of the projective type. It consists of a number of pictures which the subject must use as an illustration for a story.

Voice key. An apparatus used to measure the time required by a subject to respond with a word in answer to a stimulus word spoken by the experimenter. It consists of two microphones and a chronoscope in series with an electronic switch. The experimenter speaks into the first microphone starting the chronoscope. The responses of the subject spoken into the second microphone stop the chronoscope. The reaction time is recorded by the chronoscope.

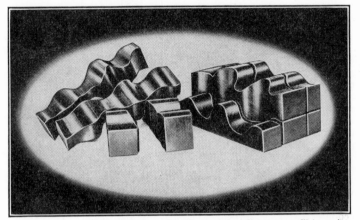

Fig. 10.24.   Wiggly block.   (*C. H. Stoelting Company, Chicago.*)

Wechsler-Bellevue Intelligence Scale. An intelligence test available for children or adults. It yields a verbal, performance, and full-scale I.Q.

Wiggly block. A cube of wood cut in several wavy pieces. The subject must assemble the pieces so as to form the cube. It sometimes yields "sudden solutions" (see Fig. 10.24).

Zöllner illusion. Used as a demonstration of visual space perception illusion. It consists of a series of parallel lines wherein alternate lines are crossed at acute angles by shorter lines, each set slanting in the opposite direction. The parallel lines then appear to slant alternately in different directions.

Apparatus Used in Specific Areas of Psychology.

The following table will allow the reader to ascertain quickly the use in different areas of psychology of the various pieces of apparatus described above. If a piece of apparatus is checked in the first column, this indicates that it can be used in psychological experiments to present a stimulus to a subject. If the piece is checked in the second column, this means it can be used to measure the response of a subject to a stimulus. The

Apparatus	Present stimulus	Measure response	Pneumatic	Mechanical	Electrical	Animal	Clinical	Emotions	General	Learning	Motivation	Perception
Activity cage		X	X		X	X					X	
Activity wheel		X		X		X					X	
Aesthesiometer	X	X		X								X
Ataximeter		X		X			X	X				
Audiometer	X	X			X		X					X
Automatograph		X		X			X	X				
Barany chair	X			X								X
Beat-frequency oscillator	X				X				X			X
Bell adjustment inventory	X	X					X					
Chronoscope		X			X				X			
Color wheel	X			X								X
Conditioning unit	X	X			X					X		
Depth-perception box	X	X	X									X
Dynamometer		X		X					X	X		
Electrocardiograph		X			X		X		X			
Electromyograph		X			X							
Electrostimulator	X			X					X			
Episcotistor	X			X								X
Erograph		X		X					X			
Eye-movement camera		X		X					X			
Eye perimeter	X	X		X								X
Galton bar	X	X		X								X
Galton whistle	X	X	X									X
Healy puzzle box	X			X						X		
Impulse counter		X		X					X			
Ishihara Test	X						X					X
Koenig bars	X	X		X								X
Kuder Preference Record	X	X					X					
Kwalwasser-Dykoma	X	X					X					X
Kymograph		X	X	X	X				X			
Memory drum	X			X	X					X		
Mirror tracing board	X			X						X		
Müller-Lyer illusion	X			X								X
Multiple-choice apparatus	X			X						X		
Multiple-T maze	X					X						
Obstruction box	X	X		X		X					X	
O'Conner Finger Dexterity Test	X					X		X			X	
O'Conner Tweezer Dexterity Test	X					X		X				

next three columns, headed Pneumatic, Mechanical, and Electrical, respectively, show, when checked, whether the apparatus operates on a pneumatic, mechanical, or electrical principle. The remaining columns, when checked for a piece of apparatus, reveal those areas of psychology where the particular apparatus is most often used.

Apparatus	Present stimulus	Measure response	Pneumatic	Electrical	Mechanical	Animal	Clinical	Emotions	General	Learning	Motivation	Perception
Olfactometer	X	X	X		X							X
One-way vision screen					X				X	X		
Oscilloscope		X		X					X	X		
Photometer		X			X				X			
Plethysmograph		X	X	X	X			X				
Pneumograph		X	X					X				
Polygraph		X	X	X	X			X	X			
Problem box	X				X					X		
Pseudophone	X		X									X
Psychogalvanometer		X		X				X				
Pupillometer		X			X		X					
Pursuit meter	X	X		X						X		
Reaction-time apparatus	X	X		X								X
Revised Stanford-Binet Test	X	X					X					
Rorschach Test	X	X					X					
Seashore Test of Musical Aptitude	X	X					X					
Singerman's color-mixture apparatus	X			X								X
Skinner box		X			X					X	X	
Sound perimeter	X	X		X								X
Spectrometer	X				X							X
Sphygmograph		X		X			X		X			
Stabilimeter		X		X	X	X	X	X				
Steadiness tester	X	X			X				X			
Stereoscope	X					X						X
Strong Vocational Interest Blank	X	X					X					
Szondi Test	X	X					X					
Tachistoscope	X			X	X					X		X
Tautophone	X			X			X					
T.A.T.	X	X					X					
Temporal maze	X				X					X		
Voice key		X		X	X				X			
Wechsler-Bellevue Test	X	X					X					
Wiggly block	X				X					X		
Zöllner illusion	X				X							X

Useful Electric Circuits in Experimentation

The experimental psychologist often finds that he needs a piece of apparatus to perform a certain function, but that such apparatus is either not readily available or else the price is too great. In analyzing these needs one finds that four basic electric circuits will perform the majority of the tasks desired. The following circuit diagrams were specially designed for inclusion here with the idea of economy, efficiency, and simplicity governing the selection.   Anyone with even an elementary knowledge of radio or electric circuits can easily construct the pieces of apparatus from these diagrams.

Electrical Stimulator.   This circuit (Fig. 10.25) will deliver an alternating current within the range of 0 to 35 milliamperes for any duration

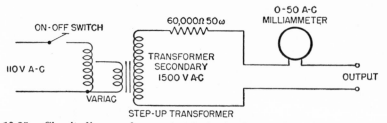

FIG. 10.25.   Circuit diagram for an electrical stimulator.   (*From a design suggested by Dr. J. F. Pierce, Western State Psychiatric Hospital, Pittsburgh, Pa.*)

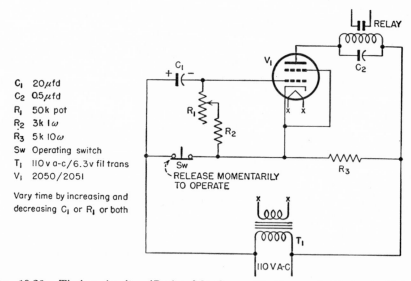

C₁ 20μfd
C₂ 0.5μfd
R₁ 50k pot
R₂ 3k 1ω
R₃ 5k 10ω
Sw Operating switch
T₁ 110v a-c/6.3v fil trans
V₁ 2050/2051

Vary time by increasing and
decreasing C₁ or R₁ or both

FIG. 10.26.   Timing circuit.   (*Designed by George W. Townsend, Electronic Maintenance, U.S. Steel Co., Irvin Works, Dravosburg, Pa.*)

desired.   It has been used by the author to deliver the unconditioned stimulus in conditioning experiments and as the shocking current in producing electroshock convulsions in rats.   The circuit has the desirable feature of delivering a preset current which is insignificantly altered by changes in a subject's resistance.

Timing Circuit. The circuit shown in Fig. 10.26 will close or open a relay (depending upon the type of relay chosen) for any preset duration of time throughout a range of 0.1 second to several minutes. This circuit may be used in conjunction with the electrical stimulator described above or anywhere where a stimulus is to be presented for a short controlled duration of time.

Photoelectric Cell Circuit. In order to allow a light stimulus to produce a mechanical response, the circuit in Fig. 10.27 is suggested. In this circuit, as drawn, each of the relays will respond to a different intensity of

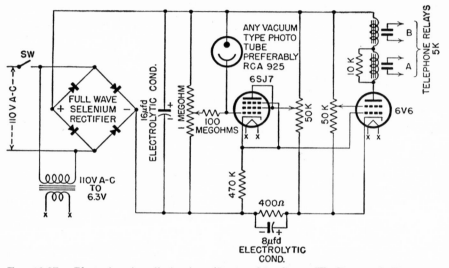

FIG. 10.27. Photoelectric cell circuit. (*Designed by George W. Townsend, Electronic Maintenance, U.S. Steel Co., Irvin Works, Dravosburg, Pa.*)

light, one of the relays closing and remaining closed at a low intensity and the other closing only when a more intense light is presented to the photocell. In this way the same light source can produce two different types of mechanical response, if desired.

Electronic Voice Key. When sound is the stimulus and it is desired to close or open a relay as the mechanical response, then the circuit in Fig. 10.28 is most adequate. The circuit as drawn is actually complete for use as a voice key in experiments involving a subject's vocal response to a word spoken by the experimenter. Speaking into one of the microphones starts the chronoscope and speaking into the other microphone stops the chronoscope.

These circuits are far more versatile than indicated here and will be found to serve in many experimental situations as some particular need arises.

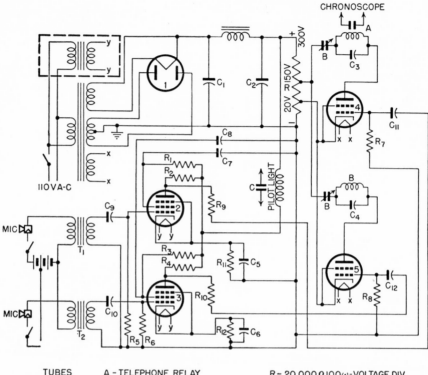

TUBES	A - TELEPHONE RELAY	R - 20,000Ω100ω-VOLTAGE DIV.
1 - "80"	B - " "	R_1- R_3-100,000Ω
2 - "6SJ7"	C - " "	R_2- R_4-250,000Ω
3 - "6SJ7"	C_1-C_2-C_3-C_4-C_7-C_8-8μfd - 350VD-C	R_5-R_6-10Ω MEG
4 - 2050 (2051)	C_5-C_6-25μfd - 50V D-C	R_7-R_8-0.5Ω MEG
5 - 2050 (2051)	C_9-C_{10}-C_{11}-C_{12}-0.001μfd	R_9-R_{10}-2000Ω
	T_1 - T_2- MIC INPUT XMFR S.B. TO S.G.	R_{11}-R_{12}-100Ω

FIG. 10.28. Electronic voice key. (*Designed by George W. Townsend and John C. Townsend, U.S. Steel Co., Irvin Works, and West Virginia University.*)

BIBLIOGRAPHY

1. Davis, R. C.: in Andrew's *Methods of Psychology*, John Wiley & Sons, Inc., New York, 1948.
2. Warren, Howard C.: *Dictionary of Psychology*, Houghton Mifflin Company, Boston, 1934.

CHAPTER 11

CONDUCTING THE EXPERIMENT

The experimenter, prior to entering the laboratory for the purpose of performing his experiment, has gone far on his way toward answering his problem. He has selected a tenable hypothesis, defined his independent and dependent variables, introduced the highest degree of control over all known relevant variables—save the one chosen for the dependent variable—provided adequate apparatus for the presentation and manipulation of the independent variable, settled upon a satisfactory procedure for conducting his experiment and collecting the results, and has reflected on all these things which constitute his research design in an effort to find an error in his plans. Satisfied that no one can voice a correctable criticism, the experimenter enters the laboratory.

The experimenter should have prepared a written prospectus for his research project. Included below is a typical form on which may be written the major points pertinent to the research design and the execution of the experiment. Space also is allocated to the statement of results and conclusions. Some laboratory directors insist that the research workers submit such a work sheet before attempting to conduct any experiment. Experiments can then be evaluated and altered if necessary, or not even attempted if the research design is poor. In some universities, the laboratory courses in psychology consist of the performance of experiments by the students as a result of some research design that either the individual student or the class as a whole has developed. The form for presenting the research design included here makes an excellent report sheet on which students may submit their original research designs for proposed experiments. Later on in this book, the reader will see such a report sheet well done in respect to containing the basic information required under each heading on the form. The following work sheet when reproduced for use should have the items separated enough to provide ample space for the inclusion of as much information as required.

Name_____
Section_____
Date_____

129

Form for Planning or Reporting Experimentation[1]

1. What is the problem?

2. State the problem in terms of a hypothesis.

3. What is the independent variable?

4. What is the dependent variable?

5. How is the dependent variable (s) to be measured?

6. What controls are necessary?

What?	How?	Why?

7. What is the procedure to be followed in conducting the experiment?
   a. Diagram the apparatus.

   b. Describe exactly what you plan to do.

   c. How do you plan to analyze the research results?

8. *Review* the research design.
   a. What results, were they obtained, would support your hypothesis?

   b. What results, were they obtained, would fail to support your hypothesis?

9. Conduct the experiment.
   a. What unplanned occurrences were present that may have influenced your results?

[1] This form represents a revision of an original form developed at the University of Pittsburgh, 1946 to 1948, by Drs. R. W. Russell, H. W. Braun, A. J. Latham, W. S. Barker, and J. C. Townsend.

b. What were your subject's reactions to the experiment (remarks, attitudes, etc.)?

c. Summarize your research results in tables, graphs, and/or other clear means of presentation.

10. Interpret the results.
   a. Describe your tables and graphs and statistical analysis from the point of view of proving or disproving the hypothesis.

   b. State your conclusions.

In the laboratory, the experimenter will spend his time observing and recording the behavior of his subjects. All through the long and often tiring experience of data collection he must remember to obey the dictates of his research design to the letter. Any variation from his design, if not justified through some judicious change, will render his results meaningless. There will be times when he will grow tired of the monotonous routine of performing the task of gathering data. It is here that research may lose some of the glamour that is often thought attached. But interest can be maintained if the experimenter develops the mental set of looking for occurrences which may lead to future hypotheses. It is not at all unusual for the trained experimenter to develop a "hunch" every time he "runs" his subjects. Such observations should be recorded for later study, and possibly later experimentation.

The collection of data moves most easily if the experimenter provides himself with a simple yet efficient means of recording his data. Research data should be collected in some neat, orderly fashion. To make the records permanent, all writing should be done in ink. Use of a hardback ledger type of data book is favored by some. In this manner, a permanent record is easily kept. Some experimenters collect their data on large sheets of graph paper on which there will be sufficient room for working the statistical analysis without the labor and chance for error involved in recopying the data. This procedure works best when a large mass of data is to be handled.

Data are meaningful only if they are identifiable. Otherwise they are just a collection of numbers standing for some quantity of an unknown quality. One way to make data meaningful is to collect them in tabular form. Generally, tables make for easy comparison of different values. Their use in place of word descriptions of data is encouraged.

An example of a skeleton tabular form for *collecting* data throughout the entire 10 trials of an experiment on one subject is given below. Such forms are often mimeographed if the number to be used is large.

Title of experiment: _____	Date: _____
Experimenter's name: _____	Place: _____
Identification of subject _____	Classification
Name (or number) _____	Experimental _____
Address (or cage) _____	Control _____
Age _____	Other _____
Sex _____	

Trial	Data (_____) units	Remarks
1		
2		
10		

Sum = _____   S. E. Mean = _____
Mean = _____
S.D. = _____

General remarks:

The above table could be altered as shown on page 133 to allow for the collection of the results of all the data on, say, 10 different subjects during an experiment.

These two tabular forms are more complete than those one would use for presenting data in a printed form, for example, in a journal article or a textbook. But the data collection period is no time for reducing the data; instead, it is the time for elaboration.

If facilities are available, data may be collected, sorted, analyzed statistically, and filed by machine sorting methods. This greatly simplifies the task of the experimenter in that once a card is punched on each subject, many desired operations can be quickly performed almost automatically. Unless a great number of subjects or a considerable amount of data are involved the machine method is unnecessary.

Title of table: _____			
Subject	Expt'l group (units)	Control group (units)	Remarks
A			
B			
J			

N_e =

Sum = _____ _____ N_c = _____
Mean = _____ _____
S.E. Mean = _____ _____

Critical ratio _____   Level of confidence _____

General remarks:

The data gathered during the performance of the experiment constitute the material from which inferences will be drawn in support or refutation of the hypothesis. Errors in data collection or its manipulation can ruin your experiment even if your research design were perfect and your interpretation of the data faultless. Data collection represents, therefore, an important link in the chain composed of hypothesis, research design, collection and manipulation of data, interpretation, and generalization. Like any chain, it is no stronger, as the saying goes, than its weakest link.

PART C
INTERPRETATIONS AND CONCLUSIONS

CHAPTER 12

CENTRAL TENDENCY AND VARIABILITY

When one surveys the literature of the entire field of science, one is impressed with the tremendous use psychologists make of statistics. Psychologists have developed this interest in the use of statistics for perhaps at least two reasons: (a) much of psychology deals with norms of behavior wherein statistical manipulation of data has been of extreme importance, and (b) psychology has been faced with the challenge of "proving" itself a science. The experimenter in psychology has been forced to be extremely critical of his results and has thus drawn heavily on the statistical methods for aid in analyzing and interpreting them. Perhaps the most severe critics of psychology have been the psychologists themselves, who have demanded the best critical thinking about the subject. To many psychologists, results of experimentation not put to statistical analysis are results not properly analyzed. This is an extreme, though characteristic, point of view.

Meaning and Use of Statistics

Statistics is a term that has many meanings for different people. Broadly speaking, a differentiation can be made between *descriptive statistics* and *statistical inference*. The difference between these two terms is, essentially, one involving the use to which statistics is put. Descriptive statistics involves summarizing and describing data by means of various devices, such as measures of central tendency, measures of variability, measures of relationship, the construction of graphs, the determination of the shape of curves representing the data, etc. Statistical inference deals with interpreting data and predicting what probably *will* happen from what *has* happened in the past. Such devices as the reliability of differences between means, the degree of correlation between two variables, etc., are used in the process of statistical inference.

Basic to the use of statistics, and particularly from the statistical inference point of view, is the concept of the *probability* of the occurrence of an event. The probability of the occurrence of an event is a ratio of how frequently the event is expected to happen to the total possible outcomes.   Thus, a coin tossed into the air has one chance of landing "heads" compared to the two possible outcomes "heads" and "tails."   A probability ratio of $\frac{1}{2}$ is then used to represent this situation.   Another example might help.   If we know that there are 100 marbles in a bag, 5 black, and 95 white, the probability of drawing a black marble is 5 chances out of 100, or written as a probability ratio, $\frac{5}{100}$.   This means that once out of each 20 times we may expect to draw a black ball by chance alone.

Probability ratios can be discovered for most events.   Two processes may be used to ascertain how frequently an event may be expected to happen in a given situation.   First, one may assume through logical means that an event will rate a given probability ratio.   This a priori method was used in the "bag of marbles" example just discussed.   Second, one may not be able to arrive by logic alone at a probability ratio in regard to a question such as the following: "What is the probability of a passenger being killed on a particular air line?"   To establish a probability ratio for this event one would use the *empirical* method, and set up a ratio of the number of individuals killed on the air line during a certain period to the total number of persons who rode the air line during that same period.

Statistical inference is greatly aided by the concept of probability. The experimenter in interpreting his data makes a decision as to the acceptance of his results by observing probability ratios.   The control group in an experiment furnishes, by an empirical method, the frequency of occurrence of a particular result in the absence of the independent variable.   The experimental group reveals the frequency of occurrence of a particular result in the presence of the independent variable.   Thus, if the experimenter finds that the probability of the occurrence of a change in his dependent variable without the presence of his independent variable is 50-50 and that when his independent variable is introduced the dependent variable changes 100 times out of 100, he has made use of probability theory in interpreting his results if he relates his independent variable to his dependent variable as cause to effect.   The first step of the experimenter is one of collecting data which will tell him how frequently certain behavior occurs as a result of his manipulation of the independent variable (experimental group) and how frequently the behavior occurs in absence of his independent variable (control group).   A comparison of the occurrence of the dependent variable in these two groups, respectively, affords him an opportunity of arriving at an inference of relationship between his independent and dependent variables.

Thus our task is (*a*) to find the simplest way of describing the frequency of occurrence of an event or a specific form of an event in our experiment, (*b*) to find the simplest way of comparing the occurrence of the event in our experiment with the probability of its occurrence by chance alone, and (*c*) to find the simplest way of quantifying our level of confidence in accepting our experimental results.

Measures of Central Tendency

The raw scores one obtains from measuring his dependent variable constitutes his data. These data are called *raw scores* because they are as yet *untreated statistically*. Ordinarily, the beginning student in psychological research does not find that his data are massive. Most often his data consist of single or paired scores on less than 30 subjects. When dealing with such small samples, it is common practice to treat the data in an ungrouped form. Ungrouped data are simply raw scores obtained on each of your subjects by your measurement of a dependent variable.

In the following example we see ungrouped data presented in the usual tabular form.

Subject	Errors in solving a maze, X
A	12
B	6
C	4
D	3
E	0
F	1
G	9
H	6
I	5
J	4

As the scores now stand they represent only a column of numbers. It would be interesting for us to know the point at their center around which they all tend to cluster. We have three commonly used statistics which will allow us to calculate this *central tendency* of a distribution (1, 2, 3).

Mode. The easiest measure of central tendency to calculate is the mode. The mode is defined as *the most often recurring score*. In general, the mode tells us just where in the data a concentration of measures exist. It is not a very reliable measure, but often serves as a quick, easy measure of central tendency.

In column *a* below, the mode is easily apparent. In column *b*, it is less obvious. In column *c*, we suddenly realize that a distribution may have two or more modes. Column *c* is called a bimodal distribution (see Fig. 12.1).

a	b	c
3	0	1
5	5	3
7	2	3
7	4	2
7	3	4
10	5	6
11	7	6
14	9	6
16	1	7
17	6	5

Mode = 7   Mode = 5   Modes = 3 and 6

The mode is often called a *terminal statistic* because it is seldom used in the calculations of further statistical analysis on a given set of data.

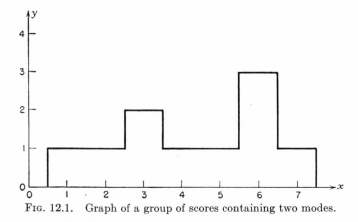

FIG. 12.1.   Graph of a group of scores containing two modes.

Median.   A somewhat better measure of central tendency is called the *median*.   The median is defined as the *mid-point of a series of numbers*. The median is quite easy to locate for ungrouped data.   One places the scores in rank order from the lowest to the highest, or vice versa, and then finds the mid-point of the series.   This is the median.   The median finds its best use when there are extreme scores in the series which might distort the true picture of central tendency.

In column *a*, below, the median is easily found because there is an odd number of scores in the series.   In column *b*, the median falls halfway between two scores because there is an even number of scores in the series.   In column *c*, to locate the median, one needs only to count halfway down or up in the series of scores, that is, 18, 10, 9, 8, 7, or 2, 3, 4, 6, 7. In column *d*, one sees that duplicated numbers are counted.

a	b	c	d
1	1	6	4
2	2	7	5
3	3	4	7
4	4	3	7
5	5	9	6
6	6	8	5
7	7	2	4
8	8	10	4
9	9	18	3
	10		

Median = 5	Median = 5.5	Median = 7	Median = 5

Mean. The most often used and most reliable measure of central tendency is the mean. The mean is defined as the average or "arithmetic mean." To calculate the mean, one adds all the scores together and divides their sum by the number of scores in the series. The statistican writes the calculation of the mean in terms of the following equation:

$$M = \frac{\Sigma X}{N}$$

where M = mean, Σ means sum of, X = scores, and N = the number of scores in the series.

The following is an example of the calculation of a mean of a series of ungrouped scores.

$$X \qquad 4 \quad 7 \quad 5 \quad 3 \quad 9 \quad 2 \quad 6 \quad 8 \quad 1 \quad 7$$
$$\Sigma X = 52$$
$$N = 10$$
$$M = \frac{\Sigma X}{N} = \frac{52}{10} = 5.2$$

The mean is calculated so that the experimenter will have one number that best represents all the other numbers in his distribution. When the experimenter wishes to compare two groups of subjects in terms of their possession of a given trait or behavior, he may do so by calculating and comparing their means. Thus the difference in the dependent variable, as it has been changed in the experimental group, as compared to the control group, where it may have changed even in the absence of the independent variable, is revealed in one manner, by subtracting the means of the two groups.

Summary. Let us conclude our discussion of central tendency by calculating the mode, median, and mean on one set of data and then showing their locations on a bar graph (Fig. 12.2). In a perfectly normal distribution, the mode, median, and mean would all fall at the same point. The data in our example are not normally distributed.

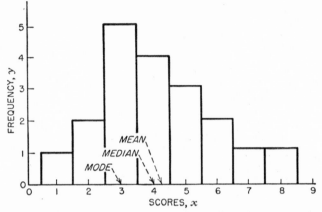

FIG. 12.2. Graph showing the relative locations of various measures of central tendency in a skewed distribution.

Measures of Variability. If one looks closely at two sets of data and compares them, he will notice that they are seldom identical. Instead he will observe that they not only differ in terms of central tendency, *i.e.*, their means, medians, and modes are different, but that they also differ in terms of variability or "spread." In the following table, distribution *a* varies or spreads less than distribution *b*.

a	b	c	d
4	2	1	1
5	2	1	1
6	16	1	2
7	19	2	2
9	38	3	2
13	72	3	3
14	104	4	3
20	119	4	3
21	120	5	3
32	133	6	10

Mean = 13.1	Mean = 62.5	Mean = 3.0	Mean = 3.0
Total range =	Total range =	Total range =	Total range =
4–32 or 29	2–133 or 132	1–6 or 6	1–10 or 10

In comparing distribution c with distribution d, we see that although the means of c and d are equal, the variability of c is less than the variability of d. Figure 12.3 shows this graphically.

Total Range. The simplest way to quantify the variability of a set of data is to calculate the total range (R_t). Usually, in reporting the range

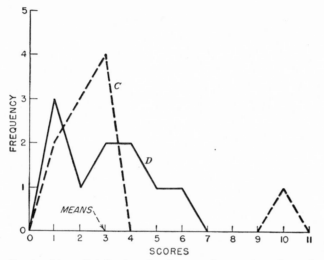

Fig. 12.3. Graph of two distributions having equal central tendency but different variability.

one simply states that the numbers go from, for example, 2–133 as in distribution b. If one wishes to use the total range in further calculations, he may use the following formula:

$$R_t = H - L + 1$$

Where R_t is the total range, H is the highest number in the series, and L is the lowest number in the series.

Thus for distribution b,

$$R_t = 133 - 2 + 1$$
$$R_t = 132$$

If we look at distribution d or Fig. 12.3, we see an example of the false impression sometimes given by the total range. Nine-tenths of the scores were no higher than 3 while only one-tenth of the scores, actually one score, was 10. In this instance we see that the range can easily conceal the real picture of a set of data. Because the presence of large gaps in a series can so greatly alter the size of the total range, particularly in small samples, the range is considered the least reliable measure of variability.   It should only be used when the scores are known to be widely scattered and when the total scatter of the scores is all that is desired.

Average Deviation (A.D.) *or Mean Deviation* (M.D.).   The best way to look at the concept of variability is in terms of how much each score deviates from the measure of central tendency of the distribution.   If one calculates how much, on the average, the scores deviate from the mean of a distribution, he has calculated the average deviation for that distribution (1, 2).   The formula for the average deviation is

$$\text{A.D.} = \frac{\Sigma d}{N}$$

where A.D. is the mean deviation, Σd is the sum of the deviations of each score from the mean, and N is the number of scores in the series.

In the following examples, we show the calculation of a average deviation.

X	d
2	6
3	5
4	4
4	4
8	0
9	1
10	2
12	4
13	5
15	7
Total = 80	Total = 38

$$M = \frac{\Sigma X}{N} \qquad \text{A.D.} = \frac{\Sigma d}{N}$$
$$M = {}^{80}\!/_{10} \qquad \text{A.D.} = {}^{38}\!/_{10}$$
$$M = 8 \qquad \text{A.D.} = 3.8$$

The average deviation is calculated without regard to sign.   That is, 4 from 8 is recorded in column d as 4, and 12 from 8 is recorded as 4.

The use of the average deviation is usually restricted to instances in which a fairly quick method is desired of arriving at a number which will serve as a basis for comparing one distribution with another in terms of variability.

If the average deviation is added to and subtracted from the mean of the series of scores, it marks off a range between the two calculated scores within which fall the middle 57.5 per cent[1] of the scores.   This is demonstrated using the data from the example of the calculation of the A.D. given above.

[1] Actually, the 57.5 per cent value holds less true if the scores are not normally distributed.

$$M = 8 \qquad \text{A.D.} = 3.8$$
$$M + \text{A.D.} = 8 + 3.8 = 11.8$$
$$M - \text{A.D.} = 8 - 3.8 = 4.2$$

Therefore, 57.5 per cent of the scores fall between 4.2 and 11.8. This is shown graphically for a normal distribution in Fig. 12.4.

Standard Deviation (S.D. or σ). The most often used, and most

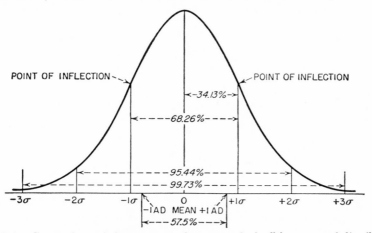

FIG. 12.4. Comparison of the per cent of cases marked off in a normal distribution by the standard and average deviations.

reliable, measure of variability is the standard deviation (1, 2, 3). If further statistics are to be calculated on a series of scores, the standard deviation will almost invariably be part of the formula. A standard deviation is calculated in the example below.

The procedure for finding the standard deviation is:

1. Find the mean of the series of scores.
2. Make a column d in which is recorded the deviation of each score from the mean of the series $(X - M)$.
3. Make a column d^2 in which is recorded the square of each deviation score in column d.
4. Find the mean of the d^2 column.
5. Take the square root of the mean of the d^2 column.

The formula for the standard deviation is

$$\text{S.D.} = \sqrt{\frac{\Sigma d^2}{N}}$$

where S.D. is the standard deviation, Σd^2 is the sum of the deviations squared column, and N is the number of scores in the series.

X	d	d^2
1	-4	16
2	-3	9
2	-3	9
3	-2	4
4	-1	1
5	0	0
6	1	1
8	3	9
9	4	16
10	5	25

$M = 5$ $\Sigma d^2 = 90$

$$\text{S.D.} = \sqrt{\frac{\Sigma d^2}{N}} = \sqrt{\frac{90}{10}}$$

$$\text{S.D.} = \sqrt{9}$$
$$\text{S.D.} = 3$$

Note: A table of squares and square roots, Table A, is to be found in the Appendix.

If the standard deviation is added to and subtracted from the mean of the series of scores, it marks off a range between the two calculated scores within which fall the middle 68.26 per cent[1] of the scores (see Fig. 12.4). As an example of the procedure for marking off the range within which fall 68.26 per cent of the scores, we draw upon the distribution above for which we calculated the standard deviation.

$$M = 5 \qquad \text{S.D.} = 3$$
$$M + \text{S.D.} = 5 + 3 = 8$$
$$M - \text{S.D.} = 5 - 3 = 2$$

Therefore, 68.26 per cent of the scores fall between 2 and 8.

BIBLIOGRAPHY

1. Garrett, Henry E.: *Statistics in Psychology and Education,* 3d ed., Longmans, Green & Co., Inc., New York, 1947.
2. Lindquist, E. F.: *A First Course in Statistics,* rev. ed., Houghton Mifflin Company, Boston, 1942.
3. Munn, Norman L.: *Psychology: The Fundamentals of Adjustment,* 2d ed., Houghton Mifflin Company, Boston, 1951.

[1] The 68.26 per cent value holds less true if the scores are not normally distributed.

CHAPTER 13

RELIABILITY OF MEASURES

Let us look into the problem of using anything less than a whole population in conducting an experiment.

Sampling

In doing an experiment, one usually makes use of what is called *sampling*. In sampling, a few, or perhaps many, measurements are made of a trait or a characteristic possessed by the thing being studied. A cook samples the soup by tasting a teaspoonful. From this teaspoonful, a generalization is made concerning the taste of all the soup in the pot. Perhaps the cook is judging a particular recipe for soup and makes the statement that not only is the particular pot of soup not "tasty" but doubts the "tastiness" of all soup past and future that depends on that particular recipe for its formula of ingredients. It is sometimes the same with experimenters other than cooks; they are tempted to make broad and loose generalizations from insignificant samples. Experimenters and cooks alike should learn to say, "I am only certain that this particular teaspoonful of soup I am tasting is unpalatable to me. I cannot go farther without the risk of error."

Suppose it became your job to report the average size of the lumps of coal in a railroad car. You would probably, because you might be lazy or to use a more innocuous adjective, efficient, decide that it would be too much trouble and thoroughly impractical to measure the size of each individual lump of coal in the car and then divide by the number of lumps to arrive at the mean. Instead you would do as is usually done and merely sample the coal. You might gather a sample of perhaps the first 24 lumps of coal within reach and calculate the average size. You would now have a mean which might be representative of the average size of all the lumps in the car. Now, suppose you recorded this mean and then decided to check it against the mean calculated from a measurement of all the lumps in the car. It is extremely likely that you would not find the mean of the 24 lumps coinciding exactly with the mean of the 20,000 lumps in the car. The mean of the size of the 24 lumps is known as the *sample mean;* the mean of the size of all the lumps in the car is known as the *true mean*. An

147

error would likely be made if you calculated only the sample mean and tried to predict the true mean from it.

In what way could the sample be improved so as to increase the chances of securing a sample mean close to the true mean without the burden of measuring all the lumps in the car?

First, you could select your sample better.   You might use a technique of sampling whereby you would in imagination divide the car into four sections: top right, top left, bottom right, and bottom left.   You might, then, from these sections select at random a half dozen lumps from each. In this way, a better sampling might be selected.   Better sample means that the sample would come nearer to having as its characteristics those aspects which are common to the population from which it was drawn. Such a sample is called an *unbiased sample.*

A second way to improve your sample would be to increase the number of lumps of coal measured.   You would probably secure a sample mean closer to the true mean if your sample were 100 rather than only 1.

Third, your prediction of the approximation of the true mean would be more reliable if the lumps of coal were more nearly the same size.   In other words, the more variation in the size of the lumps, the harder it is to find a small sample whose mean will approximate the true mean.

If one found a mean of his sample of 24 lumps, recorded it, tossed the lumps back in the car, and then repeated the process many times, he would find that he would not always arrive at the same sample mean. Instead, there would be a distribution of means produced that would resemble the normal curve.

Here is the point.   The reliability or consistency of the mean of any sample depends on the amount of variation in such a distribution of sample means.   If the means of your samples varied greatly from one another, you would not have much faith in any one sample mean as indicating the size of the true mean.   But if all your sample means hung closely around one mean then you would be more confident in accepting it as best representing the true mean.

The Standard Error

From our discussion so far, we see that the reliability of a mean of a sample depends upon (a) an unbiased sample, (b) the size of the sample, and (c) the variability of the distribution of sample means.   If we could combine as many of these points as possible into a single formula, we might have a quick, easy method for finding the reliability of a mean of a sample.   Statisticians have already done this for us.   The formula for the reliability of a sample is known as the standard error of a mean (1, 2, 3).   In reality, it is simply the standard deviation of the distribution of sample means we talked about above.   The formula for the standard error of a small random sample follows:

$$\text{S.E.}_M \text{ or } \sigma_M = \frac{\sigma}{\sqrt{N - 1}}$$

where S.E.$_M$ is the standard error of the mean, also written σ_M, σ is the standard deviation of the scores in the sample, and N is the number of scores in the distribution.

An example showing the calculation of the standard error of the mean follows.

If the mean of a sample is 100, the standard deviation is 10, and the number of cases is 26, what is the standard error or reliability of the mean?

$$\sigma_M = \frac{\sigma}{\sqrt{N - 1}}$$
$$= \frac{10}{\sqrt{26 - 1}} = \frac{10}{\sqrt{25}} = \frac{10}{5}$$
$$\sigma_M = 2$$

We see, then, that there are two ways to arrive at the standard error of a mean.   First, we could go through the laborious process of a series of, say, 200 random samples from the population and calculating the mean for each sample in the series.   If we put all the means from the samples into a distribution and calculated its standard deviation, we would have our standard error of the mean.   Suppose, for example, we found that the means we calculated were sometimes as low as 68 and sometimes as high as 80.   The mean of these means would be the best estimate of the true mean of the entire population from which the samples were drawn.   The standard deviation of this distribution of sample means might be 2, and would be the standard error of the mean.   Figure 13.1 show how the curve based on these hypothetical data would appear.   Second, we could simply take one sample from the population, find its standard deviation, and divide by $\sqrt{N - 1}$.   This would give approximately the same standard error as found in the first method.

Now that we have calculated the standard error of the sample mean, what does it allow us to say concerning the sample mean's reliability?

First, it tells us that the larger the standard error, the less reliable is the mean of our sample.   In other words, the reliability of our sample mean decreases as the size of the standard error increases.

Second, much of the interpretation of the meaning of a standard deviation is of use in interpreting the standard error of the mean of such a sample distribution.   The standard error of a mean of a sample, if added to and subtracted from the mean, marks off a range of scores within which the true mean of the population from which the sample was drawn would fall 68.26 per cent, or approximately two-thirds, of the time.   Three standard errors of the mean of a sample if added to and subtracted from the mean of the sample mark off a range of scores within which would fall the true mean of the population, from which the sample was drawn, 99.73

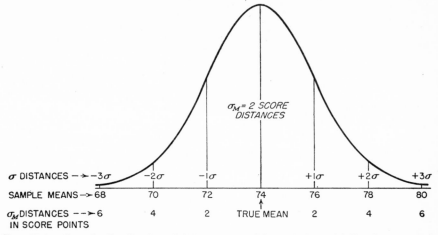

Fig. 13.1.   Sample distribution of 200 means and how their variability is measured in terms of the standard error.

per cent of the time.   An example follows which demonstrates this calculation.   The data used above in demonstrating the calculation of the standard error of the mean are used.

$$M = 100$$
$$\sigma_M = 2$$
$$M + \sigma_M = 100 + 2 = 102$$
$$M - \sigma_M = 100 - 2 = 98$$

Therefore the true mean of the population will fall between 98 and 102 68.26 per cent of the time (in a normal distribution).

$$M + 3 \times \sigma_M = 100 + 3(2) = 106$$
$$M - 3 \times \sigma_M = 100 - 3(2) = 94$$

Therefore the true mean of the population will fall between 94 and 106 (in a normal distribution) 99.73 per cent of the time.   Since the true mean is a fixed value, it might be better to say that we are 99.73 per cent sure that the true mean will fall between 94 and 106.

The calculation of the standard error of the mean is a measure of reliability in that it tells you how confident you may be that the true mean rests within a certain range. For instance, you would be wrong only 5 times out of a 100 if you said the true mean of a large sample lies within the range of sample mean plus and minus 1.96 times the standard error. You would be wrong only 1 time out of a 100 if you said that the true mean lies within the range of sample mean plus and minus 2.58 times the standard error. In the first instance you would be confident at the 5 per cent level of confidence, the second instance, the 1 per cent level.

Every mean calculated is a sample mean unless the mean based on the scores of the entire population is calculated. All sample means should have their reliability stated by attaching to them their standard errors. This is usually done as follows:

$$M = 100 \quad \sigma_M = 5$$

The correct way to report mean is $M = 100 \pm 5$.

BIBLIOGRAPHY

1. Garrett, Henry E.: *Statistics in Psychology and Education*, 3d ed., Longmans, Green & Co., Inc., New York, 1947.
2. Lindquist, E. F.: *A First Course in Statistics*, rev. ed., Houghton Mifflin Company, Boston, 1942.
3. Munn, Norman L.: *Psychology: The Fundamentals of Adjustment*, 2d ed., Houghton Mifflin Company, Boston, 1951.

CHAPTER 14

COMPUTING SIGNIFICANCE OF DIFFERENCES

In the factorial type of experiment one usually finds his data to be in the form of two means: one for the experimental group and one for the control group. Very often, these two means are close together. How is one to know whether the means of the two groups are far enough apart to allow one to say that a significant difference exists between them?

We touched on this problem before. In our discussion of the null hypothesis, we said that in the use of a null hypothesis one assumes, until shown otherwise, that any difference achieved between the experimental and control group is due to chance alone. If, then, the results indicate only a small unreliable difference, or in other words, a difference that could easily be due to chance factors, we should feel little confidence in the difference and consequently accept the null hypothesis. On the other hand, if the two means are so far apart as to almost preclude their occurrence by chance then we should, at a certain level of confidence, reject the null hypothesis.

If the experiment has been highly controlled in that the only known difference between experimental and control groups was the presence of the independent variable in the experimental group, and the results indicate that the difference in the two groups in terms of the mean of the measurements of the dependent variable was so large that it could have occurred only once in a hundred times by chance alone, then we are justified in rejecting the null hypothesis at the 1 per cent level of confidence. We then go farther, as a rule, and state that the independent variable produced a difference in the two groups significant at the 1 per cent level of confidence.

Let us now see how to go about evaluating differences between means in the search for significance.

The t Test

The name applied to the statistical techniques which allow one to deal with the significance of differences between means in small independent samples is the t test (1). In general, the t test involves the ratio of the size of the difference between two means to the size of the standard error of the difference between the two means. t may be used in dealing with either large or small samples, and is simply the evaluation of a statistic in terms of its reliability.

Assuming the true difference to be zero between the groups in respect to the trait measured, one calculates t to see how many times out of 100 a difference as large as was obtained could have happened by chance alone. To do this, one divides the difference between the means for the two groups (D) by the standard error of that difference (S.E.$_D$).   The more times S.E.$_D$ goes into D the wider is the distribution of differences between the two means.

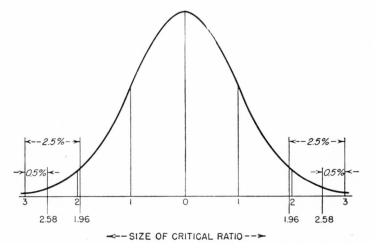

FIG. 14.1.   Size of the critical ratio as related to level of significance for a normal distribution.   (When both tails of the curve are considered, 1.96 = 5 per cent level and 2.58 = 1 per cent level.)

When the number of cases is very large, say more than 100, results of the t test very closely approximate the results of another technique of arriving at the significance of difference between means known as *critical ratio*.   Assuming, then, that one has conducted the t test on a very large sample, Fig. 14.1 shows that as the "true difference" varies from zero then the S.E.$_D$ divided into D yields larger critical ratios.   One S.E.$_D$ plus and minus the mean marks off 68.26 per cent of the cases in a normal distribution, 1.96 S.E.$_D$ plus and minus the mean marks off 95 per cent, and 2.58 S.E.$_D$ marks off 99 per cent.   Thus if the distribution is normally distributed, one would expect a critical ratio as large as 1.96 times the S.E.$_D$ five times in a hundred if the true difference between the means were zero (5 per cent level of confidence) and as large as 2.58 times the S.E.$_D$ only once in a hundred times (1 per cent of confidence).

The t test applied to *small* samples requires the use of a special table wherein a correction is made in terms of the size of the sample (see Table B in the Appendix). If one has conducted an experiment wherein he has 10 subjects in the experimental group and 8 subjects in the control group, the degrees of freedom equal $(N_1 - 1) + (N_2 - 1)$ or 16. Table B shows that he can reject the null hypothesis at the 5 per cent level of confidence if t equals 2.12, and at the 1 per cent level of confidence if t equals 2.92.

Detailed Calculation of t

In the following itemized procedure, the progression of operations necessary to arrive at t is given.

ITEMIZED PROCEDURE FOR FINDING t

Data	Group I result	Group II result
1. Find mean..	M_1	M_2
2. Find how much the mean deviates from each separate measure $(X - M)$...	d_1	d_2
3. Square each of these deviations found in (2) above.........	$d_1{}^2$	$d_2{}^2$
4. Find sum of these squared deviations found in (3) above....	$\Sigma d_1{}^2$	$\Sigma d_2{}^2$

5. Add $\Sigma d_1{}^2$ to $\Sigma d_2{}^2$ and divide by $(N_1 - 1) + (N_2 - 1)$. Note: N_1 = number of cases in group I and N_2 = number of cases in group II.
6. Take square root of result found in step 5. This equals the combined S.D. of the groups.
7. Divide the sum of N_1 and N_2 by the product of N_1 and N_2.
8. Take the square root of result found in step 7.
9. Multiply the result found in step 8 by the S.D. found in step 6. This equals S.E._D.
10. Find difference between M_1 and M_2 (neglect sign).
11. Divide difference between M_1 and M_2 found in step 10, by S.E._D found in step 9. This equals t.

In order to simplify the task of the experimenter in arriving at a t, the work sheet which appears on the following page has been developed by the author. On the page following the work sheet is a demonstration of the calculation of t, using the work sheet.

When t has been calculated for the difference between the means of the two groups, the final decision must be made as to whether to accept or reject the null hypothesis. In other words, it must be decided whether

WORK SHEET FOR COMPUTATION OF t

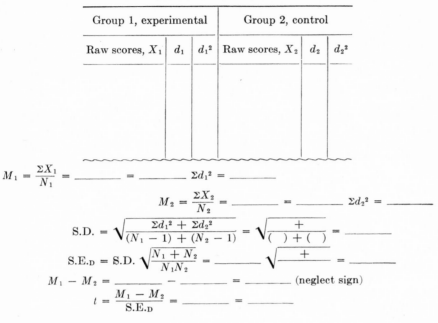

Group 1, experimental			Group 2, control		
Raw scores, X_1	d_1	$d_1{}^2$	Raw scores, X_2	d_2	$d_2{}^2$

$M_1 = \dfrac{\Sigma X_1}{N_1} = \underline{\hspace{1cm}} = \underline{\hspace{1cm}} \quad \Sigma d_1{}^2 = \underline{\hspace{1cm}}$

$M_2 = \dfrac{\Sigma X_2}{N_2} = \underline{\hspace{1cm}} = \underline{\hspace{1cm}} \quad \Sigma d_2{}^2 = \underline{\hspace{1cm}}$

$\text{S.D.} = \sqrt{\dfrac{\Sigma d_1{}^2 + \Sigma d_2{}^2}{(N_1 - 1) + (N_2 - 1)}} = \sqrt{\dfrac{+}{(\ ) + (\ )}} = \underline{\hspace{1cm}}$

$\text{S.E.}_\text{D} = \text{S.D.} \sqrt{\dfrac{N_1 + N_2}{N_1 N_2}} = \underline{\hspace{1cm}} \sqrt{\dfrac{+}{\ }} = \underline{\hspace{1cm}}$

$M_1 - M_2 = \underline{\hspace{1cm}} - \underline{\hspace{1cm}} = \underline{\hspace{1cm}}$ (neglect sign)

$t = \dfrac{M_1 - M_2}{\text{S.E.}_\text{D}} = \underline{\hspace{1cm}} = \underline{\hspace{1cm}}$

Degrees of freedom $\underline{\hspace{1cm}}$
Value of t required for significance at:
5% level of confidence $\underline{\hspace{1cm}}$
1% level of confidence $\underline{\hspace{1cm}}$

Note: In using the table to find significance, the degrees of freedom are equal to $(N_1 - 1) + (N_2 - 1)$, that is, the number of scores in the first group, minus one, are added to the number of scores in the second group, minus one.

or not the independent variable caused the difference between the two groups in respect to the behavior being studied.

On the work sheet, there is a reference to the 5 per cent and 1 per cent levels of confidence. The evaluation of the significance of your results may be made in terms of whether or not t is large enough to be at the 1 per cent level of confidence. If by going to Table B in the Appendix it is found that t in your calculation is less than the value required for significance at the 1 per cent level of confidence, then you would be following an accepted standard if you accepted your null hypothesis. If your t equals or exceeds the value required for significance at the 1 per cent level of confidence, then you may reject the null hypothesis and accept your independent variable as related significantly to the dependent variable. t's which fall short of the value required for significance at the 1 per cent level of confidence but which are equal to or larger than the

Work Sheet for Computation of t

Group 1, Experimental			Group 2, Control		
Raw scores, X_1	d_1	$d_1{}^2$	Raw scores, X_2	d_2	$d_2{}^2$
2	−3	9	3	−3	9
3	−2	4	2	−4	16
4	−1	1	4	−2	4
4	−1	1	4	−2	4
5	0	0	7	1	1
6	1	1	7	1	1
3	−2	4	8	2	4
5	0	0	9	3	9
7	2	4	10	4	16
11	6	36	6	0	0

$$M_1 = \frac{\Sigma X_1}{N_1} = \frac{50}{10} = 5 \qquad \Sigma d_1{}^2 = 60 \qquad M_2 = \frac{\Sigma X_2}{N_2} = \frac{60}{10} = 6 \qquad \Sigma d_2{}^2 = 64$$

$$\text{S.D.} = \sqrt{\frac{\Sigma d_1{}^2 + \Sigma d_2{}^2}{(N_1 - 1) + (N_2 - 1)}} = \sqrt{\frac{60 + 64}{9 + 9}} = 2.62$$

$$\text{S.E.}_\text{D} = \text{S.D.} \sqrt{\frac{N_1 + N_2}{N_1 N_2}} = 2.6 \sqrt{\frac{10 + 10}{(10)(10)}} = 1.16$$

$$M_1 - M_2 = 5 - 6 = -1 \text{ (neglect sign)}$$

$$t = \frac{M_1 - M_2}{\text{S.E.}_\text{D}} = \frac{1}{1.16} = .86$$

Degrees of freedom = 18
Value of t required for significance at:
5% level of confidence 2.10
1% level of confidence 2.88
   Note: In using the table to find significance, the degrees of freedom are equal to $(N_1 - 1) + (N_2 - 1)$, that is, the number of scores in the first group, minus one, are added to the second group, minus one.

value required for significance at the 5 per cent level of confidence are usually reported, but are only regarded as a possible indication of a trend toward disproving your null hypothesis.   Experimental results significant at less than the 5 per cent level of confidence are, in the author's opinion, too near the wheel of chance to be taken seriously.

Chi-square Technique

   This statistical technique is included here so as to allow the student to test the significance of certain results that cannot be handled by the use of the t and correlation techniques.   For the most part, the data we talked about previously were in the form of a series of numbers or paired scores representing the measurements of the variables in the study.   We could calculate means and standard deviations on such data.   Now, suppose you have decided to test the hypothesis that students at your university prefer athletic events to theatrical productions.   Your procedure would consist of questioning, perhaps, 100 students as to which they prefer and recording their preferences.   Out of the 100 students let us suppose that 63 said they preferred athletic events and 37 said they preferred theatrical productions.   Is there a significant preference for the former?

Obviously, the data are of such a nature that some technique other than t or correlation is needed to deal with the results.   The chi-square (χ^2) technique will provide the answer in this case.

In applying chi square, the observed results are compared with the results expected according to some hypothesis about the population. In our example, we would hypothesize that just as many students would prefer athletic events as would prefer theatrical productions.   This would be a 50-50 hypothesis or a null hypothesis where any deviation from this 50-50 proportion would be hypothesized as due to chance fluctuation.   In our study, we found that the split was 63–37.

Chi square will allow us to test for the significance of the divergence of our *observed frequency* from that expected on the basis of the equal probability hypothesis.   If we find that the answer to our chi-square problem indicates that a divergence as large as the one we observed could have happened by chance alone only one time in a hundred, then we can make the statement, at the 1 per cent level of confidence, that the students preferred athletic events to theatrical productions.

The formula for finding chi square is

$$\chi^2 = \sum \left[\frac{(f_o - f_e)^2}{f_e} \right]$$

where $(f_o - f_e)^2$ is the squared differences between the observed and expected frequencies, f_e is the expected frequency in terms of some hypothesis about the population, and Σ means the sum of.

Steps for Calculating χ^2

1. Record in the appropriate cells of the table that follows the observed frequencies of occurrence under the various categories.
2. Record in the appropriate cells of the table the expected frequency of occurrence under the various categories.
3. Record the totals of the observed and expected frequencies, respectively, in the space provided.
4. Find the difference between each observed and expected frequency for each category.
5. Square each of the differences found in step 4.

6. Divide each squared difference in step 5 by its corresponding expected frequency as recorded in step 2.

7. Find the sum of the items found in step 6. This is the chi square.

8. Determine the significance level of the chi square by finding the degrees of freedom by the formula $df = (r - 1)(c - 1)$, where df is the degrees of freedom, r is the number of rows, and c is the number of columns dealt with in your chi-square problem. Consult Table C in the Appendix.

In applying these steps for finding chi square to our example previously cited, we proceed as follows:

TABLE 1.   CALCULATION OF CHI SQUARE FOR AN EQUAL PROBABILITY HYPOTHESIS

	Prefer athletic events	Prefer theatrical productions	Total
Observed (f_o)	63	37	100
Expected (f_e)	50	50	100
($f_o - f_e$)	13	−13	
($f_o - f_e$)^2	169	169	
$\dfrac{(f_o - f_e)^2}{f_e}$	3.38	3.38	$\chi^2 = 6.76$

$$df = (r - 1)(c - 1) = (2 - 1)(2 - 1) = (1)(1) = 1$$

Consulting the table of chi square, Table C in the Appendix, and entering it with one degree of freedom, we find that a chi square of 6.76 could occur less than once in a hundred times by chance. Therefore we have sufficient reason for rejecting the equal probability hypothesis and can say at the 1 per cent level of confidence that the students prefer athletic events to theatrical productions.

This is the general scheme by which chi squares are calculated. Certain conditions may arise that will alter the above table. Some of these conditions follow.

1. We may be dealing with more than two categories as when a questionnaire might be given that calls for responses to be recorded as failing, poor, fair, good, and excellent. In these cases, simply use more columns headed by the descriptive terms, record the observed and expected frequencies for each, and proceed as usual. When two categories were used and it was hypothesized that a given category had a 50-50 chance of being chosen, we simply divided the total observed frequencies by 2 and recorded the quotient in each of the two cells for expected frequencies. If there

are five categories of response, then divide the total observed frequencies of response by 5, and record the quotient in each of the five cells for expected frequencies, etc.

2. It may happen that the equal probability hypothesis does not apply and some other hypothesis may be needed. This most often happens when the occurrence of an event may be normally distributed through the categories instead of equally distributed. This will occur, for example, when we force categories on a distribution of intelligence scores so as to check if our observed frequencies vary from the expected. In such a case, if we used five categories, such as borderline, low normal, normal, high normal, and superior, we would not expect each category to have the same frequency. There would be a high frequency of normals and lower frequencies at extreme categories because intelligence follows a normal distribution. When one runs into this type of chi-square problem, he should consult Garrett (1) for the correct procedure of calculating expected frequencies.

BIBLIOGRAPHY

1. Garrett, Henry E.: *Statistics in Psychology and Education*, 3d ed., Longmans, Green & Co., Inc., New York, 1947.

CHAPTER 15

TESTING FOR THE SIGNIFICANCE OF RELATIONSHIPS

In the functional type of experiment, one arrives at data in the form of paired scores. These paired scores represent the changes in a dependent variable as an independent variable is manipulated. Each step up the continuum of the value of the independent variable appears to be accompanied by a change in the dependent variable. In order to quantify the relationship which may exist between the independent and dependent variable, correlational techniques have been devised. It must be noted that one can only calculate a correlation from paired scores.

Correlations may be *negative*, to some degree, *positive*, to some degree, or *zero*. Correlational techniques have been devised so as to always provide an answer somewhere between minus one, through zero, to plus one. The correlation has been incorrectly computed if one finds it to be more than plus or minus one.

A positive correlation means that as variable A increased so did variable B. Correlational values such as $+.54$ or $+.78$ or $+1.00$, etc., are examples of the type of answers to be expected when related variables are correlated positively. It should be noted that a correlation value, or r as it is symbolized, of .50 does not mean one half or fifty-hundredths of a perfect correlation. If one wishes to convert an r into hundredths of a perfect correlation, he may do so by squaring the value of r. In our example, an r of .50 is $.50^2$ or .25 of a perfect correlation. A negative correlation means that as variable A increases variable B decreases. Negative correlation values may be revealed by an r of $-.72$ or $-.63$ or -1.00, etc.

A zero correlation means that no relationship exists between variable A and variable B. Correlations at, or not significantly different from, zero are indicative of no relationship.

A correlation does not prove a cause-and-effect relationship between the two variables involved, but when a strong significant correlation exists between changes in the independent and dependent variable, then support is felt for rejecting the null hypothesis. The null hypothesis for functional, or correlational, studies is that the true correlation is zero and that any apparent relationship between the two variables is due to chance fluctuation. If one tests the calculated r for significance and finds that a correlation as large as it can be expected only once or less than once in a hundred times by chance alone, then he may reject his null hypothesis at the 1 per cent level of confidence. A table is provided in the Appendix for testing the significance of r.

In the following treatment of methods for computing correlations, two specific techniques will be demonstrated. The first is known as the rank-difference method, the second, the product-moment method.

Rank-difference Method

The rank-difference method (1) is most applicable when dealing with scores that have been placed in a rank order of merit, and when not more than 25 paired scores constitute the data.

The following is an itemized procedure for calculating the rank-difference correlation value.

The rank-difference correlation value is represented by the symbol ρ, pronounced *rho*.

Itemized Procedure for the Calculation of the Rank-difference
Method of Measuring Correlation

1. Record the paired raw scores for the two variables in columns X and Y.
2. Assign ranks to each score in the X column. Then do the same for the Y column. Assign the number 1 to the lowest score in each column, etc. In case of duplication of scores, *i.e.*, if two or more subjects should receive the same ranks, do as indicated below.

Subject	Scores		Ranks	
	X	Y	X_1	Y_1
A	2	1	1	1
B	3	2	2	3.5
C	4	2	3.5	3.5
D	4	2	3.5	3.5
E	5	2	5	3.5
F	6	3	7.5	6
G	6	4	7.5	7
H	6	6	7.5	9
I	6	6	7.5	9
J	8	6	10	9

3. Make a D column which is filled in by subtracting the two ranks in columns X_1 Y_1 for each corresponding pair of scores.
4. Make a D^2 column which is filled in by squaring each D value in column D.

WORK SHEET FOR COMPUTING THE RANK-DIFFERENCE METHOD OF MEASURING CORRELATION

Subject	Scores		Ranks		D	D^2
	X	Y	X_1	Y_1		
A						
B						
C						
Z						

$$N = \underline{\hspace{1cm}} \qquad \Sigma D^2 = \underline{\hspace{1cm}}$$

$$\rho = 1 - \frac{6\Sigma D^2}{N(N^2 - 1)}$$

$$= 1 - \frac{6()}{(-1)}$$

$$= 1 - \underline{\hspace{1.5cm}}$$

$$= 1 - \underline{\hspace{1.5cm}}$$

$$= \underline{\hspace{1.5cm}}$$

WORK SHEET FOR COMPUTING THE RANK-DIFFERENCE METHOD OF MEASURING CORRELATION

Subject	Scores		Ranks		D	D^2
	X	Y	X_1	Y_1		
A	4	6	4	6	2	4.00
B	5	5	5	4.5	.5	.25
C	6	7	6	7	1	1.00
D	9	8	9	8.5	.5	.25
E	11	9	10	10	0	.0
F	7	8	7	8.5	1.5	2.25
G	8	4	8	2.5	5.5	30.25
H	1	2	2	1	1	1.00
I	0	4	1	2.5	1.5	2.25
J	2	5	3	4.5	1.5	2.25
Z						

$$N = 10 \qquad \Sigma D^2 = 43.50$$

$$\rho = 1 - \frac{6\Sigma D^2}{N(N^2 - 1)}$$

$$= 1 - \frac{6(43.5)}{10(100 - 1)}$$

$$= 1 - {}^{261}\!/_{990}$$

$$= 1 - .263$$

$$= .74$$

5. Find ΣD^2 by adding the D^2 column.
6. Substitute into the following formula:

$$\rho = 1 - \frac{6\Sigma D^2}{N(N^2 - 1)}$$

Note: Be sure to solve the part of the equation to the right of the minus sign and then subtract from 1.00. Negative ρ will be found when the value to the right of the minus sign is greater than the value of 1.00 at the left of the minus sign.

On the opposite page is a work sheet for use in measuring correlations by the method of rank difference. Following the work sheet is a demonstration of the calculation of ρ using a hypothetical set of data.

Product-moment Method

This method (1) is more accurate and more convenient when the number of cases is large. An itemized procedure for computing a measure of correlation by this method follows.

Itemized Procedure for Computing the Product Moment Method of Correlation

1. Find the means of the X and Y columns of raw scores.
2. Make a column d_x in which you record the deviations of each raw score in column X from the mean of column X, that is $(X - M)$. Make a column d_y in which you record the deviation of each raw score in column Y from the mean of column Y, that is $(Y - M)$. In both columns make certain that the minus sign precedes the deviation if the mean is larger than the score from which it was subtracted.
3. Multiply each number in the d_x column by each corresponding number in the d_y column, and record in a $d_x d_y$ column. Make certain that the correct sign is affixed to the products in the $d_x d_y$ column. Find the sum of the $d_x d_y$ column, and record as $\Sigma d_x d_y$.
4. Square each number in the d_x column, and record in a d_x^2 column. Square each number in the d_y column, and record in a d_y^2 column. Find the mean of each of these columns, and record as $\frac{\Sigma d_x^2}{N}$ and $\frac{\Sigma d_y^2}{N}$, respectively.
5. The standard deviation of X, or σ_x, is found by taking the square root of $\frac{\Sigma d_x^2}{N}$. The standard deviation of Y, or σ_y, is found by taking the square root of $\frac{\Sigma d_y^2}{N}$.

6. Substitute the above factors into the following formula and solve:

$$r_{xy} = \frac{\Sigma d_x d_y}{N(\sigma_x)(\sigma_y)}$$

$N(\sigma_x)(\sigma_y)$ means the number of paired scores times the standard deviation of column X times the standard deviation of column Y.

Shown below is a work sheet for calculating the product-moment method of correlation. Included on the work sheet is the formula for

WORK SHEET FOR CALCULATING THE PRODUCT MOMENT COEFFICIENT OF CORRELATION
(*Ungrouped data*)

Subject	X	Y	d_x	d_y	$d_x d_y$	$d_x{}^2$	$d_y{}^2$
A							
B							
C							
Z							

$N =$ _____ $M_X =$ _____ $M_Y =$ _____

$\Sigma d_x d_y =$ _____ $\Sigma d_x{}^2 =$ _____ $\Sigma d_y{}^2 =$ _____

$r_{xy} = \dfrac{\Sigma d_x d_y}{(N)(\sigma_x)(\sigma_y)}$ $\dfrac{\Sigma d_x{}^2}{N} =$ _____ $\dfrac{\Sigma d_y{}^2}{N} =$ _____

$= \dfrac{}{()()}$ $\sigma_x = \sqrt{\dfrac{\Sigma d_x{}^2}{N}} =$ _____ $\sigma_y = \sqrt{\dfrac{\Sigma d_y{}^2}{N}} =$ _____

$=$ _____

$=$ _____

Reliability of r_{xy}:

$\sigma_{r_{xy}} = \dfrac{(1 - r^2)}{\sqrt{N - 1}} =$ _____

Value of r_{xy} required for significance at:
5% level of confidence: _____
1% level of confidence: _____

calculating the standard error of r. The standard error of r is interpreted in the same fashion as any standard error of any statistic when r is small. Table D, Correlation Coefficients (r) Required for Significance at the 5 per cent and 1 per cent Levels of Confidence, in the Appendix will aid in establishing the significance of r. Following is a work-sheet demonstration of the product-moment method using the same set of data for which we calculated ρ. Notice that ρ differs from r in this example by only two-hundredths (.02).

WORK SHEET FOR CALCULATING THE PRODUCT MOMENT COEFFICIENT OF CORRELATION
(*Ungrouped data*)

Subject	X	Y	d_x	d_y	$d_x d_y$	$d_x{}^2$	$d_y{}^2$
A	4	6	-1.3	.2	$-$ .26	1.69	.04
B	5	5	$-$ .3	$-$ .8	.24	.09	.64
C	6	7	.7	1.2	.84	.49	1.44
D	9	8	3.7	2.2	8.14	13.69	4.84
E	11	9	5.7	3.2	18.24	32.49	10.24
F	7	8	1.7	2.2	3.74	2.89	4.84
G	8	4	2.7	-1.8	-4.86	7.29	3.24
H	1	2	-4.3	-3.8	16.34	18.49	14.44
I	0	4	-5.3	-1.8	9.54	28.09	3.24
J	2	5	-3.3	$-$ .8	2.64	10.89	.64
Z							

$N = 10$ $M_X = 5.3$ $M = 5.8$ $\Sigma d_x d_y = 54.60$ $\Sigma d_x{}^2 = 116.10$ $\Sigma d_y{}^2 = 43.60$

$$r_{xy} = \frac{\Sigma d_x d_y}{(N)(\sigma_x)(\sigma_y)} \qquad \frac{\Sigma d_x{}^2}{N} = 11.61 \qquad \frac{\Sigma d_y{}^2}{N} = 4.36$$

$$= \frac{54.60}{10(3.4)(2.1)} \qquad \sigma_x = \sqrt{\frac{\Sigma d_x{}^2}{N}} = 3.4 \qquad \sigma_y = \sqrt{\frac{\Sigma d_y{}^2}{N}} = 2.1$$

$$= .765$$
$$= .76$$

Reliability of r_{xy}:

$$\sigma_{r_{xy}} = \frac{(1 - r^2)}{\sqrt{N - 1}} - \frac{.422}{3} - .14$$

Value of r_{xy} required for significance at
5% level of confidence .632
1% level of confidence .765

Note: Degrees of freedom for correlation equals number of paired scores minus two
$(N - 2)$.

BIBLIOGRAPHY

1. Munn, Norman L.: *Psychology: The Fundamentals of Adjustment*, 2d ed., Houghton Mifflin Company, Boston, 1951.

CHAPTER 16

THE CONSTRUCTION OF GRAPHS

The presentation of the data and results collected through the process of experimentation produces a problem for the experimenter. Ordinarily, he has manipulated his data statistically so that certain trends, differences, and relationships are expressed numerically. For those who understand statistics, data and results expressed statistically are written in a common, easily understood language. Those not understanding statistics fail to derive any accurate meaning from results so expressed. It is, therefore, important that the data and results of research be expressed in some form that will be easily comprehended by all those who desire the information contained in them. Besides the need for expressing results simply and directly there is also the need for expressing results in such a manner that the information included can be used in many situations. To do these jobs, the data and results are often expressed in graphical form. Using graphs as pictures of what happened in an experiment provides the most efficient and useful way of making the data meaningful to the greatest number of people.

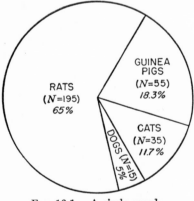

FIG. 16.1. A circle graph.

Types of Graphs

Most often only three basic types of graphs are used. Let us take a look at each of these types.

Circle Graphs. The circle graph is one of the simplest means of presenting data in graphical form. Ordinarily, this type of graph is used to portray the ratio of parts of the data collected to the total amount of data collected. Ratios may be expressed as percentages of a circle. This "pie" type of graph is shown in Fig. 16.1.

Each sector of the circle corresponds to a certain ratio or percentage of the entire circle. In Fig. 16.1 we see at a glance that there are more rats than any other kind of animal in the colony. Since 360° of the circle corresponds to the total number of animals in the colony, then a given percentage of one species of animal should be represented by a sector of the circle whose size is that per cent of 360°.   For example, 65 per cent of the total number of animals is composed of rats.   Then, a sector whose size is 65 per cent of the total area of the circle should be devoted to them. It is perfectly legitimate to include the number of animals in each section and the per cent they represent of the total colony.   This has been done in the above example.

Certain types of graphs are used to represent certain types of data.   A series of data may be either *discontinuous* or *continuous*.   A discontinuous series of data is one in which the things dealt with differ from one another qualitatively or by a given quantitative amount.   For example, dogs, cats, and rats belong to a discrete qualitative series (categories) in terms of kind of animals.   You may fire a pistol 2 or 3 times but never 2.5 times.   This would be a discrete quantitative series.   A continuous series of data is one in which the things dealt with are connected by fine intergradations of value.   For example, a stick of wood may be 2 feet 3 inches long or 2 feet 3.2 inches or 2 feet 3.25 inches long, etc.   Circle graphs may not be used to represent continuous data series.   For continuous data, the line graph, discussed later, is more appropriate.

Bar Graphs.   This type of graph has a "graph" appearance, for it looks more like the graphs one sees in textbooks and scientific publications. The bar graph is built upon a coordinate system.   The coordinates involved are two straight lines drawn at right angles to one another and intersecting at a point called the *origin*.   The horizontal line is called the *abscissa*, and the vertical line is known as the *ordinate*.   We will use these two terms repeatedly in our discussion of graphs.   As seen in the system of coordinates of Fig. 16.2, each coordinate extends from a minus value through zero to a plus value.

In most graphs utilizing a coordinate system, only the positive ends of the abscissa and ordinate are used.   These graphs start with coordinates, as shown in Fig. 16.3.

In graph *a* of Fig. 16.4 the mean of the distribution is 0, and the range of the distribution is from −4 to +6.   In graph *b*, the mean is 3, and the range is from 1 to 6.

Bar graphs of the type shown in Figs. 16.4 and 16.5 are called *histograms*.   Histograms are used when one is dealing with a frequency distribution, *i.e.*, the data have been grouped into step intervals.

As can be seen in Fig. 16.5, the histogram is drawn from an abscissa, which is divided into equal units with each unit representing one step interval distance along the base line.   The ordinate is divided into equal units representing the frequency or number of scores in a step interval.

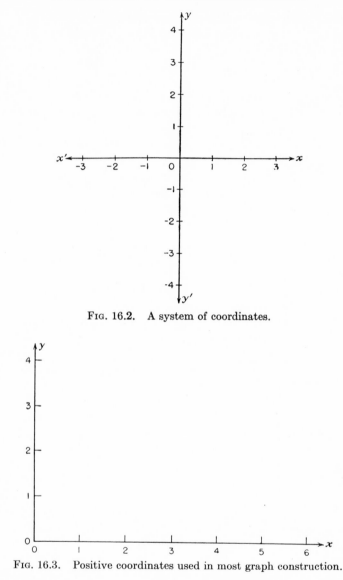

FIG. 16.2.   A system of coordinates.

FIG. 16.3.   Positive coordinates used in most graph construction.

The length of the abscissa is such that all the step intervals can be placed along it, and the ordinate is long enough so that it has as many units as necessary to represent the maximum frequency in any step interval in the distribution.   The mid-point of each unit on the abscissa is usually labeled by a number representing the mid-point of its corresponding step interval in the distribution.   Rectangles, or bars, are drawn so that the

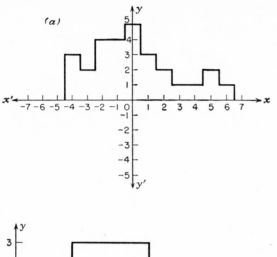

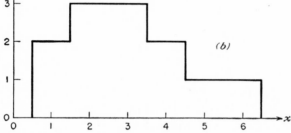

FIG. 16.4. Graphs drawn on coordinates involving positive and negative values, and positive values, respectively.

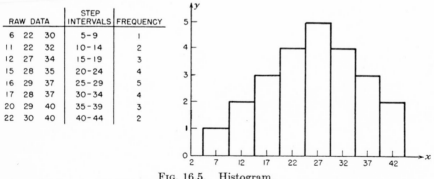

RAW DATA			STEP INTERVALS	FREQUENCY
6	22	30	5-9	1
11	22	32	10-14	2
12	27	34	15-19	3
15	28	35	20-24	4
16	29	37	25-29	5
17	28	37	30-34	4
20	29	40	35-39	3
22	30	40	40-44	2

FIG. 16.5. Histogram.

width of the bar corresponds to the width of the unit representing the step interval, and the length of the rectangle, or bar, corresponds to the unit along the ordinate representing the frequency of occurrence of scores in a particular step interval. Sometimes, the step intervals are constructed on the ordinate and the frequencies are placed on the abscissa. There is no objection to this, except that such a practice is less common than the former method of construction. A space is usually left at each end of the histogram so that one-half of the next possible, but unoccupied, step interval is shown.

The histogram in the above discussion is drawn from continuous data. This is correct, but is not ordinarily as useful as a line graph would be in representing continuous data. Figure 16.6 shows a bar graph representing discrete or "exclusive" categories. This is the more common application of the bar graph.

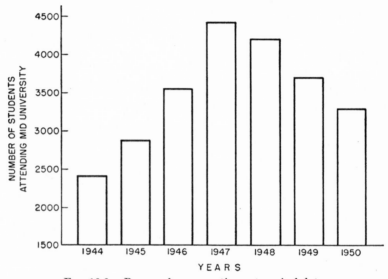

FIG. 16.6.   Bar graph representing categorical data.

The bar graph in Fig. 16.6 is read by moving out the abscissa to the year desired and going up to the top of the bar and across to the number of students indicated at the point of intersection with the ordinate.

Line Graph. This type of graph has more uses than the others mentioned in that it usually represents the relationship of two continuous variables. A line graph should not be used to represent discrete classes, since a false impression would be created by a continuous line connecting several categories.

The simplest type of line graph is shown in Fig. 16.7, where the data from Fig. 16.5 are used and the line graph is superimposed on a histogram.

One can see that the line curve is drawn in such a manner as to connect the mid-point of the step intervals at a distance above the abscissa corresponding to the frequencies of the step intervals. The line curve is drawn beyond the extreme step intervals containing a frequency to the mid-point of the next step interval. Thus, the curve is "closed" against the abscissa. A line curve of this nature is called a *frequency polygon*.

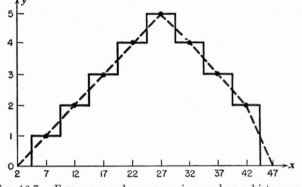

FIG. 16.7. Frequency polygon superimposed on a histogram.

Other line curves **may** begin and end "up in the air," so to speak, as shown in Fig. 16.8.

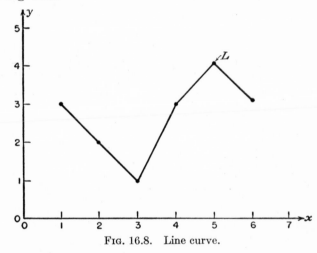

FIG. 16.8. Line curve.

Such a graph, as is true of all line graphs, relates a change in the function represented by the abscissa to a change in the function represented by the ordinate. All simple line graphs are read by locating a point on the curve in terms of rectilinear coordinates drawn from the abscissa and the ordinate. For example, in the preceding figure (Fig. 16.8) we see that point L is five units from the origin in terms of the abscissa and four units from the origin in terms of the ordinate. Thus, a value of five for the variable represented on the abscissa is related to a value of four for the variable on the ordinate.

After one has gathered his data and plotted the points on his coordinate system so that each point represents the relationship of one variable to a given value of a second variable, the problem then arises of connecting the various points so as to form a line graph.   If one merely draws a straight line from each point to its adjacent point, then he has produced a line graph showing an observed relationship (see Fig. 16.9a).

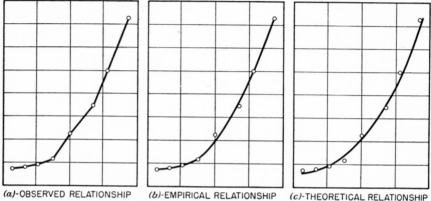

(a)-OBSERVED RELATIONSHIP   (b)-EMPIRICAL RELATIONSHIP   (c)-THEORETICAL RELATIONSHIP

FIG. 16.9.   (a) Graph of observed data; (b) graph of a "smoothed curve"; (c) graph of a theoretical curve.   (*After Engineering and Scientific Graphs for Publication, 1943, with kind permission of the American Society of Mechanical Engineers.*)

Plotting the observed relationship does not usually yield a smooth, sweeping curve.   Some believe this is due to an insufficient number of measurements because the addition of more subjects, cases, or measurements will often do away with the irregular characteristic of a line graph of an observed relationship.   One may attempt to smooth an irregular curve by drawing a smooth curve over the plotted points.   This is called *smoothing a curve by eye* (see Fig. 16.9b).

One may attempt to smooth the observed relationship by some smoothing technique such as a form of the "method of moving averages." Here, one averages the ordinate values for the first, second, and third plotted points on the graph, and plots this average; then one averages the ordinate values for the second, third, and fourth plotted points, and plots this average, etc.   One may then connect the points representing the running averages of the plots, and secure a smoother curve.

A third method of smoothing a curve is to superimpose on the observed relationship a theoretical curve that has been previously shown to represent the total population for which the present data represents a sample (see Fig. 16.9c).

A theoretical curve is usually drawn by substituting values into a formula representing the relationship of the abscissa to the ordinate.   The psychologist sometimes wishes to fit a "normal curve" on his observed data when they are in the form of a frequency polygon, and he can do this by using a direct statistical procedure.

Regardless of the method of smoothing observed data, one should *never* present a smoothed curve without also indicating the curve of the observed relationship.

The Normal Curve

Normal curve is the name applied to a particular bell-shaped curve which is produced by plotting the frequency of occurrence of successive values of a variable whose variations appear to be due to a number of independent and random conditions. It has been found that when a factor is allowed to vary in a chance manner—such as tossing a large number of coins in the air repeatedly and recording all combinations of heads and tails that appear—and the outcomes of the chance variations of the factors are plotted on a coordinate system, a curve whose shape has been given the name normal curve will be approximated. It has been found that random variation in some psychological traits produce a curve similar to the normal curve. By normal curve, we do not mean that any other shaped curve is abnormal or that we have made mistakes in collecting our data if we do not arrive at it. We simply mean that our data have formed a curve having the characteristics of the curve we call normal. The normal curve has its point of inflection (point at which it changes direction) one sigma from the mean. (See drawing of normal curve in Fig. 12.4.) In addition, the normal curve is asymptotic to the base line. This means that it continues to approach but never reaches the base line. The normal curve is approximately six standard deviations wide. If one adds and subtracts three standard deviations from the mean of a normal curve, he nearly marks off the extremes of the distribution (99.73 per cent).

Hints for Constructing Graphs

It is necessary that certain principles be accepted and maintained for the construction of graphs if standards for neatness, clarity, and practicability are desired.[1]

In the remaining pages of this chapter let us discuss the requirements for good graph construction. There are at least six interrelated topics inherent in a discussion of graph construction; these are (a) helping the

---

[1] The American Society of Mechanical Engineers in 1943 sponsored a publication entitled "Engineering and Scientific Graphs for Publication." The author has drawn heavily on this publication, and wishes to thank the ASME for their permission to do so. The student would do well to obtain this publication from the American Society of Mechanical Engineers, 29 West 39th Street, New York.

reader to understand the graph, (b) the coordinates, (c) the selection of scales for the coordinates, (d) the curve itself, (e) the lettering and line width, and (f) the title of the graph. Each of these points will be discussed separately.

Helping the Reader to Understand the Graph. Any graph should present, to the reader, information as accurately, clearly, directly, efficiently, and helpfully as possible. To do this, it is necessary to make a special appeal to the particular reader for whom the graph is primarily intended. A good rule to follow is to construct your graph so simply that it will be understandable to the most naïve person who might have need of understanding the information contained in it. Engineers should not construct graphs so that only their fellow graduate engineers can understand them, but should see to it that the graph has an appeal to all persons who, in their pursuits, might have need of the information. So it is with psychologists, where esoteric symbols and phrases coupled with decorative, clever, and unusual labels and drawings have no place in a graph. However, if certain abbreviations are common in the field and there is a need for saving space on the graph, then there is no objection to their use.

The size of a graph should be relative to its importance in the study where it appears. Large graphs presenting minor information and small graphs presenting major information may convey a false and confusing impression to the reader. This point and many similar ones of "psychological" importance should be thought about by the person constructing the graph, and he should attempt to include only the ideas and use only the methods of presentation that will aid the reader in receiving the desired impression of the significant information revealed.

Save your reader as much work in interpreting the graph as you can by using a form of presentation familiar to him. In addition, there should be a minimum of nonessentials included in the graph. Particularly should an attempt be made to keep all data, lines, scale divisions, notations, formulas, and lettering to a bare minimum. Figure 16.10 reveals how a cluttered graph (a) is simplified to a clear graph (b) by removing extraneous materials.

Rectangularly shaped graphs are recommended for two reasons: (a) graphs drawn on a rectangular pattern so that the width of the rectangle is approximately 75 per cent of the length will allow, on the average, a correct representation of the relationship between the variables in terms of relative proportion in size, and (b) rectangles of this length and width present a more pleasing appearance in print, whether placed vertically or horizontally on the page.

Often it is necessary to include more than one curve on a single graph. This may be done, but usually it is advisable to place no more than four

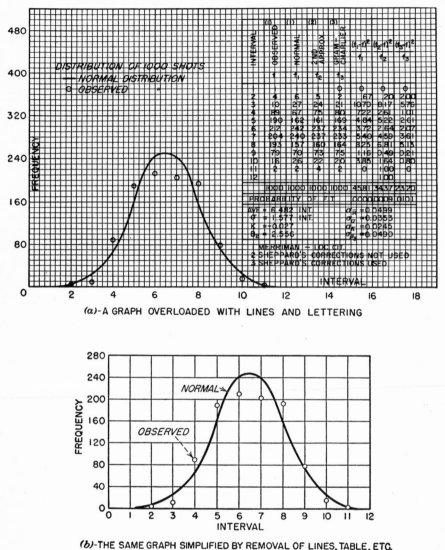

(a)-A GRAPH OVERLOADED WITH LINES AND LETTERING

(b)-THE SAME GRAPH SIMPLIFIED BY REMOVAL OF LINES, TABLE, ETC.

FIG. 16.10. Simplification by removal of material. (*After Engineering and Scientific Graphs for Publication, 1943, with kind permission of the American Society of Mechanical Engineers.*)

curves on the same graph unless they do not cross one another and are well separated.

The Coordinates. In addition to the abscissa and ordinate it is desirable to include what are called *coordinate rulings*. Coordinate rulings are additional lines placed on the graph that will guide the reader's eye from a point on a curve to its scale values on the abscissa and ordinate. If the graph is to be used as a means of accurately relating values on the abscissa to values on the ordinate, then it may be desirable to use many closely spaced coordinate rulings. However, in graphs where just the general function or relationship of one variable to another is represented by the curve, then as few coordinate rulings as needed should be included.

The coordinate rulings should form rectangles instead of squares. The rectangles may or may not have their lengths and widths positioned in a manner corresponding to the length and width of the whole graph.

Selection of Scales for the Coordinates. Scales are placed along the abscissa and ordinate so that the distance along either corresponds to some value of the variable. The scales used are in reference in the measurement of the variables. The independent variable is usually placed on the abscissa and its scale values should increase from left to right. The dependent variable, then, is placed on the ordinate and increases in scale value from bottom to top. If there are to be included two related curves on one graph, each having a different vertical scale value, then one of these scale values should be placed on the left-hand side and the other on the right-hand side.

Different choices of scale values for graphs of the same relationship will produce graphs of different appearance. False impressions may be created as to the relationship between the independent and dependent variables if the scale values are not judiciously selected (see Fig. 16.11).

In order to simplify the numbering of the scale units, one should let each unit, represented by a coordinate ruling, correspond to a value of 10, 100, 1,000, etc. Each scale should be identified by a caption indicating the variable measured, and the unit of measurement used, for example, "Age in Years."

The Curve Itself. A single curve should be drawn as one continuous solid line. If more than one curve is drawn on the same graph, then two procedures may be used: (*a*) if one of the curves is more important than the others, then it should be of a solid line and the others should be composed of dotted lines, or of lines drawn lighter than the major curve; (*b*) if more than one curve is drawn on the same graph, and the curves represent a series of observations, then symbols should be placed on each curve that would help to identify it (see Fig. 16.12). Naturally, the different symbols used to differentiate the curves and identify them should themselves be identified by use of a key placed preferably in an isolated spot within a space cleared in the grid system. If only one or two curves are drawn, it is better to identify them by labels rather than by geometric symbols. Arrows may be used to connect a label with a curve, but

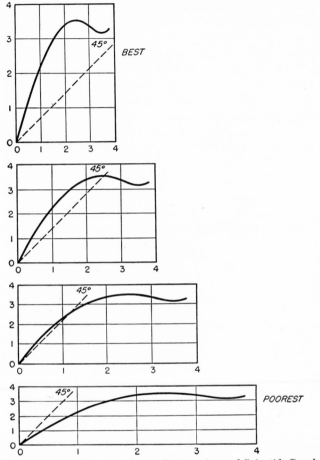

FIG. 16.11. Effect of choice of scale. (*After Engineering and Scientific Graphs for Publication, 1943, with kind permission of the American Society of Mechanical Engineers.*)

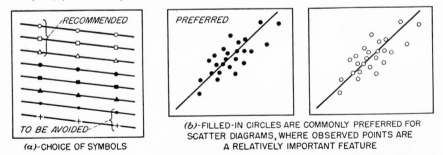

FIG. 16.12. Symbols for designating observed points. (*After Engineering and Scientific Graphs for Publication, 1943, with kind permission of the American Society of Mechanical Engineers.*)

arrows should be used sparingly and placed so as to give a pleasing appearance.

Line Width and Lettering. Line width may be varied so as to indicate the relative emphasis to be placed on a particular curve. The curve should be drawn as the widest line on the graph, the abscissa and the ordinate next widest, and the coordinate rulings should be narrowest. As the number of curves on a single graph increase, the width of the lines used for the curves should decrease. Exceptional care should be exercised to avoid drawing lines of any kind on the graph through any plotted points, designations, notations, keys, lettering, etc.

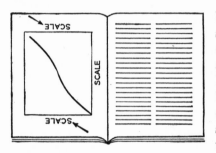

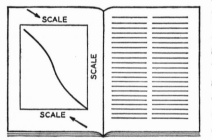

The lettering on the graph should be of a simple easy to read variety such as the so-called vertical gothic capital, and should be of uniform size and spacing throughout the graph. It is recommended that the lettering be done with the help of a commercial lettering guide. Although type stamping is sometimes successfully used to produce lettering in published works, graphs should not be lettered by use of the ordinary typewriter. All writing on and around the graph should be so placed as to enable the viewer to read it from the right-hand side and bottom of the page. Graphs designed to be read from the left side or from the top of the page are not only unpleasing in appearance but cumbersome in use (see Fig. 16.13).

Fig. 16.13. Lettering for full page illustration. (*After Engineering and Scientific Graphs for Publication, 1943, with kind permission of the American Society of Mechanical Engineers.*)

Title of the Graph. Titles of graphs should be so self-explanatory as to make almost unnecessary the reading of the particular part of the text wherein the graph is discussed. The title should be preceded by a figure number which refers the reader from the written material to the graph or from the graph to the written material. Figures should be numbered consecutively throughout the text.

The title should contain as much of the following information about the curve as needed: (*a*) a statement of the independent and dependent variable, for example, Effects of Practice on Performance; (*b*) it should be stated whether the curve plotted is based on raw or statistically treated data, for example, Means Scores by Trial for the Experimental and Control Groups at 24-hour Intervals throughout the Series of Tests; (*c*) indicate whether the curve is based on data from one set of measurements or for a combined series of measurements, for example, Combined Errors at Each Choice Point for All Subjects Who Reach the Criterion; (*d*) indicate the number of subjects, or separate measurements, yielding the data, for example, Distribution of Score Made on a Judgment Test by 1,000 women; (*e*) clarify the meaning of any separation or division made in the graph, for example, Prerest and Postrest Median Performance under the Three Experimental Conditions; (*f*) indicate if the curve is compared with, or fitted to, a theoretical curve, for example, Distribution of Intelligence Quotients on 2,000 Men and Women Compared with a Normal Distribution.

NOTES ON INTERPRETATION AND GENERALIZATION

The experiment is over and you have arrived at the last stage, the difficult stage. You have in your hands at the conclusion of the experiment certain numbers which now must be changed from the symbols they are to the things for which they stand. Here is the last chance for error, but it is one of the biggest chances for error. Here a judgment must be made by you based entirely on the results of the experiment you have just completed. Reputations are made (and lost) at this stage of the adventure into science. The experimenter is faced with the conflict of being cautious and parsimonious and yet wishing to make the most of the results. Here experience in the interpretation of data and the formulation of generalization pays dividends. It is at this point that the experimenter often wishes he had been more careful in the collection of his data, and regretfully mourns the fact that he did not use twice the number of subjects. Let us see just where the experimenter stands at the conclusion of his experiment.

The experiment was designed and performed to test the validity or truthfulness of some hypothesis. The relationship of some independent variable was suspected. All known factors whose presence might affect the dependent variable were controlled. Only one factor, the independent variable, was allowed to vary in the presence of the dependent variable. The experimenter collected results, which means he recorded the changes taking place in the dependent variable as the independent variable varied. He checked, by statistical methods, for the presence of significant changes in his dependent variable and for the presence of significant relationships between his independent and dependent variable. He may have found that these differences and relationships were such as could easily occur by chance fluctuation even if there were no significant differences or significant relationships. Perhaps he found that only once in one hundred times could he expect such differences or relationships to occur by chance. If the latter were true, he feels that the odds are in his favor if he affirms a significant difference in his dependent variable as related to the presence or absence of the independent variable. With the chances of being wrong only once in a hundred times, he may not hesitate to affirm a positive or a negative relationship between his independent and dependent variable. He has already learned the inherent errors in drawing causal sequences. He may find that his conscience rests easier if he speaks only of the degree of the relationship and couples it with a statement of the level of confidence it has earned.

He must remember that he has only been dealing with a sample of the thing under observation. He may have picked out the only piece of garlic in the pot of soup. It is not wise for him to generalize outside the confines of his experiment. If he includes, as a prefixion to his conclusions, a statement to the effect that within the limits imposed by the research design the following conclusions appear warranted, he does not himself go outside the bounds of his sample. Others may extrapolate on the results and conclusions, but they do so at their own risk, not his.

Often, in fact almost invariably, new hypotheses suggest themselves, or better means for testing the present hypothesis are discovered, as a result of his experiment and experience with the problem. This type of contribution for the edification of other experimenters in the field should most certainly be reported by an experimenter.

The simplest answer is the best. So it was in the statement of the hypothesis and so it is in the statement of generalizations from the results. The experimenter must constantly guard against "reading into" the subject's behavior. Particularly is it important to keep the level of explanations at the level of the subject. If the experimenter has performed a study using rats as the experimental animals, he should make certain that he remembers he used rats. He should not draw inferences concerning the rat's behavior that depend upon any characteristic, trait, or structure of the rat for their validity unless he is positive that the rat has such capacities. The author is reminded of a fairly recent psychoanalytic study that dealt with interpreting the behavior of a pussycat that kept attempting to crawl into a drain spout. The behavior was interpreted as caused by a "death wish" on the part of the pussycat. It seemed to the author that it is more likely that this was projection of the interpreter's own idea of what he might be wishing if he crawled into a drain spout. Perhaps Lloyd Morgan summed it all up in his famous law of parsimony wherein he said, "In no case may we interpret an action as the outcome of the exercise of a higher psychical faculty, if it can be interpreted as the outcome of the exercise of one which stands lower in the psychological scale." This law particularly applies to the anthropomorphic tendency in interpreting animal behavior. Sometimes, in the interest of new hypotheses, the law may be broken, but it should still be kept on the statute books.

PART D

APPLICATION OF THE EXPERIMENTAL METHOD

CHAPTER 17

REPORT OF TWO WELL-WRITTEN EXPERIMENTS

The write-ups of two hypothetical experiments follow. They are similar since each deals with the span of apprehension as the dependent variable, but differ in that the first experiment is conducted under a method of difference design and the second under a method of concomitant variation design. The student who wishes to plan, execute, and report an experiment under either one of these types of design will find that these write-ups provide him with an easily followed guide.

Example of an Experiment Planned, Conducted, and Reported
under a Variation of the Method of Differences
Type of Design

Name: *John Doe*
Section: *Monday*, 10:00 A. M.
Date: 24 *September*, 1951

Form for Planning or Reporting Experimentation

1. What is the problem?
   Is the span of apprehension of numbers greater when an individual is mentally set to recall them from left to right than when the individual is set to recall them from right to left?
2. State the problem in terms of a hypothesis.
   The span of apprehension of numbers is not significantly greater when an individual is mentally set to recall them from left to right than when the individual is mentally set to recall them from right to left.
   Definition of Span of Apprehension. The number of objects that can be perceived or correctly apprehended during an exposure so short as to exclude eye movements. *L-R* will refer to left to right mental set. *R-L* will refer to right to left mental set.
3. What is the independent variable?
   The mental set of the individual to recall the numbers under a particular direction of apprehension. Specifically, the mental set to recall from left to right, as compared with the second condition of being set to recall from right to left.
4. What is the dependent variable?

185

The length of the span of apprehension. Specifically, the number of digits the subject immediately recalls under each of the two conditions of the independent variable.

5. How is the dependent variable (s) to be measured?

By observing and recording the number of digits the subject can correctly recall under each condition of the independent variable.

SAMPLE TABLE TO BE USED IN THE COLLECTION OF THE DATA

Set *L-R*		Set *R-L*	
Trial	Number of digits correctly recalled	Trial	Number of digits correctly recalled
1		1	

6. What controls are necessary?

What?	*How?*	*Why?*
1. Extraneous light and sound stimuli	Lightproof and sound-deadened room (method of removal)	To exclude interference from uncontrolled stimuli
2. Exposure time for the numbers to be ½ second	Shutter attachment for projector	To maintain uniformity of stimuli presentation
3. Order of alternation of set assumed by subject	Counterbalancing method (*R-L*, *L-R*, and *L-R*, *R-L*, etc.)	To avoid constant errors due to fatigue and practice effects
4. Orders of numbers in the series presented	Systematic randomization	To avoid repetition of same sequence of numbers
5. Fixation point	Spot of light projected on screen so as to locate for the subject the area of the screen on which the digits will be projected	To allow the subject to have his eyes focused on the important area of the screen so that he will be able to have maximum opportunity for apprehending digits
6. Ready signal	Sound buzzer just before presentation of digits	To warn subject digits are about to be presented and that he should be fixating on the screen
7. Usual set of subject in apprehending the written material	Choose subjects who do not have familiarity with reading Yiddish or Chinese	Persons who read from *R-L* instead of *L-R* may favor the former set
8. Visual acuity	Must have 20-20 vision without glasses	To ensure normal sight, and avoid variable of dirty glasses, reflection, and eye strain

7. What is the procedure to be followed in conducting the experiment?
Variation of a method of difference design.

   a. Diagram the apparatus.

      (1) Slides will contain sets of numbers varying from 2 to 11 digits.

      (2) Twenty complete sets of slides will be used.

   b. Describe *exactly* what you plan to do.

      The subject will be seated and instructed as to the purpose of
the experiment.   All questions concerning the experiment will be
answered.   No written instructions will be used.   The subject
will be seated 12 feet from the screen and below the line of projection.   The projector should be focused to the subject's approval.
Three slides, not to be used in the experiment proper, will be projected to accustom the subject to the procedure.   The slides during the experiment proper will be presented so as to increase the
number of digits by one digit, each trial, starting with a two-digit
slide and increasing until the subject fails to accurately report on
two slides in series.   The highest number of digits he reports correctly is his digit span for that series.   The subject will be
instructed to change his mental set for each presentation of a new
series of slides in the following order: *L-R, R-L, R-L, L-R, L-R, R-L,
R-L, L-R.*   A 15-second interval will be maintained between the
presentation of two slides in a series, and a 1-minute interval will
be maintained between the presentation of any two series of slides.
The subject will be given 10 trials under each of the 2 conditions
of mental set.   A different set of slides will be used in each of the
20 trials.   Exposure time for each slide will be ½ second.

   c. How do you plan to analyze the research results?

      The significance of the difference between the subject's mean
digit span under the *L-R* set as compared to his mean digit span
under the *R-L* set will be determined by a *t* test.   A graph showing
the result of each direction of set as it is related to the digit span in
each series will be constructed.

8. Review the research design.

   a. What results, were they obtained, would support your hypothesis?

      If no significant difference at the 1 per cent level is found
between the means of the two digit spans, then it will be taken
to indicate that the direction of the set of the individuals is not
a significantly important variable in its relation to digit span.
Such results would force the acceptance of the null hypothesis.

   b. What results, were they obtained, would fail to support your
hypothesis?

      If a significant difference exists between the two mean digit spans significant at or above the 1 per cent level of confidence, then it will be felt that such a difference is not due to chance fluctuation but represents the influence of a variable, most likely, the direction of the set of the individual. If such results are obtained, the null hypothesis will be rejected.

9. Conduct the experiment.

a. What unplanned occurrences were present that may have influenced your results?

The projector bulb burned out during trial 3 under the set *L-R.* It was immediately replaced without the need for illuminating the room.

The subject sneezed during trial 4 under the set *L-R.* The three digit slide was projected a second time for him.

TABLE 1.   THE NUMBER OF DIGITS CORRECTLY RECALLED UNDER EACH OF THE TWO CONDITIONS OF MENTAL SET

Set *L-R*		Set *R-L*	
Trial	Number of digits correctly recalled	Trial	Number of digits correctly recalled
1	5	1	4
2	5	2	4
3	6	3	3
4	6	4	4
5	6	5	4
6	5	6	3
7	7	7	3
8	7	8	3
9	6	9	4
10	7	10	3

b. What were your subject's reactions to the experiment (remarks, attitudes, etc.)?

Reported difficulty in maintaining a *R-L* set.

Tried to light up a cigarette but was not permitted to do so.

Subject seemed anxious to cooperate at first, but looked at his watch during the last half of data collection.

c. Summarize your research results in tables, graphs, and/or other clear means of presentation.

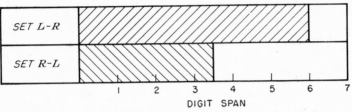

Fig. 18.1.   Relationship of digit span to direction of mental set.

10. Interpret the results.
   a. Discuss your tables and graphs from the point of view of proving or disproving the hypothesis.

   The graph in Fig. 18.1 shows a fairly large difference between the two conditions of mental set as regards digit span.   On the basis of this graph, one can see a numerical difference in favor of the *L-R* mental set as being more conducive to a longer digit span.

   In terms of bare means as indicated in Table 2, we see that the

TABLE 2.   RESULTS OF STATISTICAL MANIPULATION OF THE DATA IN TABLE 1

	Set *L-R*	Set *R-L*
N	10	10
M	6.0	3.5
S.E.$_D$	.307	
D	2.5	

$t = 8.14$

Level of confidence = 1% (much beyond)
t required for significance at:
5% of confidence 2.10
1% level of confidence 2.88

superiority of the *L-R* mental set over the *R-L* mental set is 2.5 more digits recalled correctly.   The *t* of 8.14 between these means is several times larger than necessary for significance at the one per cent level of confidence.

   It is noted that the subject was more variable under the *L-R* mental set than under the *R-L.*   However, this difference in variability may not be significant.

In summary, these data reveal a superiority of the *L-R* set over the *R-L* set significant beyond the 1 per cent level of confidence. The data gathered in this experiment offer no support for the acceptance of the null hypothesis.   On the contrary, so far as these data are concerned, the rejection of the null hypothesis is demanded.

b. State your conclusions.

Within the limits imposed by the research design the following conclusions appear warranted:

(1) In this experiment it has been demonstrated that the subject accurately recalled significantly more digits under a mental set *L-R* than under a mental set *R-L.*

(2) Further work might be undertaken to investigate the reason for the greater variability of the subject's recall under his more familiar *L-R* mental set than under the less familiar mental set. The operation of greater attention under the unfamiliar mental set is hypothesized as a possible answer.

(3) It must be noted that although the difference obtained under the two conditions of mental set was highly significant, only one subject and a series of only ten trials was used.   Whether the rejection of the null hypothesis would hold true as a generality is as yet unknown.

Example of an Experiment Planned, Conducted, and Reported
under a Method of Concomitant Variation Type of Design

Name: *John Doe*
Section: *Monday,* 10:00 A.M.
Date: 1, *October,* 1951

Form for Planning or Reporting Experimentation

1. What is the problem?

Is there a relationship between the amount of practice one has in apprehending numbers and his span of apprehension?

2. State the problem in terms of a hypothesis.

There is no significant relationship between the amount of practice one has in apprehending numbers and his span of apprehension.

Definition of Span of Apprehension.   The number of objects that can be perceived or correctly apprehended during an exposure so short as to exclude eye movements.

Definition of Practice.   The number of times the individual has his span of apprehension calculated will be taken as the amount of practice he has had.

3. What is the independent variable?

The amount of *practice* the subjects have in determining their spans of apprehension.   One determination of a subject's span of apprehension constitutes one unit of practice, two determinations constitute two units of practice, etc.

4. What is the dependent variable?

The *length of the span of apprehension.*   Specifically, the number of digits the subjects immediately recall under various amounts of practice.

5. How is the dependent variable (s) to be measured?

By observing and recording the number of digits the subjects can correctly recall under various conditions of the independent variable. Subject A's span will be based on one trial, Subject B's on his second trial, and subject C on his third trial, etc.

SAMPLE TABLE TO BE USED IN THE COLLECTION OF DATA

Subject	Number of trials	Span of apprehension
A	1	
B	2	
C	3	
G	7	

6. What controls are necessary?

7. What is the procedure to be followed in conducting the experiment?
   Variation of the method of concomitant variation design.
   a. Diagram the apparatus.
      (1) Slides will contain sets of numbers varying from 2 to 11 digits.
      (2) Ten complete sets of slides will be needed.
   b. Describe *exactly* what you plan to do.

The subject will be seated and instructed as to the purpose of the experiment.   All questions concerning the experiment will be answered.   No written instructions will be used.   The subject will be seated 12 feet from the screen and below the line of projection.   The projector should be focused to the subject's approval. Three slides, not to be used in the experiment proper, will be projected to accustom the subject to the procedure.   The slides dur-

What?	How?	Why?
1. Equation of subjects as to span of apprehension	Use only subjects who have span of apprehension of 6 digits on first determination	To exclude individual differences in length of span of apprehension, which might be differentially affected by practice
2. Control of mental set of subjects	Use mental set of left to right in determining span of apprehension	To exclude influence of direction of mental set, and keep data comparable among subjects
3. Extraneous light and sound stimuli	Lightproof and sound-deadened room	To exclude interference from uncontrolled stimuli
4. Exposure time for the numbers to be ½ second	Shutter attachment for projector	To maintain uniformity of stimuli presentation
5. Order of numbers in the series presented	Systematic randomization	To avoid repetition of same sequence of numbers
6. Fixation point	Spot of light projected on screen so as to locate for the subject the area of the screen on which the digits will be projected	To allow the subject to have his eyes focused on the important area of the screen so that he will be able to have maximum opportunity for apprehending digits
7. Ready signal	Sound buzzer just before presentation of digits	To warn subject digits are about to be presented and that he should be fixating on the screen
8. Usual set of subject in apprehending the written material	Choose subjects who do not have familiarity with reading Yiddish or Chinese	Persons who read from R-L instead of L-R may favor the former set
9. Visual acuity	Must have 20-20 vision without glasses	To ensure normal sight, and avoid variable of dirty glasses, reflection, and eye strain

ing the experiment proper will be presented so as to increase the number of digits by one digit, each trial, starting with a two-digit slide and increasing until the subject fails to accurately report on two slides in series. The highest number of digits he reports correctly is his digit span for that series. Exposure time for each slide will be ½ second.

Each subject will have his span of apprehension for digits ascertained in the manner described. The 10 subjects having the same span on this first determination will be chosen for the study. The subjects so chosen will be given different amounts of practice in determining their span of apprehension. Subject A will only be given one trial, his equating determination, Subject B, two trials or two determinations of his span of apprehension, Subject C, three trials, etc.

c. How do you plan to analyze the research results?

A Pearson product-moment coefficient of correlation will be calculated on the data representing as (X) the number of practice trials and (Y) the span of apprehension for each subject. The resulting r will be tested for significance from a zero correlation between the two variables. A graph will be constructed showing the relationship of practice to span of apprehension.

8. Review the research design.

a. What results, were they obtained, would support your hypothesis?

If there is no significant relationship between the amount of practice and span of apprehension as revealed by a coefficient of correlation significant at less than the 1 per cent level of confidence, it will be felt that no relationship exists between the two variables other than could be explained by chance fluxation. Thus the lack of a significant relationship will force the acceptance of the null hypothesis.

b. What results, were they obtained, would fail to support your hypothesis?

If a significant relationship exists between the amount of practice and span of apprehension significant at or above the one per cent level of confidence then it will be felt that a true relationship exists in the direction determined by the sign of the coefficient of correlation. In such a case, the null hypothesis would be rejected.

TABLE 3. THE SPAN OF APPREHENSION OF THE SUBJECTS UNDER VARIOUS AMOUNTS OF PRACTICE IN DETERMINING THEIR SPAN OF APPREHENSION

Subject	Number of determinations	Span of apprehension
A	1	6
B	2	7
C	3	7
J	10	11

9. Conduct the experiment:

a. What unplanned occurrences were present that may have influenced your results?

One subject who was given eight practice determinations asked if he were "dumber" than his friend who had been excused after having been given only two practice trials.

b. What were your subject's reactions to the experiment (remarks, attitudes, etc.)?

Those subjects given the greater number of trials became bored. The experimenter attempted to keep their attention on the task without introducing a variable of increased motivation by his attempts.

c. Summarize your research results in tables, graphs, and/or other clear means of presentation.

TABLE 4.   RESULTS OF STATISTICAL MANIPULATION OF THE DATA
$N = 10$
$r = .96$

r required for significance at:
5% level of confidence .632
1% level of confidence .765

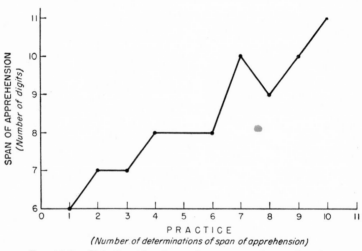

FIG. 18.2.   Relationship of practice to span of apprehension.

10. Interpret the results.

a. Discuss your tables and graphs from the point of view of proving or disproving the hypothesis.

The graph in Fig. 18.2 shows a strong trend for a lengthening of the span of apprehension of digits when opportunity for additional practice in determining the span was provided.   When a coefficient of correlation was calculated, it was found that practice was correlated with span of apprehension to the extent of $+.96$. This r is significant at the 1 per cent level of confidence.   As such, we have evidence supporting a rejection of our null hypothesis and the acceptance of the statement that in this experiment, practice was significantly and positively related to the span of apprehension.

b. State your conclusions.

Within the limits imposed by the research design the following conclusions appear warranted:

(1) As one increases the amount of practice afforded to subjects in determining their span of apprehension, the span of apprehension is significantly increased.

(2) It is suggested that future research aimed at checking these results should not only include a larger number of subjects but also should include a technique of design as control that would aid in counteracting the influence of a change in motivation during the experiment which may have influenced the results. However, if a decrease in motivation occurred in this experiment, then the results of this experiment are even more significant in favor of the influence of practice.

APPENDIX

TABLE A.   TABLE OF SQUARES AND SQUARE ROOTS OF NUMBERS FROM 1 TO 1,000*

Number	Square	Square root	Number	Square	Square root
1	1	1.0000	41	16 81	6.4031
2	4	1.4142	42	17 64	6.4807
3	9	1.7321	43	18 49	6.5574
4	16	2.0000	44	19 36	6.6332
5	25	2.2361	45	20 25	6.7082
6	36	2.4495	46	21 16	6.7823
7	49	2.6458	47	22 09	6.8557
8	64	2.8284	48	23 04	6.9282
9	81	3.0000	49	24 01	7.0000
10	1 00	3.1623	50	25 00	7.0711
11	1 21	3.3166	51	26 01	7.1414
12	1 44	3.4641	52	27 04	7.2111
13	1 69	3.6056	53	28 09	7.2801
14	1 96	3.7417	54	29 16	7.3485
15	2 25	3.8730	55	30 25	7.4162
16	2 56	4.0000	56	31 36	7.4833
17	2 89	4.1231	57	32 49	7.5498
18	3 24	4.2426	58	33 64	7.6158
19	3 61	4.3589	59	34 81	7.6811
20	4 00	4.4721	60	36 00	7.7460
21	4 41	4.5826	61	37 21	7.8102
22	4 84	4.6904	62	38 44	7.8740
23	5 29	4.7958	63	39 69	7.9373
24	5 76	4.8990	64	40 96	8.0000
25	6 25	5.0000	65	42 25	8.0623
26	6 76	5.0990	66	43 56	8.1240
27	7 29	5.1962	67	44 89	8.1854
28	7 84	5.2915	68	46 24	8.2462
29	8 41	5.3852	69	47 61	8.3066
30	9 00	5.4772	70	49 00	8.3666
31	9 61	5.5678	71	50 41	8.4261
32	10 24	5.6569	72	51 84	8.4853
33	10 89	5.7446	73	53 29	8.5440
34	11 56	5.8310	74	54 76	8.6023
35	12 25	5.9161	75	56 25	8.6603
36	12 96	6.0000	76	57 76	8.7178
37	13 69	6.0828	77	59 29	8.7750
38	14 44	6.1644	78	60 84	8.8318
39	15 21	6.2450	79	62 41	8.8882
40	16 00	6.3246	80	64 00	8.9443

* Portions of Table A have been reproduced from J. W. Dunlap and A. K. Kurtz: *Handbook of Statistical Nomographs, Tables, and Formulas*, World Book Company, New York (1932), by permission of the authors.

TABLE A. TABLE OF SQUARES AND SQUARE ROOTS OF NUMBERS
FROM 1 TO 1,000.* (*Continued*)

Number	Square	Square root	Number	Square	Square root
81	65 61	9.0000	121	1 46 41	11.0000
82	67 24	9.0554	122	1 48 84	11.0454
83	68 89	9.1104	123	1 51 29	11.0905
84	70 56	9.1652	124	1 53 76	11.1355
85	72 25	9.2195	125	1 56 25	11.1803
86	73 96	9.2736	126	1 58 76	11.2250
87	75 69	9.3274	127	1 61 29	11.2694
88	77 44	9.3808	128	1 63 84	11.3137
89	79 21	9.4340	129	1 66 41	11.3578
90	81 00	9.4868	130	1 69 00	11.4018
91	82 81	9.5394	131	1 71 61	11.4455
92	84 64	9.5917	132	1 74 24	11.4891
93	86 49	9.6437	133	1 76 89	11.5326
94	88 36	9.6954	134	1 79 56	11.5758
95	90 25	9.7468	135	1 82 25	11.6190
96	92 16	9.7980	136	1 84 96	11.6619
97	94 09	9.8489	137	1 87 69	11.7047
98	96 04	9.8995	138	1 90 44	11.7473
99	98 01	9.9499	139	1 93 21	11.7898
100	1 00 00	10.0000	140	1 96 00	11.8322
101	1 02 01	10.0499	141	1 98 81	11.8743
102	1 04 04	10.0995	142	2 01 64	11.9164
103	1 06 09	10.1489	143	2 04 49	11.9583
104	1 08 16	10.1980	144	2 07 36	12.0000
105	1 10 25	10.2470	145	2 10 25	12.0416
106	1 12 36	10.2956	146	2 13 16	12.0830
107	1 14 49	10.3441	147	2 16 09	12.1244
108	1 16 64	10.3923	148	2 19 04	12.1655
109	1 18 81	10.4403	149	2 22 01	12.2066
110	1 21 00	10.4881	150	2 25 00	12.2474
111	1 23 21	10.5357	151	2 28 01	12.2882
112	1 25 44	10.5830	152	2 31 04	12.3288
113	1 27 69	10.6301	153	2 34 09	12.3693
114	1 29 96	10.6771	154	2 37 16	12.4097
115	1 32 25	10.7238	155	2 40 25	12.4499
116	1 34 56	10.7703	156	2 43 36	12.4900
117	1 36 89	10.8167	157	2 46 49	12.5300
118	1 39 24	10.8628	158	2 49 64	12.5698
119	1 41 61	10.9087	159	2 52 81	12.6095
120	1 44 00	10.9545	160	2 56 00	12.6491

* Portions of Table A have been reproduced from J. W. Dunlap and A. K. Kurtz: *Handbook of Statistical Nomographs, Tables, and Formulas*, World Book Company, New York (1932), by permission of the authors.

TABLE A. TABLE OF SQUARES AND SQUARE ROOTS OF NUMBERS
FROM 1 TO 1,000.* *(Continued)*

Number	Square	Square root	Number	Square	Square root
161	2 59 21	12.6886	201	4 04 01	14.1774
162	2 62 44	12.7279	202	4 08 04	14.2127
163	2 65 69	12.7671	203	4 12 09	14.2478
164	2 68 96	12.8062	204.	4 16 16	14.2829
165	2 72 25	12.8452	205	4 20 25	14.3178
166	2 75 56	12.8841	206	4 24 36	14.3527
167	2 78 89	12.9228	207	4 28 49	14.3875
168	2 82 24	12.9615	208	4 32 64	14.4222
169	2 85 61	13.0000	209	4 36 81	14.4568
170	2 89 00	13.0384	210	4 41 00	14.4914
171	2 92 41	13.0767	211	4 45 21	14.5258
172	2 95 84	13.1149	212	4 49 44	14.5602
173	2 99 29	13.1529	213	4 53 69	14.5945
174	3 02 76	13.1909	214	4 57 96	14.6287
175	3 06 25	13.2288	215	4 62 25	14.6629
176	3 09 76	13.2665	216	4 66 56	14.6969
177	3 13 29	13.3041	217	4 70 89	14.7309
178	3 16 84	13.3417	218	4 75 24	14.7648
179	3 20 41	13.3791	219	4 79 61	14.7986
180	3 24 00	13.4164	220	4 84 00	14.8324
181	3 27 61	13.4536	221	4 88 41	14.8661
182	3 31 24	13.4907	222	4 92 84	14.8997
183	3 34 89	13.5277	223	4 97 29	14.9332
184	3 38 56	13.5647	224	5 01 76	14.9666
185	3 42 25	13.6015	225	5 06 25	15.0000
186	3 45 96	13.6382	226	5 10 76	15.0333
187	3 49 69	13.6748	227	5 15 29	15.0665
188	3 53 44	13.7113	228	5 19 84	15.0997
189	3 57 21	13.7477	229	5 24 41	15.1327
190	3 61 00	13.7840	230	5 29 00	15.1658
191	3 64 81	13.8203	231	5 33 61	15.1987
192	3 68 64	13.8564	232	5 38 24	15.2315
193	3 72 49	13.8924	233	5 42 89	15.2643
194	3 76 36	13.9284	234	5 47 56	15.2971
195	3 80 25	13.9642	235	5 52 25	15.3297
196	3 84 16	14.0000	236	5 56 96	15.3623
197	3 88 09	14.0357	237	5 61 69	15.3948
198	3 92 04	14.0712	238	5 66 44	15.4272
199	3 96 01	14.1067	239	5 71 21	15.4596
200	4 00 00	14.1421	240	5 76 00	15.4919

* Portions of Table A have been reproduced from J. W. Dunlap and A. K. Kurtz: *Handbook of Statistical Nomographs, Tables, and Formulas*, World Book Company, New York (1932), by permission of the authors.

TABLE A. TABLE OF SQUARES AND SQUARE ROOTS OF NUMBERS FROM 1 TO 1,000.* (*Continued*)

Number	Square	Square root	Number	Square	Square root
241	5 80 81	15.5242	281	7 89 61	16.7631
242	5 85 64	15.5563	282	7 95 24	16.7929
243	5 90 49	15.5885	283	8 00 89	16.8226
244	5 95 36	15.6205	284	8 06 56	16.8523
245	6 00 25	15.6525	285	8 12 25	16.8819
246	6 05 16	15.6844	286	8 17 96	16.9115
247	6 10 09	15.7162	287	8 23 69	16.9411
248	6 15 04	15.7480	288	8 29 44	16.9706
249	6 20 01	15.7797	289	8 35 21	17.0000
250	6 25 00	15.8114	290	8 41 00	17.0294
251	6 30 01	15.8430	291	8 46 81	17.0587
252	6 35 04	15.8745	292	8 52 64	17.0880
253	6 40 09	15.9060	293	8 58 49	17.1172
254	6 45 16	15.9374	294	8 64 36	17.1464
255	6 50 25	15.9687	295	8 70 25	17.1756
256	6 55 36	16.0000	296	8 76 16	17.2047
257	6 60 49	16.0312	297	8 82 09	17.2337
258	6 65 64	16.0624	298	8 88 04	17.2627
259	6 70 81	16.0935	299	8 94 01	17.2916
260	6 76 00	16.1245	300	9 00 00	17.3205
261	6 81 21	16.1555	301	9 06 01	17.3494
262	6 86 44	16.1864	302	9 12 04	17.3781
263	6 91 69	16.2173	303	9 18 09	17.4069
264	6 96 96	16.2481	304	9 24 16	17.4356
265	7 02 25	16.2788	305	9 30 25	17.4642
266	7 07 56	16.3095	306	9 36 36	17.4929
267	7 12 89	16.3401	307	9 42 49	17.5214
268	7 18 24	16.3707	308	9 48 64	17.5499
269	7 23 61	16.4012	309	9 54 81	17.5784
270	7 29 00	16.4317	310	9 61 00	17.6068
271	7 34 41	16.4621	311	9 67 21	17.6352
272	7 39 84	16.4924	312	9 73 44	17.6635
273	7 45 29	16.5227	313	9 79 69	17.6918
274	7 50 76	16.5529	314	9 85 96	17.7200
275	7 56 25	16.5831	315	9 92 25	17.7482
276	7 61 76	16.6132	316	9 98 56	17.7764
277	7 67 29	16.6433	317	10 04 89	17.8045
278	7 72 84	16.6733	318	10 11 24	17.8326
279	7 78 41	16.7033	319	10 17 61	17.8606
280	7 84 00	16.7332	320	10 24 00	17.8885

* Portions of Table A have been reproduced from J. W. Dunlap and A. K. Kurtz: *Handbook of Statistical Nomographs, Tables, and Formulas,* World Book Company, New York (1932), by permission of the authors.

TABLE A.   TABLE OF SQUARES AND SQUARE ROOTS OF NUMBERS
FROM 1 TO 1,000.*   (Continued)

Number	Square	Square root	Number	Square	Square root
321	10 30 41	17.9165	361	13 03 21	19.0000
322	10 36 84	17.9444	362	13 10 44	19.0263
323	10 43 29	17.9722	363	13 17 69	19.0526
324	10 49 76	18.0000	364	13 24 96	19.0788
325	10 56 25	18.0278	365	13 32 25	19.1050
326	10 62 76	18.0555	366	13 39 56	19.1311
327	10 69 29	18.0831	367	13 46 89	19.1572
328	10 75 84	18.1108	368	13 54 24	19.1833
329	10 82 41	18.1384	369	13 61 61	19.2094
330	10 89 00	18.1659	370	13 69 00	19.2354
331	10 95 61	18.1934	371	13 76 41	19.2614
332	11 02 24	18.2209	372	13 83 84	19.2873
333	11 08 89	18.2483	373	13 91 29	19.3132
334	11 15 56	18.2757	374	13 98 76	19.3391
335	11 22 25	18.3030	375	14 06 25	19.3649
336	11 28 96	18.3303	376	14 13 76	19.3907
337	11 35 69	18.3576	377	14 21 29	19.4165
338	11 42 44	18.3848	378	14 28 84	19.4422
339	11 49 21	18.4120	379	14 36 41	19.4679
340	11 56 00	18.4391	380	14 44 00	19.4936
341	11 62 81	18.4662	381	14 51 61	19.5192
342	11 69 64	18.4932	382	14 59 24	19.5448
343	11 76 49	18.5203	383	14 66 89	19.5704
344	11 83 36	18.5472	384	14 74 56	19.5959
345	11 90 25	18.5742	385	14 82 25	19.6214
346	11 97 16	18.6011	386	14 89 96	19.6469
347	12 04 09	18.6279	387	14 97 69	19.6723
348	12 11 04	18.6548	388	15 05 44	19.6977
349	12 18 01	18.6815	389	15 13 21	19.7231
350	12 25 00	18.7083	390	15 21 00	19.7484
351	12 32 01	18.7350	391	15 28 81	19.7737
352	12 39 04	18.7617	392	15 36 64	19.7990
353	12 46 09	18.7883	393	15 44 49	19.8242
354	12 53 16	18.8149	394	15 52 36	19.8494
355	12 60 25	18.8414	395	15 60 25	19.8746
356	12 67 36	18.8680	396	15 68 16	19.8997
357	12 74 49	18.8944	397	15 76 09	19.9249
358	12 81 64	18.9209	398	15 84 04	19.9499
359	12 88 81	18.9473	399	15 92 01	19.9750
360	12 96 00	18.9737	400	16 00 00	20.0000

* Portions of Table A have been reproduced from J. W. Dunlap and A. K. Kurtz: *Handbook of Statistical Nomographs, Tables, and Formulas*, World Book Company, New York (1932), by permission of the authors.

TABLE A. TABLE OF SQUARES AND SQUARE ROOTS OF NUMBERS
FROM 1 TO 1,000.* (Continued)

Number	Square	Square root	Number	Square	Square root
401	16 08 01	20.0250	441	19 44 81	21.0000
402	16 16 04	20.0499	442	19 53 64	21.0238
403	16 24 09	20.0749	443	19 62 49	21.0476
404	16 32 16	20.0998	444	19 71 36	21.0713
405	16 40 25	20.1246	445	19 80 25	21.0950
406	16 48 36	20.1494	446	19 89 16	21.1187
407	16 56 49	20.1742	447	19 98 09	21.1424
408	16 64 64	20.1990	448	20 07 04	21.1660
409	16 72 81	20.2237	449	20 16 01	21.1896
410	16 81 00	20.2485	450	20 25 00	21.2132
411	16 89 21	20.2731	451	20 34 01	21.2368
412	16 97 44	20.2978	452	20 43 04	21.2603
413	17 05 69	20.3224	453	20 52 09	.21.2838
414	17 13 96	20.3470	454	20 61 16	21.3073
415	17 22 25	20.3715	455	20 70 25	21.3307
416	17 30 56	20.3961	456	20 79 36	21.3542
417	17 38 89	20.4206	457	20 88 49	21.3776
418	17 47 24	20.4450	458	20 97 64	21.4009
419	17 55 61	20.4695	459	21 06 81	21.4243
420	17 64 00	20.4939	460	21 16 00	21.4476
421	17 72 41	20.5183	461	21 25 21	21.4709
422	17 80 84	20.5426	462	21 34 44	21.4942
423	17 89 29	20.5670	463	21 43 69	21.5174
424	17 97 76	20.5913	464	21 52 96	21.5407
425	18 06 25	20.6155	465	21 62 25	21.5639
426	18 14 76	20.6398	466	21 71 56	21.5870
427	18 23 29	20.6640	467	21 80 89	21.6102
428	18 31 84	20.6882	468	21 90 24	21.6333
429	18 40 41	20.7123	469	21 99 61	21.6564
430	18 49 00	20.7364	470	22 09 00	21.6795
431	18 57 61	20.7605	471	22 18 41	21.7025
432	18 66 24	20.7846	472	22 27 84	21.7256
433	18 74 89	20.8087	473	22 37 29	21.7486
434	18 83 56	20.8327	474	22 46 76	21.7715
435	18 92 25	20.8567	475	22 56 25	21.7945
436	19 00 96	20.8806	476	22 65 76	21.8174
437	19 09 69	20.9045	477	22 75 29	21.8403
438	19 18 44	20.9284	478	22 84 84	21.8632
439	19 27 21	20.9523	479	22 94 41	21.8861
440	19 36 00	20.9762	480	23 04 00	21.9089

* Portions of Table A have been reproduced from J. W. Dunlap and A. K. Kurtz:
Handbook of Statistical Nomographs, Tables, and Formulas, World Book Company,
New York (1932), by permission of the authors.

TABLE A. TABLE OF SQUARES AND SQUARE ROOTS OF NUMBERS
FROM 1 TO 1,000.*   (Continued)

Number	Square	Square root	Number	Square	Square root
481	23 13 61	21.9317	521	27 14 41	22.8254
482	23 23 24	21.9545	522	27 24 84	22.8473
483	23 32 89	21.9773	523	27 35 29	22.8692
484	23 42 56	22.0000	524	27 45 76	22.8910
485	23 52 25	22.0227	525	27 56 25	22.9129
486	23 61 96	22.0454	526	27 66 76	22.9347
487	23 71 69	22.0681	527	27 77 29	22.9565
488	23 81 44	22.0907	528	27 87 84	22.9783
489	23 91 21	22.1133	529	27 98 41	23.0000
490	24 01 00	22.1359	530	28 09 00	23.0217
491	24 10 81	22.1585	531	28 19 61	23.0434
492	24 20 64	22.1811	532	28 30 24	23.0651
493	24 30 49	22.2036	533	28 40 89	23.0868
494	24 40 36	22.2261	534	28 51 56	23.1084
495	24 50 25	22.2486	535	28 62 25	23.1301
496	24 60 16	22.2711	536	28 72 96	23.1517
497	24 70 09	22.2935	537	28 83 69	23.1733
498	24 80 04	22.3159	538	28 94 44	23.1948
499	24 90 01	22.3383	539	29 05 21	23.2164
500	25 00 00	22.3607	540	29 16 00	23.2379
501	25 10 01	22.3830	541	29 26 81	23.2594
502	25 20 04	22.4054	542	29 37 64	23.2809
503	25 30 09	22.4277	543	29 48 49	23.3024
504	25 40 16	22.4499	544	29 59 36	23.3238
505	25 50 25	22.4722	545	29 70 25	23.3452
506	25 60 36	22.4944	546	29 81 16	23.3666
507	25 70 49	22.5167	547	29 92 09	23.3880
508	25 80 64	22.5389	548	30 03 04	23.4094
509	25 90 81	22.5610	549	30 14 01	23.4307
510	26 01 00	22.5832	550	30 25 00	23.4521
511	26 11 21	22.6053	551	30 36 01	23.4734
512	26 21 44	22.6274	552	30 47 04	23.4947
513	26 31 69	22.6495	553	30 58 09	23.5160
514	26 41 96	22.6716	554	30 69 16	23.5372
515	26 52 25	22.6936	555	30 80 25	23.5584
516	26 62 56	22.7156	556	30 91 36	23.5797
517	26 72 89	22.7376	557	31 02 49	23.6008
518	26 83 24	22.7596	558	31 13 64	23.6220
519	26 93 61	22.7816	559	31 24 81	23.6432
520	27 04 00	22.8035	560	31 36 00	23.6643

* Portions of Table A have been reproduced from J. W. Dunlap and A. K. Kurtz: *Handbook of Statistical Nomographs, Tables, and Formulas*, World Book Company, New York (1932), by permission of the authors.

TABLE A.   TABLE OF SQUARES AND SQUARE ROOTS OF NUMBERS
FROM 1 TO 1,000.*   (*Continued*)

Number	Square	Square root	Number	Square	Square root
561	31 47 21	23.6854	601	36 12 01	24.5153
562	31 58 44	23.7065	602	36 24 04	24.5357
563	31 69 69	23.7276	603	36 36 09	24.5561
564	31 80 96	23.7487	604	36 48 16	24.5764
565	31 92 25	23.7697	605	36 60 25	24.5967
566	32 03 56	23.7908	606	36 72 36	24.6171
567	32 14 89	23.8118	607	36 84 49	24.6374
568	32 26 24	23.8328	608	36 96 64	24.6577
569	32 37 61	23.8537	609	37 08 81	24.6779
570	32 49 00	23.8747	610	37 21 00	24.6982
571	32 60 41	23.8956	611	37 33 21	24.7184
572	32 71 84	23.9165	612	37 45 44	24.7385
573	32 83 29	23.9374	613	37 57 69	24.7588
574	32 94 76	23.9583	614	37 69 96	24.7790
575	33 06 25	23.9792	615	37 82 25	24.7992
576	33 17 76	24.0000	616	37 94 56	24.8193
577	33 29 29	24.0208	617	38 06 89	24.8395
578	33 40 84	24.0416	618	38 19 24	24.8596
579	33 52 41	24.0624	619	38 31 61	24.8797
580	33 64 00	24.0832	620	38 44 00	24.8998
581	33 75 61	24.1039	621	38 56 41	24.9199
582	33 87 24	24.1247	622	38 68 84	24.9399
583	33 98 89	24.1454	623	38 81 29	24.9600
584	34 10 56	24.1661	624	38 93 76	24.9800
585	34 22 25	24.1868	625	39 06 25	25.0000
586	34 33 96	24.2074	626	39 18 76	25.0200
587	34 45 69	24.2281	627	39 31 29	25.0400
588	34 57 44	24.2487	628	39 43 84	25.0599
589	34 69 21	24.2693	629	39 56 41	25.0799
590	34 81 00	24.2899	630	39 69 00	25.0998
591	34 92 81	24.3105	631	39 81 61	25.1197
592	35 04 64	24.3311	632	39 94 24	25.1396
593	35 16 49	24.3516	633	40 06 89	25.1595
594	35 28 36	24.3721	634	40 19 56	25.1794
595	35 40 25	24.3926	635	40 32 25	25.1992
596	35 52 16	24.4131	636	40 44 96	25.2190
597	35 64 09	24.4336	637	40 57 69	25.2389
598	35 76 04	24.4540	638	40 70 44	25.2587
599	35 88 01	24.4745	639	40 83 21	25.2784
600	36 00 00	24.4949	640	40 96 00	25.2982

* Portions of Table A have been reproduced from J. W. Dunlap and A. K. Kurtz: *Handbook of Statistical Nomographs, Tables, and Formulas*, World Book Company, New York (1932), by permission of the authors.

TABLE A. TABLE OF SQUARES AND SQUARE ROOTS OF NUMBERS FROM 1 TO 1,000.* *(Continued)*

Number	Square	Square root	Number	Square	Square root
641	41 08 81	25.3180	681	46 37 61	26.0960
642	41 21 64	25.3377	682	46 51 24	26.1151
643	41 34 49	25.3574	683	46 64 89	26.1343
644	41 47 36	25.3772	684	46 78 56	26.1534
645	41 60 25	25.3969	685	46 92 25	26.1725
646	41 73 16	25.4165	686	47 05 96	26.1916
647	41 86 09	25.4362	687	47 19 69	26.2107
648	41 99 04	25.4558	688	47 33 44	26.2298
649	42 12 01	25.4755	689	47 47 21	26.2488
650	42 25 00	25.4951	690	47 61 00	26.2679
651	42 38 01	25.5147	691	47 74 81	26.2869
652	42 51 04	25.5343	692	47 88 64	26.3059
653	42 64 09	25.5539	693	48 02 49	26.3249
654	42 77 16	25.5734	694	48 16 36	26.3439
655	42 90 25	25.5930	695	48 30 25	26.3629
656	43 03 36	25.6125	696	48 44 16	26.3818
657	43 16 49	25.6320	697	48 58 09	26.4008
658	43 29 64	25.6515	698	48 72 04	26.4197
659	43 42 81	25.6710	699	48 86 01	26.4386
660	43 56 00	25.6905	700	49 00 00	26.4575
661	43 69 21	25.7099	701	49 14 01	26.4764
662	43 82 44	25.7294	702	49 28 04	26.4953
663	43 95 69	25.7488	703	49 42 09	26.5141
664	44 08 96	25.7682	704	49 56 16	26.5330
665	44 22 25	25.7876	705	49 70 25	26.5518
666	44 35 56	25.8070	706	49 84 36	26.5707
667	44 48 89	25.8263	707	49 98 49	26.5895
668	44 62 24	25.8457	708	50 12 64	26.6083
669	44 75 61	25.8650	709	50 26 81	26.6271
670	44 89 00	25.8844	710	50 41 00	26.6458
671	45 02 41	25.9037	711	50 55 21	26.6646
672	45 15 84	25.9230	712	50 69 44	26.6833
673	45 29 29	25.9422	713	50 83 69	26.7021
674	45 42 76	25.9615	714	50 97 96	26.7208
675	45 56 25	25.9808	715	51 12 25	26.7395
676	45 69 76	26.0000	716	51 26 56	26.7582
677	45 83 29	26.0192	717	51 40 89	26.7769
678	45 96 84	26.0384	718	51 55 24	26.7955
679	46 10 41	26.0576	719	51 69 61	26.8142
680	46 24 00	26.0768	720	51 84 00	26.8328

* Portions of Table A have been reproduced from J. W. Dunlap and A. K. Kurtz: *Handbook of Statistical Nomographs, Tables, and Formulas*, World Book Company, New York (1932), by permission of the authors.

TABLE A.   TABLE OF SQUARES AND SQUARE ROOTS OF NUMBERS
FROM 1 TO 1,000.*   (*Continued*)

Number	Square	Square root	Number	Square	Square root
721	51 98 41	26.8514	761	57 91 21	27.5862
722	52 12 84	26.8701	762	58 06 44	27.6043
723	52 27 29	26.8887	763	58 21 69	27.6225
724	52 41 76	26.9072	764	58 36 96	27.6405
725	52 56 25	26.9258	765	58 52 25	27.6586
726	52 70 76	26.9444	766	58 67 56	27.6767
727	52 85 29	26.9629	767	58 82 89	27.6948
728	52 99 84	26.9815	768	58 98 24	27.7128
729	53 14 41	27.0000	769	59 13 61	27.7308
730	53 29 00	27.0185	770	59 29 00	27.7489
731	53 43 61	27.0370	771	59 44 41	27.7669
732	53 58 24	27.0555	772	59 59 84	27.7849
733	53 72 89	27.0740	773	59 75 29	27.8029
734	53 87 56	27.0924	774	59 90 76	27.8209
735	54 02 25	27.1109	775	60 06 25	27.8388
736	54 16 96	27.1293	776	60 21 76	27.8568
737	54 31 69	27.1477	777	60 37 29	27.8747
738	54 46 44	27.1662	778	60 52 84	27.8927
739	54 61 27	27.1846	779	60 68 41	27.9106
740	54 76 00	27.2029	780	60 84 00	27.9285
741	54 90 81	27.2213	781	60 99 61	27.9464
742	55 05 64	27.2397	782	61 15 24	27.9643
743	55 20 49	27.2580	783	61 30 89	27.9821
744	55 35 36	27.2764	784	61 46 56	28.0000
745	55 50 25	27.2947	785	61 62 25	28.0179
746	55 65 16	27.3130	786	61 77 96	28.0357
747	55 80 09	27.3313	787	61 93 69	28.0535
748	55 95 04	27.3496	788	62 09 44	28.0713
749	56 10 01	27.3679	789	62 25 21	28.0891
750	56 25 00	27.3861	790	62 41 00	28.1069
751	56 40 01	27.4044	791	62 56 81	28.1247
752	56 55 04	27.4226	792	62 72 64	28.1425
753	56 70 09	27.4408	793	62 88 49	28.1603
754	56 85 16	27.4591	794	63 04 36	28.1780
755	57 00 25	27.4773	795	63 20 25	28.1957
756	57 15 36	27.4955	796	63 36 16	28.2135
757	57 30 49	27.5136	797	63 52 09	28.2312
758	57 45 64	27.5318	798	63 68 04	28.2489
759	57 60 81	27.5500	799	63 84 01	28.2666
760	57 76 00	27.5681	800	64 00 00	28.2843

* Portions of Table A have been reproduced from J. W. Dunlap and A. K. Kurtz: *Handbook of Statistical Nomographs, Tables, and Formulas*, World Book Company, New York (1932), by permission of the authors.

TABLE A. TABLE OF SQUARES AND SQUARE ROOTS OF NUMBERS
FROM 1 TO 1,000.* (*Continued*)

Number	Square	Square root	Number	Square	Square root
801	64 16 01	28.3019	841	70 72 81	29.0000
802	64 32 04	28.3196	842	70 89 64	29.0172
803	64 48 09	28.3373	843	71 06 49	29.0345
804	64 64 16	28.3049	844	71 23 36	29.0517
805	64 80 25	28.3725	845	71 40 25	29.0689
806	64 96 36	28.3901	846	71 57 16	29.0861
807	65 12 49	28.4077	847	71 74 09	29.1033
808	65 28 64	28.4253	848	71 91 04	29.1204
809	65 44 81	28.4429	849	72 08 01	29.1376
810	65 61 00	28.4605	850	72 25 00	29.1548
811	65 77 21	28.4781	851	72 42 01	29.1719
812	65 93 44	28.4956	852	72 59 04	29.1890
813	66 09 69	28.5132	853	72 76 09	29.2062
814	66 25 96	28.5307	854	72 93 16	29.2233
815	66 42 25	28.5482	855	73 10 25	29.2404
816	66 58 56	28.5657	856	73 27 36	29.2575
817	66 74 89	28.5832	857	73 44 49	29.2746
818	66 91 24	28.6007	858	73 61 64	29.2916
819	67 07 61	28.6082	859	73 78 81	29.3087
820	67 24 00	28.6356	860	73 96 00	29.3258
821	67 40 41	28.6531	861	74 13 21	29.3428
822	67 56 84	28.6705	862	74 30 44	29.3598
823	67 73 29	28.6880	863	74 47 69	29.3769
824	67 89 76	28.7054	864	74 64 96	29.3939
825	68 06 25	28.7228	865	74 82 25	29.4109
826	68 22 76	28.7402	866	74 99 56	29.4279
827	68 39 29	28.7576	867	75 16 89	29.4449
828	68 55 84	28.7750	868	75 34 24	29.4618
829	68 72 41	28.7924	869	75 51 61	29.4788
830	68 89 00	28.8097	870	75 69 00	29.4958
831	69 05 61	28.8271	871	75 86 41	29.5127
832	69 22 24	28.8444	872	76 03 84	29.5296
833	69 38 89	28.8617	873	76 21 29	29.5466
834	69 55 56	28.8791	874	76 38 76	29.5635
835	69 72 25	28.8964	875	76 56 25	29.5804
836	69 88 96	28.9137	876	76 73 76	29.5973
837	70 05 69	28.9310	877	76 91 29	29.6142
838	70 22 44	28.9482	878	77 08 84	29.6311
839	70 39 21	28.9655	879	77 26 41	29.6479
840	70 56 00	28.9828	880	77 44 00	29.6648

* Portions of Table A have been reproduced from J. W. Dunlap and A. K. Kurtz: *Handbook of Statistical Nomographs, Tables, and Formulas,* World Book Company, New York (1932), by permission of the authors.

TABLE A.   TABLE OF SQUARES AND SQUARE ROOTS OF NUMBERS
FROM 1 TO 1,000.*   (*Continued*)

Number	Square	Square root	Number	Square	Square root
881	77 61 61	29.6816	921	84 82 41	30.3480
882	77 79 24	29.6985	922	85 00 84	30.3645
883	77 96 89	29.7153	923	85 19 29	30.3809
884	78 14 56	29.7321	924	85 37 76	30.3974
885	78 32 25	29.7489	925	85 56 25	30.4138
886	78 49 96	29.7658	926	85 74 76	30.4302
887	78 67 69	29.7825	927	85 93 29	30.4467
888	78 85 44	29.7993	928	86 11 84	30.4631
889	79 03 21	29.8161	929	86 30 41	30.4795
890	79 21 00	29.8329	930	86 49 00	30.4959
891	79 38 81	29.8496	931	86 67 61	30.5123
892	79 56 64	29.8664	932	86 86 24	30.5287
893	79 74 49	29.8831	933	87 04 89	30.5450
894	79 92 36	29.8998	934	87 23 56	30.5614
895	80 10 25	29.9166	935	87 42 25	30.5778
896	80 28 16	29.9333	936	87 60 96	30.5941
897	80 46 09	29.9500	937	87 79 69	30.6105
898	80 64 04	29.9666	938	87 98 44	30.6268
899	80 82 01	29.9833	939	88 17 21	30.6431
900	81 00 00	30.0000	940	88 36 00	30.6594
901	81 18 01	30.0167	941	88 54 81	30.6757
902	81 36 04	30.0333	942	88 73 64	30.6920
903	81 54 09	30.0500	943	88 92 49	30.7083
904	81 72 16	30.0666	944	89 11 36	30.7246
905	81 90 25	30.0832	945	89 30 25	30.7409
906	82 08 36	30.0998	946	89 49 16	30.7571
907	82 26 49	30.1164	947	89 68 09	30.7734
908	82 44 64	30.1330	948	89 87 04	30.7896
909	82 62 81	30.1496	949	90 06 01	30.8058
910	82 81 00	30.1662	950	90 25 00	30.8221
911	82 99 21	30.1828	951	90 44 01	30.8383
912	83 17 44	30.1993	952	90 63 04	30.8545
913	83 35 69	30.2159	953	90 82 09	30.8707
914	83 53 96	30.2324	954	91 01 16	30.8869
915	83 72 25	30.2490	955	91 20 25	30.9031
916	83 90 56	30.2655	956	91 39 36	30.9192
917	84 08 89	30.2820	957	91 58 49	30.9354
918	84 27 24	30.2985	958	91 77 64	30.9516
919	84 45 61	30.3150	959	91 96 81	30.9677
920	84 64 00	30.3315	960	92 16 00	30.9839

* Portions of Table A have been reproduced from J. W. Dunlap and A. K. Kurtz: *Handbook of Statistical Nomographs, Tables, and Formulas,* World Book Company, New York (1932), by permission of the authors.

TABLE A. TABLE OF SQUARES AND SQUARE ROOTS OF NUMBERS FROM 1 TO 1,000.* (*Concluded*)

Number	Square	Square root	Number	Square	Square root
961	92 35 21	31.0000	981	96 23 61	31.3209
962	92 54 44	31.0161	982	96 43 24	31.3369
963	92 73 69	31.0322	983	96 62 89	31.3528
964	92 92 96	31.0483	984	96 82 56	31.3688
965	93 12 25	31.0644	985	97 02 25	31.3847
966	93 31 56	31.0805	986	97 21 96	31.4006
967	93 50 89	31.0966	987	97 41 69	31.4166
968	93 70 24	31.1127	988	97 61 44	31.4325
969	93 89 61	31.1288	989	97 81 21	31.4484
970	94 09 00	31.1448	990	98 01 00	31.4643
971	94 28 41	31.1609	991	98 20 81	31.4802
972	94 47 84	31.1769	992	98 40 64	31.4960
973	94 67 29	31.1929	993	98 60 49	31.5119
974	94 86 76	31.2090	994	98 80 36	31.5278
975	95 06 25	31.2250	995	99 00 25	31.5436
976	95 25 76	31.2410	996	99 20 16	31.5595
977	95 45 29	31.2570	997	99 40 09	31.5753
978	95 64 84	31.2730	998	99 60 04	31.5911
979	95 84 41	31.2890	999	99 80 01	31.6070
980	96 04 00	31.3050	1000	100 00 00	31.6228

* Portions of Table A have been reproduced from J. W. Dunlap and A. K. Kurtz: *Handbook of Statistical Nomographs, Tables, and Formulas*, World Book Company, New York (1932), by permission of the authors.

TABLE B.* LEVEL OF CONFIDENCE FOR t
(Table of t)

Degrees of freedom $(N_1 - 1) + (N_2 - 1)$	5% level	1% level
1	12.71	63.66
2	4.30	9.92
3	3.18	5.84
4	2.78	4.60
5	2.57	4.03
6	2.45	3.71
7	2.36	3.50
8	2.31	3.36
9	2.26	3.25
10	2.23	3.17
11	2.20	3.11
12	2.18	3.06
13	2.16	3.01
14	2.14	2.98
15	2.13	2.95
16	2.12	2.92
17	2.11	2.90
18	2.10	2.88
19	2.09	2.86
20	2.09	2.84
21	2.08	2.83
22	2.07	2.82
23	2.07	2.81
24	2.06	2.80
25	2.06	2.79
26	2.06	2.78
27	2.05	2.77
28	2.05	2.76
29	2.04	2.76
30	2.04	2.75
40	2.02	2.71
50	2.01	2.68
100	1.98	2.63
500	1.96	2.59
1000	1.96	2.58

* Table B is abridged from Table IV of Fisher: *Statistical Methods for Research Workers*, published by Oliver and Boyd, Ltd., Edinburgh, by permission of the author and publishers. Supplementary entries were taken, by permission, from Snedecor: *Statistical Methods*, published by Collegiate Press, Ames, Iowa.

TABLE C.* TABLE OF CHI SQUARE (χ^2)

(Chi squares appear in the body of the table)

Degrees of freedom	P = .99	.98	.95	.90	.80	.70	.50	.30	.20	.10	.05	.02	.01
1	.000157	.000628	.00393	.0158	.0642	.148	.455	1.074	1.642	2.706	3.841	5.412	6.635
2	.0201	.0404	.103	.211	.446	.713	1.386	2.408	3.219	4.605	5.991	7.824	9.210
3	.115	.185	.352	.584	1.005	1.424	2.366	3.665	4.642	6.251	7.815	9.837	11.341
4	.297	.429	.711	1.064	1.649	2.195	3.357	4.878	5.989	7.779	9.488	11.668	13.277
5	.554	.752	1.145	1.610	2.343	3.000	4.351	6.064	7.289	9.236	11.070	13.388	15.086
6	.872	1.134	1.635	2.204	3.070	3.828	5.348	7.231	8.558	10.645	12.592	15.033	16.812
7	1.239	1.564	2.167	2.833	3.822	4.671	6.346	8.383	9.803	12.017	14.067	16.622	18.475
8	1.646	2.032	2.733	3.490	4.594	5.527	7.344	9.524	11.030	13.362	15.507	18.168	20.090
9	2.088	2.532	3.325	4.168	5.380	6.393	8.343	10.656	12.242	14.684	16.919	19.679	21.666
10	2.558	3.059	3.940	4.865	6.179	7.267	9.342	11.781	13.442	15.987	18.307	21.161	23.209
11	3.053	3.609	4.575	5.578	6.989	8.148	10.341	12.899	14.631	17.275	19.675	22.618	24.725
12	3.571	4.178	5.226	6.304	7.807	9.034	11.340	14.011	15.812	18.549	21.026	24.054	26.217
13	4.107	4.765	5.892	7.042	8.634	9.926	12.340	15.119	16.985	19.812	22.362	25.472	27.688
14	4.660	5.368	6.571	7.790	9.467	10.821	13.339	16.222	18.151	21.064	23.685	26.873	29.141
15	5.229	5.985	7.261	8.547	10.307	11.721	14.339	17.322	19.311	22.307	24.996	28.259	30.578
16	5.812	6.614	7.962	9.312	11.152	12.624	15.338	18.418	20.465	23.542	26.296	29.633	32.000
17	6.408	7.255	8.672	10.085	12.002	13.531	16.338	19.511	21.615	24.769	27.587	30.995	33.409
18	7.015	7.906	9.390	10.865	12.857	14.440	17.338	20.601	22.760	25.989	28.869	32.346	34.805
19	7.633	8.567	10.117	11.651	13.716	15.352	18.338	21.689	23.900	27.204	30.144	33.687	36.191
20	8.260	9.237	10.851	12.443	14.578	16.266	19.337	22.775	25.038	28.412	31.410	35.020	37.566
21	8.897	9.915	11.591	13.240	15.445	17.182	20.337	23.858	26.171	29.615	32.671	36.343	38.932
22	9.542	10.600	12.338	14.041	16.314	18.101	21.337	24.939	27.301	30.813	33.924	37.659	40.289
23	10.196	11.293	13.091	14.848	17.187	19.021	22.337	26.018	28.429	32.007	35.172	38.968	41.638
24	10.856	11.992	13.848	15.659	18.062	19.943	23.337	27.096	29.553	33.196	36.415	40.270	42.980
25	11.524	12.697	14.611	16.473	18.940	20.867	24.337	28.172	30.675	34.382	37.652	41.566	44.314
26	12.198	13.409	15.379	17.292	19.820	21.792	25.336	29.246	31.795	35.563	38.885	42.856	45.642
27	12.879	14.125	16.151	18.114	20.703	22.719	26.336	30.319	32.912	36.741	40.113	44.140	46.963
28	13.565	14.847	16.928	18.939	21.588	23.647	27.336	31.391	34.027	37.916	41.337	45.419	48.278
29	14.256	15.574	17.708	19.768	22.475	24.577	28.336	32.461	35.139	39.087	42.557	46.693	49.588
30	14.953	16.306	18.493	20.599	23.364	25.508	29.336	33.530	36.250	40.256	43.773	47.962	50.892

* Table C is reprinted from Table III of Fisher: *Statistical Methods for Research Workers*. Oliver & Boyd, Ltd., Edinburgh, by permission of the author and publishers.

TABLE D.*   CORRELATION COEFFICIENTS (r) REQUIRED FOR SIGNIFICANCE AT THE
5% AND 1% LEVELS OF CONFIDENCE

Degrees of freedom	5% level	1% level
1	.997	1.000
2	.950	.990
3	.878	.959
4	.811	.917
5	.754	.874
6	.707	.834
7	.666	.798
8	.632	.765
9	.602	.735
10	.576	.708
11	.553	.684
12	.532	.661
13	.514	.641
14	.497	.623
15	.482	.606
16	.468	.590
17	.456	.575
18	.444	.561
19	.433	.549
20	.423	.537
21	.413	.526
22	.404	.515
23	.396	.505
24	.388	.496
25	.381	.487
26	.374	.478
27	.367	.470
28	.361	.463
29	.355	.456
30	.349	.449
40	.304	.393
50	.273	.354
100	.195	.254
500	.088	.115
1000	.062	.081

* Table D is abridged from Table V.A. of Fisher: *Statistical Methods for Research Workers*. Oliver and Boyd, Ltd., Edinburgh, by permission of the author and publishers. Supplementary entries were taken, by permission, from Snedecor: *Statistical Methods*, published by Collegiate Press, Ames, Iowa.

INDEX